A Troubled Dream

A Troubled Dream

*The Promise and Failure
of School Desegregation
in Louisiana*

Carl L. Bankston III
and Stephen J. Caldas

Vanderbilt University Press
NASHVILLE

This book is printed on acid-free paper.
Manufactured in the United States of America

Library of Congress Cataloging-in-Publication Data

Bankston, Carl L. (Carl Leon), 1952–
A troubled dream : the promise and failure of school desegrega-
tion in Louisiana / Carl L. Bankston III and Stephen J. Caldas.
    p. cm.
Includes bibliographical references.
ISBN 0-8265-1388-3 (cloth: alk. paper)
ISBN 0-8265-1389-1 (pbk.: alk. paper)
    1. School integration—Louisiana—History.
2. Segregation—Louisiana—History.
I. Caldas, Stephen J., 1957–   II. Title.

LC214.22.L8 B35 2001
379.2'63'09763—dc21   2001006528

To Cynthia and Suzanne,
both public school teachers

Contents

Figures

Tables

Acknowledgments

So many people have helped us in the writing of this book that thanking specific individuals puts us in danger of overlooking and slighting one of our benefactors. Nevertheless, we would like to express our gratitude to Evelyn Bullard, Rebecca Christian, Roslyn Growe, Scott Norton, Sam Pernici, Jean Kiesel, Fen Chou, Horace Olivier, Kay Eichler, Reasie Henry, Judith Singer, Chris Fero, David Thibodaux, Scott Feld, Min Zhou, Jim Elliott, and the parents, teachers, and students who made this book possible. We apologize to all those we have inadvertently left off this list.

A Troubled Dream

The Problem of Writing about Race

It is difficult for Americans, black or white, to write or think objectively about the role of race in our public institutions. Socially imposed racial inequality has permeated our history from its very beginning, and it continues to be intertwined with most of the controversial issues of the present. Discussions of the disturbing topic of race touch a painful and long-festering wound and are usually characterized more by guilty defensiveness, self-justification, anger, and expressions of moral outrage than by careful, detached analysis.

Race is our national neurosis. Like the neuroses of individuals, it stems from the traumas of early childhood. The first major export crops of the Americas, tobacco and sugar, were plantation crops depending heavily on the exploitation of forced labor, most of it ripped violently out of Africa. When the United States came into existence, race-based slavery was the great unacknowledged force in the shaping of our nation. Enlightenment sage, slave owner, and probable miscegenator Thomas Jefferson initially attempted in an early draft of the Declaration of Independence to blame slavery on English King George III. His fellow slaveholders required that this section be dropped from the Declaration, having no desire to give up slavery after gaining independence.

Slavery made its way into the Constitution of the United States as the great unmentionable. At the time the Constitution was adopted, approximately one out of every five people in the United States was of African ancestry, and almost all of those of African descent were held in bondage. Two of the key constitutional disputes concerned the distribution of power among the states and the relative power accorded to the states or to the central government—disputes rooted in the "slave question." Although slaves were held throughout the United States in the late eighteenth century, southern economies had already become specialized in agriculture, and the southern states therefore contained more nonvoting, enslaved residents. If political representation had been distributed among the states according to population, the comparatively few voters in the southern states would have had a much greater voice than those in the North. If slaves were not counted at all, states with large free populations would have predominated. As a compromise, Article I, Section 2, of the Constitution obliquely recognized slavery by apportioning representatives in the House of Representatives according to the number of free persons in each state and "three fifths of all other Persons." The Constitution also refers in an evasive and indirect manner to human beings held in bondage in Article IV, Section 2, which declares that "No Person held to Service or Labour in one State, under the Laws thereof, escaping to another, shall, in Consequence of any Law or Regulation therein, be discharged from such Service or Labour, But shall be delivered up on Claim of the Party to whom such Service or Labour may be due." The fundamental law of the nation was shaped by an institution that the lawmakers could not bring themselves to name openly.

The United States matured in a manner dictated by racial subjugation. The developing merchant and factory economies of the North differed from the agricultural economy of the South because the former benefitted from a strong central government and high tariffs, both of which would foster nascent industries and infrastructure. Agricultural southern economies, on the other hand, benefitted from low tariffs that would enable them to purchase imported manufactured goods cheaply and from the ability to manage local affairs without outside interference. Since the large-scale agriculture of the politically powerful in the South was based on exploitation of slaves, slavery became inseparable from the central economic and political issues of the new nation. Although tariffs would eventually become a much less divisive national question, the "states' rights" issue continued to be closely associated with North-South regional politics and with racial inequality in the South. Twentieth-century southern presidential candidates Strom Thurmond and George Wallace both ran on states' rights platforms that essentially promoted the freedom of states to maintain systems of racial inequality.

Over the course of the first half of the nineteenth century, racial politics became even more deeply ingrained in American national life. The invention and use of the cotton gin made exploitation of slaves in cotton production increasingly important to the southern economy. As cotton exports generated wealth, profits from slavery also generated much of the surplus that made industrial development possible in the North and created the preconditions for the industrial takeoff of the late nineteenth century. The people that the American Constitution could not name, then, were central to the creation of America.

While race-based slavery helped to build the entire nation, it also produced two different social and economic systems. The abolitionist movement, attacking the ownership of human chattel as evil and morally unjustifiable, took root in the nonslave states. In those states where slavery was widespread, the practice was defended as rooted in nature or in religion. American discourse about race, then, became a matter of attack and defense by people on opposite sides. While slavery was not the only cause of the Civil War, it was the root cause. It was behind the other issues, such as tariff levels and state sovereignty, and it was the one issue that could not be compromised or negotiated. The Republican administration of Abraham Lincoln apparently did not intend to eliminate slavery when Lincoln won the 1860 election, but Southern fears that Republican power would lead to slavery's end sparked secession and the formation of the Confederacy. Racial subjection, that unspoken presence behind the Constitution, had shaped the American political structure and then threatened to break it into two.

Racial stratification profoundly affected American social structure, as well as American political structure. The caste system of the southern economy meant that blacks constituted a category of disenfranchised, drastically disadvantaged people. Historian Eric Foner has argued that Reconstruction offered the possibility of breaking down the system of racial inequality by providing true economic opportunity to the freed slaves. This goal was never achieved. With the end of Reconstruction, black Americans were largely returned to a state of serfdom in the South, where nine out of ten of them still lived at the opening of the twentieth century.[1]

The Great Migration to northern cities that began about the time of the

First World War and continued through the 1960s established large black populations in many northern cities. But even by 1997, the South continued to be home to 55% of black Americans.[2] The South, with its large and openly oppressed black populace, was the focal point of the Civil Rights movement of the 1950s and 1960s. In this movement, blacks aimed at completing the unfinished business of the Reconstruction and at taking a full place as citizens in the nation their ancestors had helped to build.

One of the successes of the Civil Rights movement lay in altering the accepted moral values that guided thought and talk about race in America. From the end of Reconstruction to the middle of the twentieth century, racial questions generally received either the silence of the pre–Civil War Constitution or the sometimes brutal self-justifications of those who had benefitted directly or indirectly from racial subjugation. The drama of the Civil Rights era provided a televised morality play that redefined what would be acceptable in American society. The women's movement, the anti–Vietnam War protests, the demands of the disabled, and other new facets of society were shaped by the Civil Rights model. The language of moral outrage at inequality began to eclipse the language of racist self-justification in most public discourse.

Racial inequality did not disappear with the Civil Rights movement, though. Although the black middle class grew in the years following the 1960s, gaps in income, education, and living circumstances continued to separate black and white Americans into "two nations," to use Andrew Hacker's term.[3] Although the political vocabulary of the post–Civil Rights period did not permit the openly racist populism that flourished earlier in the century, political issues such as welfare, crime, and urban poverty had strong racial connotations.

One of the greatest difficulties in dealing realistically with problems of racial inequality has been the morally charged nature of the language used to discuss these problems. Because of our long history of racial subjection and brutalization, self-righteous insistence on moral absolutes presents itself as the easiest alternative to racism. Thinking in terms of right and wrong, of social justice and injustice, does have its advantages. There is a moral dimension to any set of relations within a society, and emphasizing this dimension can mobilize and motivate people. This type of approach can also, however, lead us to overlook some of the complexities of social existence.

Human societies are not composed of abstract principles, but of groups of people pursuing their own interests and goals. Any time people are divided into different groups, they also acquire different interests. These interests may sometimes coincide, but they may also conflict. People are especially eager to pursue goals that benefit their children—their personal contributions to society and the future. In a mobility-oriented society such as the United States, this means that families relentlessly seek opportunities to secure advantageous futures for their own children.

Our painful racial history has left us with two legacies. First, it has divided black and white Americans into two separate groups, which frequently do not share identical interests. Second, the emotions provoked by the topic of race have made it hard for us to talk about racial groups as having legitimate conflicts of interest that do not lend themselves to simple, moralistic solutions.

In this book, we attempt to consider the limited success of racially desegregating schools in one state. We believe that our analysis can be applied to other states and to the United States in general. Our close study of racial composition in the schools of Louisiana has led us to conclude that desegregation has often been self-defeating precisely because activists, the courts, and others seeking laudable social change have seen the racial makeup of schools almost exclusively from the perspective of social injustice and have failed to consider the sometimes differing interests and perspectives of black and white families. Moreover, even the social justice theories driving school desegregation have often been flawed and have delivered results that are just the opposite of what these theories promised—educational quality and equality.

Looking at racial groups as interest groups does not mean defending racial inequality. Indeed, we see racial stratification as the source of racial conflicts of interest. Although there are certainly privileged black Americans and underprivileged white Americans, race continues to be strongly associated with socioeconomic advantage. Race also, we will argue here, continues to be closely related to other aspects of social existence, most notably family structure, that greatly affect children's lives and influences on one another. By failing to deal with the problems connected to race that exist outside of the schools, we have undermined efforts to deal with racial disparities inside the schools.

The Dilemma of Desegregation

In a scholarly article that we published in 1996, we argued that desegregation has posed a complicated philosophical dilemma for American social policy.[4] We cited an insightful essay by James S. Coleman in which Coleman points out that the pursuit of social justice can be seen from two angles, one exemplified by the work of John Rawls and the other by the work of Rawls' fellow philosopher and adversary Robert Nozick. In his classic work, *A Theory of Justice,* Rawls essentially argued that a society's goods belong to the society as a whole and inequality can only be justified insofar as it benefits the least advantaged. Replying to Rawls, Nozick pointed out that individuals produce the wealth of societies by their own efforts and that goods belong to those individuals. Rawls' view was redistributionist, since he assumed that any inequalities in distribution of resources or opportunities are open to question and require justification. Nozick's stance was anti-redistributionist, since he assumed that the resources people hold or the opportunities open to them are rightfully theirs.

Few people are pure Rawlsians or pure Nozickians. Most of us would accept that human communities are collaborative efforts that depend on the contributions of all and that inequality in distribution does not necessarily reflect differences in those contributions. Applying this to the role of race in American history, black labor occupied a key place in building the nation. It hardly seems justifiable, then, that today's national wealth is unequally distributed according to race or that black schoolchildren are at a systematic disadvantage in entering our socioeconomic system. Today's opportunities are rigged by yesterday's injustices.

At the same time, though, we do live in a competitive society. Individuals may receive unequal opportunities for achievement, but they usually still need to do something with those opportunities. The very word *opportunity* suggests something peculiar about American ideas of equality. A belief in equal opportunity is a belief in inequality of outcome. Most of us do not believe that differences in wealth or prestige should be abolished, even in principle. We accept the Nozickian idea that the fruits of effort belong to individuals and that individuals should be allowed to keep and enjoy those fruits. Most of us would also agree that part of our enjoyment consists in being able to provide our family members with the means to thrive in the competitive American arena.

Our public school system, on the other hand, largely represents the redistributionist version of social justice. Every child has the right to an education that is equal to the education of every other child. We support schools with taxes in order to take wealth out of private pockets and put it in the public domain. School desegregation is entirely consistent with the redistributionist character of public education. As desegregation expert Gary Orfield has eloquently argued, segregated schools deny black children an equal education by isolating them in disadvantaged communities, in which they do not have the same access as white children to the common store of skills and knowledge.

Families, however, tend to represent the anti-redistributionist version of social justice, the belief that justice consists of not dispossessing people of the fruits of their labor. Just as individuals create wealth, families create educational achievement. The children of parents with advanced educational degrees, the children of parents with relatively high incomes, and the children of parents from two-parent homes are all consistently found to do better in schools than children who do not come from these kinds of family circumstances. Families foster performance in schools, and some families are better suited to foster performance than others.

In a sense, then, public schools and families have opposite goals. Schools exist to promote equality of opportunity. Families exist to promote the competitive interests of their own children. The better the ability of families to promote the interests of their children, the more likely they are to act on Nozickian principles. Families that have social resources to pass on to their children have no interest in seeing those resources socialized. Especially in the American middle class, which depends heavily on educational credentials, the overriding family goal is to maximize the competitive advantages of children in schooling.

In these pages, we argue that continuing racial inequality outside of the schools has created a fundamental contradiction for desegregation policy. As a consequence of centuries of enslavement, followed by the discriminatory Jim Crow system, today's African American young people are, on the average, systematically disadvantaged in the American educational system. As the articles in *The Black-White Test Score Gap,* edited by Christopher Jencks and Meredith Phillips, point out, the gap in measurable performance between whites and blacks continues to be substantial and to have far-reaching implications.[5] Black Americans as a group grow up in lower-income families and communities than white Americans do. Alfonso Pinkney of the City University of New York has recently remarked that "observers of the status of black citizens are eager to point out that government statistics show that about one-third of black families in the United States are now 'middle class,' but there is little to celebrate when the other two-thirds represent some of the most disadvantaged people in the world, including the one-third who live below the government's poverty threshold. A significant number of these people are children who see no prospect for a better life."[6] As we detail in the chapters of this book, in the site of our study, Louisiana, there is a great gap in income between black and white in every school district that we consider.

Low income means more than simply a lack of money. It also means that black American young people have parents who have less educational experience. There are consequently fewer books in their homes. Living in neighborhoods in which the majority of people have limited educational backgrounds means that minority youth have little guidance from adults with intimate knowledge of how to excel in schools.

Income and family educational background are both widely accepted to put minority young people at risk for low achievement. There is another influence, though, closely associated with both income and race, that we have found to be even more important than socioeconomic factors. Black children are far more likely than whites to live in single-parent homes, most often headed by women. In 1993, well over half of black children in the United States (58.3%) were living in households headed by single women, compared with fewer than one out of five (18.7%) white children. Although single-parent households increased in both racial groups over the course of the late twentieth century, the rate of increase was greater among black Americans, and more importantly, it was among black Americans that this became the dominant family form.[7]

There is a great deal of debate about why the percentage of single-parent families, especially those headed by never-married mothers, is so much higher among blacks than among whites.[8] We will touch on this debate in these pages, but our primary interest lies in the consequences of black family structure rather than in its cause. Single-parent families not only put children at risk for low achievement, but there is also substantial evidence that they are associated with higher incidences of behavioral and emotional problems.

It is not clear to what extent contemporary black family structure is a cause of chronic social problems among young black Americans and to what extent it is a reflection of those problems. Nevertheless, it is undeniable that these problems do exist. In 1996, blacks were only about 13% of the U.S. population, but black teenagers accounted for 58% of all juvenile arrests for murder and nonnegligent manslaughter, 43% of juvenile arrests for forcible rape, 58% of robbery arrests, and 40% of arrests for aggravated assault.[9]

All of the risk factors that show close statistical associations with race can create difficulties for individuals in schools. In addition, we argue, based on common sense, theoretical logic, observations in schools, and statistical evidence, that these risk factors also create difficulties for schools, and for all students in schools. Students do not sit in isolation throughout the school day. The academic atmosphere of each institution is largely set by those who attend it. The more students in a school who are at risk for low educational achievement, the lower the overall level of performance among all students. This is precisely the motivation for desegregating schools. The astute desegregation proponent Gary Orfield describes the problems of segregated minority-dominated schools as "low levels of competition and expectation, less qualified teachers who leave as soon as they get seniority, deteriorated schools in dangerous neighborhoods, more limited curricula, peer pressure against academic achievement and supportive of crime and substance abuse, high levels of teen pregnancy, few connections with colleges and employers who can assist students, little serious academic preparation for college, and powerless parents who themselves failed in school and do not know how to evaluate or change schools."[10]

Desegregation, then, represents a strategy of striving for equity in education by redistributing the social resources of predominantly white schools, which Orfield identifies as overwhelmingly middle class.[11] The predominantly white schools are generally assumed (correctly in our view) to enjoy comparatively high levels of competition and expectation. In these schools, according to most observers, there is less "peer pressure against academic achievement and supportive of crime and substance abuse," though to be sure, these problems do exist in predominantly white, middle class schools. Schools, however, do not create the social resources that constitute the academic environment. Students bring their expectations, their competitive orientations, their patterns of behavior, and their attitudes from their homes and communities into their schools. Good schools are those that bring together pupils who will share the benefits of supportive communities and families with each other. If predominantly white schools are overwhelmingly middle class, it is because they contain students from middle class backgrounds. Essentially, the aim of desegregating schools has been to share these backgrounds with minority students.

This aim of desegregation faces a dilemma that is rarely acknowledged. Although there is a growing black middle class, the racial statistics of contemporary America mean that increasing the African American population of a school is also, in most cases, increasing the proportion of students from low-income families, single-parent families, and disruptive neighborhoods. As we will point out in the following pages, the authorities on school desegregation have frequently assumed that redistribution of social resources involves no sacrifice on the part of the "haves." We do not take it as a given that placing more at-risk children in a school necessarily imposes sacrifices on children from two-parent, middle class families with strong orientations toward upward mobility through education. We regard this as a question to be addressed empirically. However, it does seem to us a logical contradiction to argue that black children can benefit from access to the social advantages that white children bring from their families to schools, but white children will not in any way share in the historically imposed disadvantages of their black classmates.

The evidence that we will examine in this book strongly supports the commonsensical view that parents generally do not want their children to go to school with low-income children, with children who are not adequately prepared for school work, or with children who come from family backgrounds that are inconsistent with high levels of school performance. Moreover, our evidence suggests that, from the Nozickian point of view, parents are correct in wanting to avoid schools with large proportions of at-risk children—if the highest possible academic outcome is their goal. Families want their children in schools where the children can maximize their own educational opportunities, not in schools where those opportunities are redistributed to those who are less advantaged.

Both black and white parents, in general, want the best for their own children. The continuing existence of racial inequality outside of the schools, though, means that whites tend to have more power to seek what is best for their own children; i.e., to avoid the "bad" schools, the schools with large percentages of at-risk students. Given the close correlation between the racial composition of schools and all of the at-risk factors, this means that white parents, prejudiced and nonprejudiced alike, have strong motivations to avoid schools with large minority student populations.

As we explain in Chapter 2, studies of "white flight" frequently concentrate on the objection of whites to particular strategies for achieving desegregation, such as busing. We agree that some desegregation strategies can indeed alienate white families and intensify the movement out of school systems. Still, our study of Louisiana has led us to conclude that the problem is more fundamental than opposition to busing or to judicial usurpation of the power of local school districts. It is essentially a problem created by continuing racial inequality outside of the schools and by the efforts of white parents to act in the best interests of their own children. Good schools are those with students who are, on average, high achievers. High achievers tend to come from families that are not poor and that contain both mothers and fathers and from neighborhoods that do not have the characteristics that Gary Orfield, in the quotation above, identifies as the characteristics of de facto segregated, majority-black schools. Some schools may indeed contain middle class black majorities. In theory, there is no reason that a majority-black school cannot be far superior to a majority-white school, and, in some cases, this does happen. For the most part, though, the association between the proportion of African American students and the proportion of at-risk students is so close that efforts to seek good schools and avoid bad schools mean efforts to avoid schools with concentrations of black students. Desegregation, then, bears its own self-contradiction. The very inequalities that lead policy makers to try to achieve racial balances in schools promote imbalances.

Not only do we argue that white reactions to racial compositions of schools present a much more complicated problem than is generally recognized, we also maintain that these reactions can be more varied than many authorities acknowledge. In these pages, we identify three major types of reactions. First, there is the classic form of white flight, movement from one school district to another. This has indeed been a common occurrence in the school systems we consider here. Second, movement from public to private schools, a long-recognized but understudied form of white flight, can often be found. Third, the desegregation of schools can actually lead to shifts in student populations within school districts. As overall school quality appears to decline in a school system, the number of "good schools" becomes smaller, and these schools become more intensely sought by parents in the system from relatively advantaged backgrounds. As we will see throughout the districts that we examine here, magnet schools, honors programs, and foreign language immersion programs frequently become desperately sought commodities in school districts in which minority students predominate. Thus, in New Orleans, for example, over 90% of the students are black, and the small proportion of white students remaining in the district are largely clustered in very few schools.

We realize that the argument we will present in this book may touch some nerves; as we said, race is a painful subject in the United States and many black Americans continue to suffer from the long heritage of systematic oppression. We are concerned, then, that some readers may interpret our argument as somehow presenting a justification for racial stratification, or as blaming the victims of racial inequality for their own circumstances. We reject any such interpretations. Our intention in this book is not justification or blame, but a clear and accurate explanation, as uncomfortable as that may be for some.

Louisiana as a Case Study

While we look at desegregation in Louisiana in this volume, we also intend this to be a book about desegregation in the United States. The state of Louisiana is an important area for race relations in its own right. Like other southern states, it has a large black population and therefore racial issues in Louisiana have an urgency that they may not have in, say, Idaho. Louisiana is also historically important for race relations in America. Legal segregation in the United States received Supreme Court approval in 1890 with *Plessy v. Ferguson,* a case from Louisiana. The integration of schools in New Orleans in the early 1960s became a national focus of attention. The Louisiana gubernatorial campaign of former Ku Klux Klan Grand Wizard David Duke brought not only national attention, but given his surprisingly broad conservative support, international attention as well to bear on questions of race in this state.[12] From a national as well as a local perspective, then, the desegregation of Louisiana schools deserves close attention.

While we look specifically at one state, though, our intention is to uncover the dynamics of school racial composition throughout the country.

This can best be done, we believe, by looking closely at one state, and even more closely at particular districts within that state. One of the peculiarities of the American school system is its combination of highly localized school systems with centralized federal interventions. Under normal circumstances, public education is locally controlled in the United States and largely funded by local and state governments by means of property taxes. Each state has its own department of education, which sets the guidelines for the schools within its boundaries. In turn, implementation of state guidelines is in the hands of local elected school boards. As we will discuss in Chapter 2, federal intervention for the sake of desegregation has largely taken the form of judicial involvement in local school districts. This means that even the involvement of the central government in this matter has had a highly localized character and can best be understood by focusing on specific localities.

There are good theoretical reasons, then, for looking primarily at selected districts in a single state. There are also good practical reasons. As social scientists, one of our goals is to produce generalizations that are broadly, and perhaps even universally, applicable. The Rawls-Nozick dilemma that we have mentioned is an example of such a generalization. Generalizations, though, are the common characteristics and trends that we find running through specific cases, and it is by looking at specific cases that we can best understand generalizations, as well as generate new ones.

The more we look at specific locations, the more detail we can obtain to support—or challenge—generalizations. In this book, concerning ourselves with a single state, Louisiana, has enabled us to martial a wide variety of both quantitative and qualitative sources of evidence. Since we are both from this state and have worked for years in its educational system, we are also able to draw on literally decades of fieldwork and personal observations.

We have made use of a wide variety of statistical sources in our scrutiny of school desegregation and its consequences. By compiling data on the state and on selected school districts published in the Louisiana Department of Education's *Annual Financial and Statistical Report* from 1965 through 2000, we have been able to look at trends over a thirty-five-year period, during which most of the desegregation struggles took place. This long-term view gives us a perspective on school changes that has rarely appeared in the literature on school desegregation. We have also obtained data sets on school performance from the state Department of Education, including school-level data from the 1999 Louisiana Educational Assessment Program test of fourth- and eighth-grade students and individual-level data from the 1990, 1994, and 1999 versions of the Graduation Exit Examination, a test of major subject areas, some taken in tenth grade and some taken in eleventh grade, that must be passed by all Louisiana public school students to obtain a high school diploma. Focusing on specific school districts makes it possible for us to use more localized data sets as well, such as the 1996 Lafayette Survey of Educators, in which one of the authors (Bankston) surveyed the entire population of public school teachers in a single district. We also draw on data from the U.S. Census Bureau in order to describe the populations under consideration.

While statistical data provide the objective framework of our examination, we flesh out this framework with extensive fieldwork and archival materials. Here again, the localized nature of our research gives it a depth and richness that a nationwide study would not have. We have conducted interviews with state and district school officials, principals, teachers, parents, and teachers in order to interpret our statistical findings in terms of the lives and experiences of those involved in public education in Louisiana. Our fieldwork has involved years of participation in public schools at a variety of levels. Carl L. Bankston III is a sociologist with an interest in public education who served as a substitute teacher in New Orleans in 1993 and 1994 while doing fieldwork. Bankston has also devised and administered surveys of public school teachers during the research for this book. Stephen J. Caldas is a certified teacher in Louisiana who taught in three school districts in the state from 1981 through 1987. Caldas worked as psychometrician for the Louisiana Department of Education and had primary responsibility for developing instruments and interpreting educational statistics relating to student and school accountability. As a member of the faculty of the College of Education at the University of Louisiana at Lafayette (formerly the University of Southwestern Louisiana) from 1994 to the present, he has trained public school teachers, an activity that has required constant observations of public school classes in urban, suburban, and rural schools in several school districts. Though we consider ourselves Louisianians and graduated from the state's public high schools, both of us have a somewhat unique perspective on Louisiana, fostered by years of living from one coast of the United States to the other, and residing collectively in Africa, Japan, Laos, Thailand, the Philippines, and Canada. Therefore, assuming (hopefully) that we have benefitted from our extensive exposure to other peoples and cultures, we cannot truly be characterized as typical "parochials" with the tunnel vision that parochialism can sometimes engender.

Much of the interpretation of the historical trends that we offer in these pages is based on archival work, drawing from decades of newspaper articles on school desegregation and related issues. The New Orleans *Times-Picayune* provided the most valuable source of archival material, since this is the newspaper of Louisiana's largest city, and it therefore functions as the newspaper of the entire state, in somewhat the same way that the *New York Times* may be regarded as a national newspaper. We also use the archives of other newspapers, most notably the Baton Rouge *Morning Advocate,* the principal news publication of the state's capital city, and the *Daily Advertiser,* Lafayette's daily paper.

The Plan of the Book

The struggle for the desegregation of schools and the practical self-contradictions of that struggle cannot be understood without a clear view of the historical context. For this reason, in Chapter 1 we begin with an examination of Louisiana's schools before desegregation. We examine how slavery and the Jim Crow system that followed slavery in Louisiana and elsewhere in the South created a heritage of racial inequality. We look at how separate black and white school systems emerged as part of the creation of this heritage. Separate schools helped to maintain the subjugation of blacks to whites, and these schools helped to keep black Louisianians in economic and social positions that were systematically disadvantaged. We argue that the dream of breaking down racial separation in the schools was the morally compelling dream of breaking down the walls of the racial caste system.

In Chapter 2, we continue the task of placing the desegregation of Louisiana schools in broader context by describing the struggle to desegregate schools throughout the United States. Judicial intervention in Louisiana school districts concerned specific localities, but variations of the same sort of intervention were based on national policy and were occurring in localities throughout the nation. Therefore, we discuss the evolution of desegregation policies at the national level. In this chapter, we consider the reactions to desegregation policies that have emerged since the 1970s. We consider the growing challenges to desegregation in light of the rationale for desegregating American schools. We also look at the debate over white flight and suggest a rational choice approach that we believe may help clarify the nature of the problem of white flight.

Chapters 3, 4, and 5 focus on three school districts in Louisiana in order to probe the dynamics of desegregation and reaction in schools. We select the Orleans school district, the East Baton Rouge school district, and the Lafayette school district as localities that exemplify three stages in the process of desegregation. These three districts are shown in Figure I.1. Note that where we provide counts and percentages of white students in our analyses, these figures actually represent "nonblack" unless we specifically state otherwise. We refer to nonblacks as "whites" is because of the demographic makeup of the state and because of how the state has reported race over time. First, in most school districts it is still true that almost all nonblacks are indeed white. Secondly, in the state records we analyzed for this work, the state itself reported all nonblacks as "whites" until 1979. Since we do many longitudinal comparisons beginning with the year 1965, we wanted to include as many years as possible, rather than truncate our analysis. Most nonblack and nonwhite students in Louisiana are Asian, and in terms of academic achievement, these students are much more like whites than blacks, which conceptually justifies their inclusion in the "white" grouping. Moreover, they are concentrated in just a few parishes, which we duly note in the body of this book.

The Orleans Parish school district, which is the same as the city of New Orleans, is the largest urban area in Louisiana. New Orleans was the site of a widely publicized desegregation struggle in the 1960s. The proportion of its students who are black has increased steadily over the past thirty years, and at present black students make up over 90% of the public school pupils in the district. During this period, white students have largely moved to suburban districts surrounding the city. Those remaining in New Orleans are now primarily located in the private schools. The relatively few white students in the public school system of the city are heavily concentrated in the few magnet schools that are still considered "acceptable."

Critics of the concept of "white flight" have often argued that white movement to suburban areas is a consequence of demographic change and not a response to school situations. Our interviews with parents around the New Orleans area, though, indicate that one of the primary reasons middle class families choose to settle in suburban areas is that the schools of urban areas are perceived as unsafe and academically poor. Our descriptions of the situation in New Orleans schools suggest that these perceptions do not spring from prejudice alone but are, in fact, well founded. Moreover, in the New Orleans area, there is such a close correlation between the academic quality of schools and the racial composition of schools that parents seeking good educational institutions will of necessity avoid the minority-dominated schools of the city.

From New Orleans, we move to the East Baton Rouge Parish school system, dominated by the city of Baton Rouge, capital of Louisiana. Unlike New Orleans, which has gradually moved toward an almost all-black public school system, Baton Rouge had a stable majority-white public school student population until the early 1980s, when a period of intense, judicially imposed desegregation began. A white exodus from the public schools of Baton Rouge began at precisely this time, into both the nonpublic schools of the district and into the school systems of nearby suburban parishes. Unlike New Orleans, Baton Rouge did not have a substantial private educational sector until these changes began, but this sector grew rapidly. By the late 1990s, nearly two-thirds of the students in the public schools of Baton Rouge were minority students, and the trend seemed to be continuing—and accelerating. Examining this trend in the light of interviews and archival evidence, we conclude that the desegregation of Baton Rouge schools had a result that was precisely the opposite of its intention. Instead of putting black students and white students together, the desegregation of Baton Rouge resulted in there being too few white students to distribute throughout the district. As the unfortunate association between race and social class has continued, Louisiana's capital has quickly lost middle class participation in its educational system.

Having looked at the two largest cities in the state, we next turn our attention to a smaller district, that of Lafayette Parish, which consists of the city of Lafayette and its surrounding suburbs and rural areas. One advantage of looking closely at Lafayette is that it provides us with an opportunity to see to what extent the trends that we have noted in New Orleans and Baton Rouge are big-city trends. Another advantage, as we point out, is that Lafayette is, in a sense, at the beginning stage in the desegregation

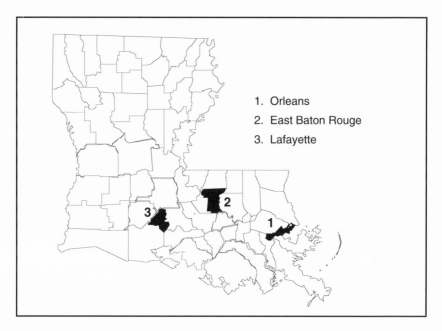

Figure I.1. Orleans, East Baton Rouge, and Lafayette Parishes and School Districts

process. The desegregation of schools in Louisiana largely began in New Orleans and it has now reached a logical impasse—the racial composition of most of the schools is essentially set because it is almost a one-race district. Baton Rouge has been going through intense efforts at desegregation and only became a majority-black district in the mid to late 1980s. In Lafayette, desegregation has proceeded much more slowly until now and has, at the time of this writing, just begun a controversial program of judicially mandated school rezoning, school closures, busing—and the attendant white flight.

By concentrating on the smaller district of Lafayette, we are able to look at racial composition on a school-by-school basis. We can look more closely at the consequences of racially identifiable schools and at the connection between racial composition and academic environment. We give special attention to the role of family structure in shaping academic environments.

Chapter 6 turns from our three focal school districts to desegregation around the state. Here, our interest is to demonstrate that the trends and processes we have identified in these three districts are widely applicable. In this chapter, we look first at the problem of the racial composition of schools in the state of Louisiana in general. We describe the socioeconomic inequalities that continue to separate black and white. We point out that de facto segregation still characterizes public schools in Louisiana and that the black student population is growing steadily.

To illustrate the dynamics of desegregation and resistance to it throughout the state, we present several short discussions of these issues in suburban, rural, and urban school districts. Again, our goal is to emphasize both the local character of school desegregation and the generalizable tendencies created by school desegregation. In all districts, black students are, on average, systematically disadvantaged socially and economically. This means that whenever minority student populations increase, the proportions of the socially and economically disadvantaged in schools increase.

Chapter 7 deals more closely with the academic consequences of desegregation. We look closely at the questions of whether the racial composition of schools is related to school performance and at why this relation might exist. Here, we look closely at a problem we have seen throughout the book: the connection between race and family structure. The socioeconomic status of black families, as commonly measured, is much lower than that of white families. Therefore, if the socioeconomic level of families matters in establishing school quality, the proportion of black families in schools will be closely associated with the academic quality of schools. Beyond this, however, it is important to realize that our racially unequal past has had cultural consequences. The correlation between race and family structure is so close that increases in the minority student population almost by definition mean increases in the proportion of students from single-parent families. We discuss why this might have a negative influence on the overall quality of schools. We provide evidence that minority-dominated schools result in lower levels of achievement for both black and white students and that the prevalence of single-parent families in minority-dominated schools can help to explain why this is the case.

Finally, in Chapter 8, we turn to the question of policy. We are not describing the troubles of desegregation simply to engage in wilful pessimism or to discourage efforts to improve American school systems for all participants. We do believe that realistic assessment provides a better basis than wishful thinking for educational policies. In this concluding chapter, we present a set of carefully considered compromises, dedicated to promoting the long-term interests of all public school students. Some of the recommendations that we offer are quite broad in character, and we suggest that many of the black and white disparities in schools can only be dealt with after we address the disparities outside of the schools. We do not think that the black-white gap in American schools and in American society can be easily closed, but we do not despair of substantially narrowing this gap. The dream of racial equality should not be abandoned, but it can only be carefully and gradually realized in the hard light of day.

Chapter 1

Louisiana's Schools Prior to Desegregation

The Roots of a Racially Divided Society

Throughout the late nineteenth and early twentieth centuries, black and white Americans lived lives that were separate and unequal, in law as well as in fact. This was especially true in the former slave states of the South, home to nine out of ten African Americans in 1900, and still home to a majority of African Americans one hundred years later. Historians have often argued that this racial concentration was the source of the long-lasting repression of black southerners by white southerners. During the years of slavery, between 1790 and 1860, people of African ancestry made up about one-third of the population of the southern states. In some of these states, including Louisiana, the majority of people were black under the regime of slavery.

Louisiana was originally established as a French colony, and its laws regarding race and slavery were somewhat different from those of the English colonies of North America. In 1724, Louisiana's colonial government published the *code noir,* or "Black Code." This set of laws required that slaves be instructed in Roman Catholicism and be baptized, and that they be allowed ownership of property and have the right to marry. These laws were changed when the French ceded Louisiana to Spain in 1763, but by that time the unique situation of black people in Louisiana had allowed the development of a different class of people in a social situation between that of slaves and whites. After the United States purchased Louisiana in 1803, legal restrictions on slaves became more stringent, and the rights of free people of color *(gens de couleur libre)* were increasingly limited. Moreover, the free people of color were always a small minority of those of African ancestry, and for most blacks slavery in American Louisiana was as harsh as in any of the other slave states (e.g., see Solomon Northup's *Twelve Years a Slave*).[1] Slavery was particularly brutal in the southwestern part of the state, where large numbers of slaves were employed in the hard work of growing sugar cane, a labor intensive crop.

The years before the Civil War saw several slave revolts, most notably the famous revolt led by Nat Turner in 1831. These revolts sparked fear on the part of white southerners and led them to sharply limit the rights of blacks. It became illegal in all southern states to teach slaves to read or write. Black people were not allowed to gather together, even for religious services, without a white person present. "Even before the war," wrote the author of one classic history of the era, "white Southerners had frequently entertained a wild, nightmarish fear that the Negroes would rise up, slay them, and overthrow the institution of slavery."[2]

After the Civil War, northern troops occupied the South, and the former slaves were freed. With the backing of the U.S. government, some blacks were elected to public office. Blacks were most influential in Louisiana and in South Carolina, since those were the only two states with substantial numbers of well-educated people of African ancestry. In Louisiana, the small group of free people of color made up the core of the black political leadership during Reconstruction, when about one-third of the state's governmental leaders were black.

Black political involvement, however, was opposed by most southern whites, and it was only made possible by the presence of federal troops. The white ruling class of the South attempted to control the freed slaves and force them to continue doing plantation-type labor through laws known as "Black Codes." The first states to pass Black Codes, in 1865, were Mississippi and South Carolina. Under the Mississippi law, all blacks were required to show proof of employment for the coming year each January. Blacks were forbidden to leave their jobs before the end of a contract. Those who were unemployed or judged to be "disorderly" could be prosecuted for vagrancy. The South Carolina law forbade blacks to hold any job except farmer or servant, and it required them to sign annual contracts and to work from sunup until sundown. As in Mississippi, unemployed blacks were guilty of vagrancy. Almost all of the states of the former Confederacy enacted similar laws. Louisiana law required work from all family members of former slave families and gave employers complete control over labor disputes.

The southern states were forced to repeal the Black Codes by the end of 1866, as a result of northern opposition and the Civil Rights Act of 1866. Still, most southern states, including Louisiana, retained strict vagrancy laws based on the Black Codes and enforced almost exclusively against blacks. By these kinds of legal strategies, the former slaves were retained as cheap agricultural labor even after the formal end of slavery. Reestablishing the status of the black population as a source of labor subordinate to whites became a primary goal of white southern Redemptionist politics, and the southern Democratic Party became the chief legitimate vehicle for achieving this goal.[3] Either whites would rule, in this view, or blacks would rule, and black rule was to be opposed by all possible means.

We may date the end of Reconstruction in Louisiana from the 1876 election, in which the Democrat and former Confederate general Francis T. Nicholls ran for governor against Republican Stephen B. Packard. Results of the Nicholls-Packard contest followed the racial distribution of the state's population. In parishes with majority-black populations, Packard was victorious. In parishes with majority-white populations, Nicholls was the clear winner.[4] Although Packard won and initially took office, with the withdrawal of federal troops the Republican administration crumbled. Nicholls and the Democrats came to power.

The Ku Klux Klan and similar organizations emerged during Reconstruction as the terrorist wing of the Democratic Party, sharing the party's dedication to white people as a group with objective interests that were in conflict with the interests of blacks.[5] The division of the political universe according to skin color was codified during the Jim Crow period of the late nineteenth and early twentieth centuries. Legally, the division was maintained by segregation and by laws forbidding miscegenation. Illegally, it was maintained by lynchings and other forms of violence.[6]

Life and politics in the South were driven by the perception of the world as divided into mutually incompatible interest groups along lines of race. By 1877, when President Rutherford B. Hayes withdrew all remaining federal troops from the southern states, the racial subordination of slavery was replaced by the racial subordination of segregation. Whites in Louisiana and the other southern states saw the world as divided into black and white, and they saw black public involvement as a permanent threat to white interests. The Louisiana free people of color, whose positions had grown increasingly tenuous even before the Civil War, were redefined as black. Property and educational qualifications, poll taxes, grandfather clauses, and other means of restricting voting practically eliminated blacks from voting in Mississippi by 1890, in South Carolina by 1895, and in Louisiana by 1898. These laws also often had the effect of limiting participation by poorer whites. Mississippi, for example, cut back the total number of voters in the state by about 70% between the end of Reconstruction and the early 1890s. In 1897, Louisiana had 130,000 registered black voters and 164,000 registered white voters. By 1904, there were only a little over 1,000 registered black Louisianians and 92,000 registered white voters.

In 1896, segregation law in Louisiana became the legal basis of segregation throughout the South and in the territories of Oklahoma and Arizona. In that year, the U.S. Supreme Court ruled that a Louisiana law requiring the racial segregation of railroad cars was constitutional, establishing the "separate but equal" doctrine. In the racially charged atmosphere of Louisiana and the other southern states, though, separate meant unequal in virtually every respect, including education.

Before Reconstruction, formal education for slaves was forbidden by Louisiana state law. Free black children, including the children of the mixed-race elite, were generally educated either at home, in small private schools, or in parochial schools, although some light-skinned children of African ancestry attended public schools by passing for white *(passer pour blanc)*. Some of the Catholic religious orders, especially the French Ursulines and Carmelites, offered separate classes for free blacks.[7]

The defeat of the South in the Civil War saw the tenuous beginnings of public education for most black Louisianians. On March 22, 1864, Nathaniel Banks, the general commanding Union troops occupying Louisiana, set up a separate board of education for Louisiana's black population under the direction of an abolitionist Quaker Union soldier, B. Rush Plumly.[8] These separate schools gave way to efforts to integrate the school system in the late 1860s, efforts that were supported by many white as well as black civic leaders sympathetic to the northern presence in Louisiana. The state's 1868 constitution went so far as to forbid the establishment of schools for any specific race.

The end of Reconstruction meant the end of these first efforts at the desegregation of Louisiana schools, as well as the beginning of the end of black political participation. Even though school desegregation had received the endorsement of some enlightened whites, it was extremely unpopular with the white population in general. The admission of black students to the elite Upper Girls High School in New Orleans resulted in three days of rioting, resulting in the deaths of a black man and child.[9]

Local school boards began to resegregate schools in 1877, in spite of the 1868 constitution. The new constitution of 1879, written after the return to power of the southern Democrats, dropped both the prohibition of officially single-race schools and the requirement that every parish establish a public school system. By the end of the nineteenth century, black and white schools were entirely separate, as an ideology of white supremacy became firmly established in the state's political structure. Official policies, such as the 1900 decision of the New Orleans school board to limit black education to the first five grades,[10] clearly reflected this ideology.

The U.S. Supreme Court gave judicial sanction to separate and unequal education in the case *Cumming v. Richmond County Board of Education,* in which the court ruled that a school district could provide schools for whites only even if the district provided no schools at all for blacks. Louisiana's white supremacist educational policies, like those of other states, therefore operated with the approval of the nation's highest court. As in the rest of the South, educational separation meant educational inequality in Louisiana. Until 1940, more money for black public education came from private charitable organizations than from the Louisiana state government.[11] Black communities often raised their own money for schools or voluntarily paid extra taxes in order to establish schools. The lack of funding made one-room, one-teacher schools common for blacks in the state: in 1910, 89% of the "Negro schools" in Louisiana were one-teacher schools. Black education did improve slightly during the early 1930s, when Governor and later Senator Huey P. Long quietly included black children in the distribution of free textbooks in Louisiana schools. However, black schools still usually received the used textbooks that had been discarded by the white schools, a practice that continued well into the 1960s.[12]

The teachers for the segregated minority school system received their training in separate institutions of higher education. Under Reconstruction, the Freedman's Bureau had provided funds for Straight University in 1869. Four years later, the State of Louisiana established New Orleans University, which merged with Straight in 1935 to form Dillard University. The

Louisiana state legislature provided a charter to Southern University, the state's largest black university system, in 1879. The Catholic Church established the elite Xavier University in New Orleans in 1915. Grambling University first came into existence as the Colored Industrial and Agricultural School, and it became a four-year college in 1940.

The existence of a separate black system of higher education did not ensure equal educational opportunities, even at the highest level. As we will see below, these institutions produced very few graduates. In addition, there have long been serious questions about the quality of education received in segregated colleges.

Racial Inequality on the Eve of the Civil Rights Movement

By the mid-twentieth century, Jim Crow laws mandated segregation in virtually every area of life in Louisiana and the other southern states. Hotels, restaurants, theaters, playgrounds, parks, drinking fountains, restrooms, bars, barbershops, and even cemeteries were only a few of the facilities that were segregated by state law. In cosmopolitan New Orleans, streetcars had a movable sign reading "colored" to indicate the area in the back of the car where all identifiable African Americans were required to sit. If more whites entered the car than the white section could comfortably fit, the sign was moved back, and the black passengers would have to crowd into fewer seats. Washington Parish, in the far eastern part of the state, had one of the region's best parish fairs. One day of the fair was the "colored" day; on other days only whites could attend.

After two generations of segregation, the legal separation was accepted as the natural order of things by many. A seventy-year-old white woman told us in 1999, "That was just the way it was. We didn't think anything about it. They had their place and we had ours."[13] A black man of seventy-five observed, "I can't say that I liked being told that I couldn't go into the best places or do things that I wanted to do. Where I sat on the bus didn't bother me. But even if it did, there wasn't much you could do about it."[14] An African American from Vermillion Parish remarked, "Whites and blacks were afraid of each other and really did not want to be around the other. Blacks chose to remain with other blacks and whites did the same."[15] Indeed, once firmly established, traditions die hard.

As recently as 1999, a French-speaking twenty-year-old white Cajun farmer in St. Martin Parish, where Catholic churches and public high school proms are still segregated by race, pointed out a bar in rural Cecilia where blacks still enter by the back door. "That's just the way it's always been," he shrugged nonchalantly.[16] A reporter for the St. Martin Parish weekly newspaper *Teche News* told us that St. Martinville, the parish seat of St. Martin Parish, was a backwater, "a throwback to plantation days," where racial attitudes were very hardened and traditional, and not necessarily overt or obvious to the casual visitor. He said it was as if there were an ever present "undercurrent" of racist feelings between blacks and whites.[17] The reporter pointed out that there had not been an election for city council in St. Martinville in over ten years, ostensibly because of conflict surrounding reapportionment, but actually the consequence of underlying issues of racial politics. At the other end of the parish, a young black teacher at the high school in rural Cecilia, who was originally from Miami, Florida, told one of the authors that she had never seen such blatant racism in her entire life: "I feel that being here in Louisiana has made me a racist. . . . I am extremely disgusted with the educational system here. I don't feel everyone is included."[18]

There were elites and middle classes within both the black and the white castes. As in John Dollard's classic study of "Southerntown,"[19] Louisiana's separate black communities had their own social structures. There was an upper class composed of small business owners who served black customers, some professionals, and members of the clergy. At the Washington Parish fair, for example, decisions relating specifically to "Colored Day" were made by a black fair committee, with officers who were the elite in their community. New Orleans had a thriving black market district located on Dryades Street, which was in many ways the "Canal Street" of the New Orleans black community.

Looking back nostalgically to the days before integration, some African American men and women lament the loss of their separate institutions. "The black businesses and black colleges were flourishing back then," a middle-aged man mused, "and I think we lost something when blacks stopped going to their own stores and supporting their own. Sometimes I'm not sure integration was entirely a good thing."[20] An African American who lived in southern Louisiana during the desegregation of the schools also had regrets: "In retrospect, I do not feel it was in the best interest of the black community to integrate. Through integration we lost the caring and compassion of teachers who took a vital interest in each black student. We were thrust into a school system that demonstrated a lack of tolerance, in short, we got the message that you are now in a white man's world and you will have to live by white man's rules."[21]

Racial segregation undoubtedly did have some positive aspects, such as black businesses, black colleges, and close-knit personal relations among minority group members. It was also, however, the enforcement of disadvantage and deprivation. Table 1.1 gives selected census data from the year 1950 to shed some light on the comparative socioeconomic situations of whites and blacks. The category "nonwhite" here also includes Asians and recognized Native Americans, but these were sufficiently few in number that we can essentially take these statistics as representing the conditions of African Americans.

The white median income in Louisiana in 1950 was two and a half times that of the nonwhite median income. While only about one in five whites had incomes of less than $1,000 in the previous year, almost half of the nonwhites had incomes below this level. To be black in Louisiana was to be much poorer than your white neighbors. It also meant having nearly twice the likelihood of being out of work, since the nonwhite unemployment rate was 6.5%, while the white unemployment rate was only 3.7%. These are not terribly high unemployment rates by contemporary standards, but we should remember that low-skilled, low-paid jobs were much more widely available in1950. Poor people at that time were more likely to be the working poor than they are today.

Whites and nonwhites show marked differences in occupational distribution. Those who lament the passing of segregated black businesses and black professions serving a black clientele should be aware that the black middle class in Louisiana, as in the rest of the United States, was tiny. Author Bart Landry has observed that the black middle class grew rapidly in the years that followed the Civil Rights struggle, from under 14% of all African Americans in 1960 to 38% in 1981.[22] Table 1.1 also shows that there were few middle class jobs for nonwhites in the economic structure of Louisiana at the middle of the century. Over 20% of whites were in professional or technical careers or were managers or proprietors of businesses. Fewer than 5% of nonwhites were in similar positions. Segregated black communities may have provided customers for some black professionals and business owners, but the latter were very few in number. Insofar as many nonwhites did own their own businesses, these were often farms, which were usually quite small and frequently barely above subsistence level. These farms were much more likely than those of whites to rely on unpaid family labor, as reflected by the fact that 4.1% of nonwhites worked at unpaid family farm labor, compared with only 1.5% of whites. Almost one in ten nonwhites worked on a farm owned by someone else. More than one out of every four nonwhites in Louisiana in 1950 was a farmer or farm laborer.

The modal occupational category for nonwhites in 1950 was that of laborer. After laborer, the next most frequent occupational concentration of nonwhites was private household worker (fewer than 1% of whites were in this occupational category). Throughout Louisiana, middle class white households of even modest incomes could afford child care workers, maids, cooks, and laundry women because black workers were so widely available and inexpensive. This statistic is the numerical artifact of a pervasive irony of life under segregation. Blacks and whites were not totally separated. In many ways, their lives were intimately intertwined. They were connected as patron and servant, a relationship that perpetuated many of the aspects of slavery.

Even in the days before the service-oriented, white collar economy, more than 22% of Louisiana whites were in clerical work or sales. Very few nonwhites were in this white collar area. At the upper range of blue collar work, the position of craftsman or foreman, nonwhites were also greatly underrepresented.

In 1950, then, most black Louisianians were unskilled laborers, domestic workers, or small farmers. They were not business owners, professionals, clerical workers, or salespeople. They had much lower incomes than whites, in a state in which even white incomes were fairly low. Why did these socioeconomic differences exist? Discrimination in hiring is certainly part of the answer. If one had asked a white Louisianian in 1950 to explain these patterns, she or he might well have maintained that blacks were simply not sufficiently well educated to hold better jobs. Although such an answer would have failed to acknowledge the pervasive, systematic racism behind racial inequalities in employment, there would have an element of truth in this response.

Table 1.1 shows dramatic differences in education between white and

Table 1.1. Selected Economic and Educational Characteristics of White and Nonwhite Louisianians, 1950

	White	*Nonwhite*
Median per capita income	$2,674	$1,074
Percent with yearly income less than $1,000	20.2	49.2
Percent over 14 years of age unemployed	3.7	6.5
Occupational distribution (%)		
Professional, technical	10.1	3.1
Farmers and farm managers	9.1	12.7
Managers, proprietors	11.6	1.6
Clerical	13.6	1.3
Sales	8.8	1.1
Craftsmen and foremen	14.5	4.9
Operatives	15.2	14.5
Private household workers	0.5	14.9
Other service workers	6.0	12.4
Unpaid family farm laborers	1.5	4.1
Farm laborers and farm foremen	2.1	9.1
Laborers other than farm	5.5	18.7
Unreported	1.4	1.4
Percent high school graduates (over 25)	22.6	3.8
Percent college graduates (over 25)	6.2	1.2
Median school years completed (over 25)	8.8	4.6

Source: U.S. Bureau of the Census, *Census of the Population,* 1950, vol. 2, part 18, Characteristics of the Population: Louisiana.

nonwhite Louisianians. High school graduation had not yet become the norm in the state: more than 70% of whites over twenty-five years of age had not completed high school in 1950. However, fully 95% of Louisiana's nonwhite adults had not completed high school. College was even less common: only 6% of the state's whites were college graduates. A college education was rare indeed among minority group members, as only about 1% had graduated from college. Blacks had no access to Louisiana State University, Tulane University, or the state's other white institutions of higher learning. Most of them also had little access to Dillard University, Xavier University, or Southern University.

The median in years of education for whites in 1950 was just under nine years. For nonwhites, the median was less than five years. This means that half of all the nonwhite adults in Louisiana had less than a fifth-grade education. Clearly, in the years before integration, blacks in Louisiana had very little formal education.

If we take educational differences as at least a partial explanation of socioeconomic inequality in segregated Louisiana, we must then ask what produced those educational differences. This leads us to an examination of racial inequality in the schools in the years before school integration became the law of the land. We should, however, also reflect on the self-perpetuating nature of education. In their classic work, *The American Occupational Structure,* Peter Blau and Otis D. Duncan found that the education of fathers was the single greatest determinant of the education of sons.[23] As general educational levels rise, succeeding generations will finish more years of schooling than their parents did, but the children of the relatively less educated will also be less educated, compared to their own generation. Once a caste system is created, then, it tends to perpetuate itself unless a society takes conscious measures to break it down. Indeed, as we will argue throughout this book, the remnants of a caste system can even undermine the very efforts to abolish caste.

Racial Inequality in Louisiana Schools Before Integration

Inequality in educational opportunity helps to perpetuate inequality throughout a society. Table 1.2 gives some idea of the systematic denial of educational opportunity to black Louisianians in the school year 1950–51, when segregation was still the legally enforced norm. We have noted that one-teacher schools became common for blacks as Louisiana created its segregated educational system. Four years before the U.S. Supreme Court ruled that segregated education was unconstitutional, over one-third of the black schools in Louisiana were still schools with only one teacher. Only 3% of the white schools were one-teacher institutions. The greater percentage of one-teacher black schools was not due to there being fewer black students, because there was actually a greater number of black pupils per teacher. Moreover, these teachers were less likely than the white teachers to have advanced educational credentials. Only 68% of teachers in black public schools held college degrees, compared with 77% of teachers in white public schools. The former also made less money: white teachers had an average salary of $3,160 per year, while black teachers had an average salary of only $2,726 per year. While this salary was above the median income for all blacks, seen in Table 1.1 above, it was below the median income for all whites, over 70% of whom were not even high school graduates.

Louisiana's black students had fewer resources, as well as less-trained and lower-paid teachers. The state spent $147.15 on the instructional services of each white pupil, but only $95.80 on the instructional services of each black pupil. The value of school plant and equipment per pupil was over three and one-third times greater in the schools for whites. The black schools, disadvantaged in almost every measurable way, produced less than half as many graduates as a percentage of daily attendance.

These numbers are cold reflections of the frustrated dreams and ambitions of human beings. Statistics are only indicators of the failure of the segregated school system to meet the needs of Louisiana's minority population. Those who remember the system testify more vividly to this failure. One former student who attended school in Louisiana's Vermillion Parish in the 1950s recalled: "I remember not being able to use the 'white library.' Having read all of the few books in the library for blacks, I had to steal from the 'white library' and hide the books, just to have the opportunity to read new material."[24] Another black former student observed: "The main concern of the black community at the time [of the beginning of integra-

Table 1.2. Selected Statistics on Louisiana White and Black Public Schools, 1950

	White	Black
Percent of schools with only one teacher	3.3	34.1
Percent of teachers with college degrees	76.8	68.1
Average teacher salary	$3,160	$2,726
Per pupil cost of instructional services	$147.15	$95.80
Per pupil value of school plant and equipment	$577.86	$171.52
High school graduates as percent of daily attendance	4.1	1.9

Source: Public Affairs Research Council of Louisiana, *Improving Quality during School Desegregation* (Baton Rouge, Louisiana, 1969), Table 4.

tion] was equality. The black schools basically received the left overs from the white schools. The main thrust of the black community's complaints had to do with receiving current classroom materials."[25] A woman who was in her fifties when she returned to school to work on a college degree in the 1990s declared, "Kids today don't remember what it was like in the segregation days. They gave us nothing. Old books, a classroom with no fan and too many kids in it. I tell you, it was just bad."[26]

The systematic exclusion of blacks from positions of influence in the post-Reconstruction order of Louisiana society meant that minorities could not even effectively run "their" schools. A community leader in Eunice, Louisiana, remembered that "when integration first came there were no blacks on the school boards."[27] Because black teachers and administrators had been trained in the Jim Crow educational system, even those who had degrees did not necessarily have educational backgrounds equivalent to those of comparably educated whites. A white former student said of the early days of integration: "Most of the black teachers were very ill-prepared. They all came from traditionally black universities and they didn't have the same standards as white teachers."[28] A professor at one of Louisiana's historically black universities made a similar observation, allowing us to quote her on condition of anonymity: "Even today, most of the graduates of the black colleges aren't up to the same level as graduates of other schools. Back in the old days, you had people who were themselves products of disadvantaged schools struggling to do the best they could with students who came from poor homes and schools that didn't even have libraries."[29] Along similar lines, a 1969 report of the Public Affairs Research Council of Louisiana stated:

Some authorities in education in Louisiana feel that the degrees held by Negro teachers who have received their schooling in Negro public schools and colleges in this state do not represent the same level of educational achievement as the degrees held by most white teachers. They base this belief on the fact that Negro public schools have been neglected in the past and hence the quality of education provided by these schools has been inferior to that provided by many white schools. They argue that the same lower quality has necessarily characterized Negro institutions of higher learning in the state, which have had to work with the product of the Negro elementary and secondary schools.

There has been some substantiation of this belief in the experience of two large public school systems in Louisiana which have required teachers applying for employment to submit their scores on the National Teachers Examination. These systems have found that Negro applicants, with degrees usually from predominantly Negro colleges, have performed less satisfactorily as a group on the examination than white applicants, who have their degrees from predominantly white colleges.[30]

The relatively weak educational preparation of many black teachers is also indicated by statistics compiled by James Coleman during the years of struggle to integrate American schools.[31] Table 1.3 gives test scores of southern white and black teachers on a verbal competency test in the mid-1960s. At every level of experience, the scores of black teachers were substantially lower. Over 75% of the most experienced black teachers scored below the white mean. Over 80% of the least experienced black teachers scored below the mean of whites with comparable experience.

Note that a majority of whites scored above the white mean, a result of the fact that a relatively small number of low-scoring whites pulled the mean below the median, the point at which half of the whites scored lower and half of the whites scored higher. These gaps in test scores could be due to causes other than the training of black teachers in segregated black colleges. Nevertheless, all the evidence indicates that black teachers were weaker than others in measurable academic skills. Students who are taught by teachers with less academic mastery tend to show less academic mastery themselves. Therefore, a segregated school system does, logically, tend to pass on educational disadvantages.

There are many qualities that cannot be measured by test scores. The

Table 1.3. Comparison of Mean Test Scores on Verbal Competence Test Given White and Black Southern Teachers, 1965

	Black Mean	White Mean	Percent of Blacks Exceeding White Mean	Percent of Whites Exceeding White Mean
>10 years experience	18.87	23.45	23.79	65.89
5–9 years experience	19.37	23.50	26.47	64.10
<5 years experience	18.59	24.38	17.11	60.92

Source: James S. Coleman et al., *Equality of Educational Opportunity* (Washington: U.S. Office of Education, 1966).

great moral drama of the Civil Rights era attested to qualities that existed in abundance among African Americans of the South. This drama continues to be compelling today because of the deep courage and profound wisdom displayed by its actors, many of whom were black teachers and students. Nevertheless, it should not be forgotten that the Civil Rights struggle was a response to a condition of imposed limitations and deprivations. African Americans in Louisiana and other southern states were not simply deprived of political power and socioeconomic position. They were deprived of the opportunity to prepare themselves for preferred places in American society.

Louisiana emerged from Reconstruction a racially polarized state in which one group, the whites, had seized virtually all of the power. By the middle of the twentieth century, black children grew up with parents who had low incomes and low-status jobs. Half of all black adults had less than a fifth-grade education, and black high school graduates were rare. This meant that there were few role models who could communicate the skills or habits needed for upward mobility, even if the Jim Crow system were dismantled.

Black schools not only had fewer resources, but by most objective measures, they had less educationally prepared teachers. Many of these teachers may have been admirable people, capable of passing on valuable lessons to their students, but the teachers were themselves products of Louisiana's separate and unequal system of training people for participation in the state's society and economy. Even with greatly improved funding and resources, with filled libraries and new textbooks and classrooms, black students in a segregated school structure would still be systematically deprived. These students would come from families that owned few books and had little formal education. They would associate only with other students from similar backgrounds. In school, they would be taught exclusively by teachers with comparatively weak educational preparation, who were themselves products of the same educational system. The racial caste system was self-perpetuating.

Sociologist James S. Coleman, in much of his work on education, has argued that schools are not just places where people acquire skills; they are also social groups in which people shape one another's behavior, attitudes, ambitions, and perceptions. In a word, schools are cultures. In the influential report *Equality of Educational Opportunity,* Coleman and his coauthors found that the greatest influence on student academic performance was the social influence. They found that educational outcomes could be predicted best from the socioeconomic status of those around an individual.[32] Since black students tended to occupy the lowest socioeconomic positions, going to exclusively black schools in the days before integration meant going to school with the economically and educationally deprived. Even teachers, who had often overcome great obstacles to obtain their own credentials, were locked into the cycle of disadvantage. Outstanding individuals could still become great writers, thinkers, and community leaders. Ordinary people might be able to draw from their hardships a moral vision that was less obvious to the more privileged. Still, the average black student was circumscribed by the range of personal contacts and experiences.

Today, many have begun to question policies of integration. White critics maintain that forced integration denies freedom of choice. Black critics argue that it weakens black cultural traditions and racial solidarity. As we look at the efforts to integrate Louisiana schools, though, it is important to recognize the historical context of these efforts. The dream of integration was a dream of breaking down the walls of segregation that surrounded young black Louisianians on all sides and of dissolving a historically imposed caste system. If it was a troubled dream, it was also a dream made necessary by a long history of intolerable social injustice.

While the dream of integration was necessary, integration's morally and emotionally compelling character has also made it difficult to take a critical or questioning stance toward strategies and policies aimed at breaking down the barriers between black and white. Given the long heritage of stark racial repression, pointing out problems caused by the desegregation of schools often seems like taking the side of moral wrong against moral right. Our own sympathies lie entirely with the long struggle to overcome the remnants of slavery and the Jim Crow system. We also think, however, that even the noblest human endeavors can have unintended consequences, consequences that can be self-defeating if left unexamined. However, before we look more closely at those consequences, we will first examine the development of the movement to make public schools into arenas of struggle against racial injustice.

Chapter 2

The Struggle
to Desegregate the Schools

Overcoming Injustice through the Schools

In order to rectify the injustices of racial segregation and discrimination, the United States embarked on a massive social and educational experiment in the latter half of the twentieth century. This experiment involved a dedicated commitment to desegregating one of the institutions at the heart of the social and economic inequality between whites and blacks: the public school system. As noted in the previous chapter, before 1954 virtually all southern schools were racially segregated by law. However, most of the rest of the nation's schools were also racially segregated—white and black—though the separation of the races in nonsouthern schools was *mostly* de facto rather than de jure. To understand what transpired in Louisiana during the era of desegregation, it is first necessary to view school desegregation from the larger national perspective, considering the social, legal, and historical circumstances within which school racial desegregation has evolved in the United States as a whole.

In the landmark 1954 U.S. Supreme Court decision of *Brown v. Topeka Board of Education,* the high court unanimously ruled that the doctrine of "separate but equal," established by the same court in 1896, was unconstitutional. This momentous decision immediately made outlaws of every public school district in the South that had refused to allow black school children to attend white schools. Initially, however, nothing happened. Public officials in the South, from school principals to state governors, simply refused to comply with the court's decision. Therefore the court followed up the "Brown I" decision with what is called "Brown II" a year later in 1955, when it ordered southern school districts to desegregate with "all deliberate speed."

Even following the strict admonition of Brown II, nothing happened immediately, other than the mobilization of segregationist forces determined to resist desegregation at all costs. In 1956, for example, 101 southern senators and congressmen boldly affixed their signatures to a manifesto declaring that the high court itself had made an illegal declaration by ordering racial integration.[1] Any questions about southern determination to resist racial integration were put to rest in 1957. In that year, President Eisenhower was forced to activate the Arkansas National Guard to escort seven black children through an angry white mob to integrate all-white Little Rock Central High School. Moreover, the anti-integration forces in Arkansas were lead by none other than the state's highest elected public official, Governor Orval Faubus. The desegregation of the public schools of New Orleans, the first district in Louisiana to desegregate, was no less dramatic, as we will see in the next chapter. The city attracted national and international attention in 1961 when Louisiana governor Jimmie Davis threatened to close down the entire system rather than allow one black student to enter an all-white school. For months most whites boycotted the Crescent City's public schools, and some organized into groups like the notorious "cheerleaders," who taunted black elementary school children who dared enter white schools with chants like "Two, four, six, eight, we don't want to integrate!"[2]

One of the most extreme examples of white defiance of orders to desegregate occurred in Prince Edward County, Virginia, in 1959. Rather than integrate their schools, the white county leaders did more than just threaten to close down all of the county's schools. They actually carried through on their threat and shut down all schools—black and white—for five years. Whites who could afford it sent their children to the newly formed (and still in existence) Prince Edward Academy—complete with swimming pool. Some who could not afford tuition educated their children in basements, but the majority of both white and black children simply were not educated at all. When the schools were forced to reopen in 1964, almost no whites attended, and the school system was so neglected by the all-white school board that even the 1,700 blacks who did attend eventually walked out because of the deplorable conditions. When Ronald Perry was appointed superintendent of Prince Edward County Schools by the courts in 1969 to repair the damage caused by years of little or no county public education, he was constantly harassed by local whites, and his wife was continually threatened with death and bodily injury. Perry estimates that even today, most middle class whites still attend the local segregationist academy.[3]

By the mid-1960s, the first significant integration of southern schools began to take place at last. However, it was not as a result of the good-will of southern whites that black students were finally admitted to white schools. Their admission was an unexpected side-effect of the 1964 Civil Rights Amendment, which stated that "No person in the United States shall, on the ground of race, color, or national origin, be excluded from participation in, be denied the benefits of, or be subjected to discrimination under any program or activity receiving *Federal financial assistance*" (emphasis added).

Federal authorities soon realized that they could legally withhold funds from schools and school systems that discriminated based on race. Withholding federal monies provided tremendous leverage to federal authorities overseeing desegregation efforts. This was especially true in light of the passage of the Elementary and Secondary Education Act (ESEA) of 1965. The ESEA legislation provided billions of federal dollars to schools and school districts nationwide through new initiatives such as Head Start, the free and reduced lunch program, and other Title I programs for disadvantaged students. Few schools or school systems were able to resist the lure of so much money, even if it meant foregoing segregated educational facilities.

Thus, from the mid through late 1960s, most de jure school segregation in the South came to an end as schoolhouse doors across the former Confederacy opened to black students for the first time. However, this did not mean that school populations were suddenly racially balanced to reflect the communities within which they were located. This first phase of school integration is often referred to as "freedom of choice" or "voluntary integration," since blacks and whites were theoretically "free" to attend the other race's schools if they so desired. If not allowing complete freedom to choose schools, other districts had "majority to minority" desegregation policies, allowing any student in a school in which his or her race was in the majority to transfer to a school in which that race was in the minority. Thus, although blacks and whites were in theory free to attend racially integrated schools, the overwhelming majority of whites chose to continue attending mostly white or all-white schools, while most blacks continued attending either mostly black or all-black schools. One reason for the continued de facto segregation of southern school systems in the 1960s and the perceived need to forcibly integrate was a tremendous social pressure in white communities to avoid black schools. It was also true, though, that many blacks were not willing to attend all-white schools (as many as 79% according to one poll).[4] Indeed, by the mid-1960s, fully 99% of all American black students were still in segregated schools.[5]

At first, courts went along with the freedom of choice plans, as they seemed reasonable responses to ending de jure segregation. However, when it became obvious that meaningful integration was not going to take place voluntarily, the courts began to change their tactics. In the celebrated *Green v. County School Board* case of 1968, the U.S. Supreme Court ruled that the New Kent County, Virginia, school board's freedom of choice plan was unconstitutional. The court noted that not one single white had volunteered to attend the all-black county school, thus maintaining a "dual-race" system. The court ordered the school board to come up with a plan, such as geographic zoning, that would realistically lead to integrated district schools. Following *Green,* the courts increasingly ruled against freedom of choice plans, and began to favor geographic zoning without reference to neighborhood racial concentrations, as a more forceful approach to school racial integration.

It became increasingly common throughout the late 1960s and into the early 1970s for districts to consolidate black and white schools—which often meant closing black schools—and to assign students to schools based on where they lived (geographic zoning). However, this tactic proved almost as troublesome as the previous freedom of choice plans, because blacks and whites tended to live in segregated neighborhoods. Thus school zones and the schools within them tended to be either predominantly white or predominantly black. The fact remained that blacks tended to be much poorer than whites, and therefore, even if they wanted to move, many blacks could often not afford homes in the often wealthier all-white school districts.

The stage was therefore set in the early 1970s for courts to enter their period of maximum intrusiveness into school desegregation matters. Drastic, and in some cases quite draconian, attempts were made not only to ensure the abstract right to attend a school without regard to race, but to ensure that schools *actually* enrolled both white and black students. Essentially two proactive methods of school integration were used, often referred to as the "command and control approaches."[6] The method that received the most public attention was busing: attempting to achieve racial balance by moving students to districts where members of other races were. The rationale behind busing developed primarily in the early 1970s, when desegregation came to be seen as a matter of increasing the actual numbers of blacks in schools, jobs, and neighborhoods, and not simply as a matter of ending legal discrimination. In the 1971 court case *Swann v. Charlotte-Mecklenburg,* the Supreme Court recognized that de facto segregation in schools was linked to residential segregation, since, as already noted, children attended schools in the areas in which they lived.[7] The court ruled that the practice of busing students in order to achieve desegregation was a legitimate remedy. The Swann case was, in a sense, the high water mark in American school desegregation legislation.

Not long after the highest court in the land sanctioned busing as a desegregation tool, it also made another extremely important ruling in the area of school desegregation, in effect extending the remedy of busing to systems outside the South. For the first time, the Supreme Court turned its attention northward, where racial segregation was, according to the court, often every bit a prolific as it was in the South. In the historic 1973 Supreme Court case of *Keyes v. School District No. 1, Denver,* the court found that Denver, Colorado, officials had intentionally been maintaining a dual school system, segregated by race. The Colorado state capital was ordered by the court to desegregate its public school system. Thus began the slow, painful process of school desegregation outside of the South, from California to Massachusetts.

Throughout the1970s, many districts, North, South, East, and West, embarked on massive and ambitious busing programs aimed at distributing white students in black schools and vice versa. Bus ridership was up, and school systems were spending larger and larger amounts of money to operate, maintain, and expand their bus fleets. Some students spent as much as three hours a day riding to and from schools on the other side of their districts, rather than walking to neighborhood schools across the street from their homes. For reasons such as these, busing to desegregate schools sparked vehement protests across the country. For the first time, it was not the intransigence of the South that attracted nationwide attention, but rather the violent demonstrations in northern cities against forced integration that riveted Americans to their television sets in the early and mid-1970s. In Boston, the hotbed of abolition prior to the Civil War, white parents and their children overturned and burned buses destined to carry black children to all-white South Boston ("Southie") schools. Other communities outside the Deep South ordered by the courts to bus as a means of forcibly integrating students included Seattle, Tulsa, Oklahoma City, Louisville, Austin, Dallas, Dayton, San Francisco, Los Angeles, Pontiac, and Indianapolis.[8] In both North and South, busing became a common means of seeking racial balances in schools. Though the response was not quite as violent as in Boston, busing was not well received in Louisiana schools, particularly in places like Baton Rouge, an issue we subsequently address in more detail.

Another method of active integration aimed at reducing the effects of residential segregation was school redistricting. This time, however, redistricting was no longer color blind, but rather involved redrawing school lines or gerrymandering school districts to include a mixture of residences from both races. In some ways, school busing was the right hand of redistricting, since some gerrymandered districts could be quite large, requiring that students be transported long distances to their new schools. Yet another related court-sanctioned method was "pairing" or "clustering" schools and distributing students among them with the goal of achieving racial balance.[9] This method was also utilized in Louisiana schools in both New Orleans and Baton Rouge and, like redistricting, often required transporting students long distances as well.

Limits to Busing

It soon became evident that drastic efforts to ensure that black and white students attended the same schools often failed. Indeed, they may well have backfired. Many parents, white and black, simply refused to enroll their children in majority-black schools, which were often impoverished. To those who had the financial means, there were essentially two options. One was to withdraw from the public schools altogether, as those staunch segregationists of the early 1960s had done. A second, and more popular option, was to flee the school district for another district that contained a smaller black population. In some cases, school districts or entire municipalities intentionally broke away from larger, integrated districts. There is some debate about whether the suburbanization process was taking place anyway and was not primarily the result of whites and middle class blacks fleeing urban school districts (we address this momentarily). However, the fact remains that many urban districts throughout the 1970s grew increasingly poor and black, whereas their suburbs grew increasingly prosperous and white. The federal courts were well aware of this trend and in several instances intervened to merge predominantly white and black school districts, which they contended developed as a result of deliberate efforts by residents to avoid desegregation.

However, the Supreme Court finally drew the line in the case of *Milliken v. Bradley* (1974). This case dealt with the Detroit, Michigan, school district, which was already majority black by 1970. Both the lower federal courts and the court of appeals ruled that it was impossible to integrate Detroit's schools without taking into account the surrounding metropolitan area, which was majority white. Therefore, they ordered the Detroit district merged with the fifty-four predominantly white districts surrounding the city, in effect creating a "super district." On appeal, however, the U.S. Supreme Court ruled that since there was no evidence or legacy of intentional de jure segregation in the governmental actions creating the surrounding white districts, there was no obligation to dissolve those districts. The integrity of their boundaries was to remain inviolate. In a sense, the Milliken case represented the first important limit on school desegregation established by the high court. It was the proverbial line in the sand over which zealous courts and prosecutors were not to transgress. From 1974 on, school desegregation efforts were limited to within school districts. All the while, suburban districts boomed, and in most cases remained more affluent—and white.

Unitary Systems

For many districts diligently employing every remedy at their disposal to satisfy court desegregation orders, the inevitable question eventually arose, "When are we integrated and freed from court supervision?" In *Green,* the Supreme Court suggested that school systems had achieved this goal when discrimination had completely vanished. In *Swann,* the high court elaborated a bit more by adding that once desegregation was achieved, school systems would be freed from judicial oversight and the continual racial balancing act, provided that any subsequent racial imbalances in schools were purely demographic—and not discriminatory—in nature.

Though there had been some activity in district and appellate courts on this issue, the first important Supreme Court decision on unitary status was not handed down until 1991. In the case of *Dowell v. Oklahoma City,* the high court overturned a lower court's ruling and declared that the Oklahoma City school system was at last "unitary." The court disagreed with the appellate court ruling that stated a district could be under court-ordered desegregation for an "indefinite future" and declared that once a system had achieved unitary status, it no longer needed court approval for student assignment policies (provided it did not violate the Fourteenth Amendment equal protection clause). Furthermore, the Supreme Court delineated more clearly than in the earlier *Swann* decision those conditions that school systems must meet prior to being granted unitary status. It stipulated that these conditions were (1) the demonstration of good faith with the consent decree from the beginning and (2) the elimination of all traces of past discrimination to the fullest "extent practicable." Thus, Oklahoma City was freed from a mandatory busing policy and allowed to return to a neighborhood school concept.

The second major Supreme Court decision with regard to unitary status was handed down a year later in the 1992 case of *Freeman v. Pitts.* This case involved the large Atlanta suburban district of DeKalb County. The school district filed for unitary status in 1988, which a district court declared had been achieved in the areas of student assignment, transportation, facilities, and extracurricular activities. The district court maintained, however, that the DeKalb County schools needed to do more work in the area of teacher and principal assignment before it could be declared unitary in these two areas. An appellate court overturned the lower court's decision, saying that the school district must be unitary in all six areas before it could be granted any measure of unitary status. The U.S. Supreme Court overturned the court of appeals ruling, stating that a district could be declared unitary on a piecemeal basis. Moreover, it reiterated its position in the earlier *Swann* decision that a school district could not be held responsible for racial imbalances caused by demographic factors beyond a school board's control.

The Challenge to Forcible Desegregation

At the end of the twentieth and beginning of the twenty-first century, school desegregation continued to be a major political and legal goal. Nevertheless, serious challenges to this goal began to appear. According to Gary Orfield, one of the nation's foremost authorities on school desegregation, the limitations on desegregation that began with judicial limitations on busing in 1974 turned into the actual dismantling of desegregation by the 1990s. In Orfield's view, the emergence of the concept of unitary status early in that decade expressed a philosophical shift away from the principles of *Brown v. Board of Education.*[10]

With many school districts moving away from busing, the school district most closely associated with the beginning of the practice appeared once again on center stage. In September of 1999, U.S. District Judge Robert Potter ruled that the Charlotte-Mecklenburg system had achieved desegregation, and he decreed that race could no longer be considered in school assignments.[11] This meant that not only busing, but virtually all desegregation strategies would henceforth be abandoned in Charlotte-Mecklenburg. This was in spite of the fact that, as the Charlotte League of Women Voters concluded in a study of schools from 1991 to 1993, "the system appears to be continuing to drift toward blacker and whiter schools. Across the three-year period, with few exceptions, the whitest schools got whiter and the blackest schools got blacker, whether they were elementary, middle or high schools."[12]

The growing challenge to desegregation was a result of the increasing unpopularity of many desegregation policies, particularly among the nation's white population. Busing may have been a particularly objectionable practice for many, but other practices such as redistricting were also widely opposed. In this book we will argue that opposition to desegregation was less a consequence of unpopular strategies than it was a consequence of a fundamental contradiction in school desegregation itself. The rationale for mandatory, coercive desegregation in the schools was the existence of racial inequality outside of the schools. However, the continuing existence of racial inequality in the larger American society made it in the interest of the relatively advantaged to avoid desegregation policies when in force and to abandon these policies as soon as the law would allow. A closer examination of the reasoning behind school desegregation may help to clarify this point.

Why School Desegregation?

Why did the movement to desegregate schools continue to be such a prominent part of the struggle against racial inequality? Why couldn't systems simply redistribute resources in order to equalize the gross disparity that undeniably existed between predominantly white and predominantly black schools? In the days prior to desegregation, the education of blacks was not only separate but vastly unequal in almost every respect. However, with the massive inflow of federal monies beginning in the mid-1960s, the gross resource inequities between white and black schools diminished markedly. In the minds of many experts, it was not the resource disparity between white and black schools that provided the strongest rationale for school integration, but rather the philosophical justification provided by one of the most influential educational studies in the twentieth century, *Equality of Educational Opportunity,* published by James Coleman and his associates in 1966. Coleman et al. looked at what influenced educational outcomes. Their research indicated that the most readily measurable educational outcome—school achievement—was actually least influenced by resources, was only somewhat influenced by teacher qualifications and experience, but was substantially affected by family socioeconomic status. Further, Coleman found that school achievement was affected by the socioeconomic levels of schoolmates and not just by students' own backgrounds. Coleman and his coauthors contended that students brought social resources from families to schools, where those resources were pooled and magnified. These social resources included familiarity with middle class norms, reading habits, and high educational expectations.[13]

Thus it was widely agreed that segregated minority schools, even those with the best physical resources and the best-trained teachers, could not completely overcome the damaging socioeconomic consequences of isolation from the majority population. Active desegregation was therefore seen as redistributive in character—a means not just of equalizing schools, but of redistributing the social resources students brought from their homes to the schools.[14] Following this logic, James Coleman initially became one of the original proponents of busing and other forms of active desegregation.

Coleman's social theory is really an elaborated version of the earlier "harm and benefit" thesis, first developed in the 1930s, which stated that black students are harmed by social isolation in predominantly black schools but would benefit from attending racially integrated schools.[15] A related "contact theory" postulated that an additional benefit of interaction between blacks and whites in school would be a reduction in racial prejudice in both races and raised self-esteem among blacks. Both theories were presented to and used by the Supreme Court in arriving at its historic 1954 ruling.

The research findings either supporting or critical of the "harm and benefit" and "contact theory" positions are mixed, with no real consensus. While there are many studies showing that blacks in predominantly white schools show some improvement academically over blacks in predominantly black schools, there are many others that find few or no benefits associated with integrated education. The findings regarding reduced racial prejudice among blacks and whites and increased self-esteem among blacks in integrated schools are even less clear.[16] We will deal at greater length with the practical academic consequences of shifting racial compositions in schools in Chapter 7. For the present, though, we turn to a related issue, the possible demographic consequences of aggressive desegregation.

White Flight

By the mid-1970s, James Coleman underwent an intellectual crisis and changed his mind on the issue of busing. He did not change his position on the theoretical virtues and benefits of integrated schools for blacks. Rather, he argued that though it had been a worthwhile experiment, forced integration had had other unfortunate consequences.[17] Chief among these negative consequences, he argued, was "white flight" from the schools and an increasing white exodus from urban areas to suburban areas. Thus, he argued that busing was counterproductive, causing the very problem it was supposed to be rectifying: resegregation.

Busing was a highly controversial strategy, and Coleman attracted media attention when he came out publicly against this remedy to segregation in 1975. He argued that white parents would not support a policy they did not see as being in the interest of their own children and that busing and other efforts at desegregation were exacerbating white flight out of urban school districts, where most black students were located, and out of public schools into private schools.[18]

Coleman's change of heart set off a major debate. Thomas F. Pettigrew and Robert L. Green responded to Coleman's opposition to forcible desegregation with a detailed critique of the white flight thesis. Drawing on four studies of white flight, Pettigrew and Green came up with six generalizations that seemed to contradict Coleman's argument that whites would leave urban public schools in response to forcible integration. First, Pettigrew and Green pointed out that there had been a long-term trend toward the movement of whites to suburbs and blacks to central cities and that the segregation of residential areas and school districts was not necessarily a consequence of school desegregation policies. Second, they observed that their studies indicated little or no effect of desegregation on small and medium-sized cities. Third, they maintained that desegregation had little effect on white flight in metropolitan school districts. Fourth, they argued that court-ordered desegregation did not promote white flight any more than desegregation not ordered by courts. Fifth, Pettigrew and Green held that declines in both black and white enrollment in public schools were related to the proportion of the school system that is black. Sixth, although school desegregation may hasten a white exodus from the largest nonmetropolitan school districts in the first year of the process, this exodus may cease in later years.[19]

Flight to Nonpublic Schools

Despite the arguments against Coleman, the weight of empirical research seemed increasingly to justify his white flight thesis more than Pettigrew and Green's stance against white flight. One of the problems with the critique offered by Pettigrew and Green was their failure to address, aside from a brief footnote, the issue of white movement to nonpublic schools.[20] If white students do not disappear from a school district but are found in greater proportions in religious or private schools than in public schools, this cannot be attributed to the suburban settlement of whites and the urban settlement of blacks. Further, Coleman did indeed argue that strategies for desegregation were likely to provoke less opposition under some circumstances than under others. Parents were much less likely to object strongly to busing, for example, when their children were being bused to schools with schoolmates from high socioeconomic levels than when their children were being bused to schools in which underprivileged children predominate.[21]

The frequent success of gifted magnet programs, for example, is arguably due to white parents' ready and even eager willingness to send their children to largely minority inner-city schools—if their children will then be placed in accelerated programs. In other words, parents objected less to any specific desegregation policy or means of achieving desegregation than to school placements resulting from desegregation that were disadvantageous to their children.

There was no reason to expect, then, that white parents would flee from the court-ordered placement of their children in low-income, minority-dominated schools any more than they would flee from placement of children in such schools resulting from demographic shifts or voluntary desegregation by school boards. It would still be legitimate, though, to see court-ordered desegregation as a stimulus for white flight.

Although both white and black school populations may decline as the proportion of the school system that is black increases, by definition the decline in the white population that decreases is much greater. This phenomenon, too, can be seen as entirely consistent with the white flight thesis: as whites leave a school system, taking their social and financial assets with them, the school system becomes less attractive to black families who can also afford to place their children elsewhere.

A final issue regarding Pettigrew and Green's critique of Coleman deals with diminishing white flight in later years of desegregation. In fact, once a school system has become minority dominant, there may be few white students left to flee. This was the case in Pasadena, California; Detroit, Michigan; and as we subsequently investigate in some detail, in New Orleans. Thus white movement out of a desegregating system may naturally decline over time to a point where only increases in the white student population may be possible.

The debate over desegregation and white flight continued long after the initial flurry over Coleman's work. Sociologist David Armor in the 1980s advised against busing precisely because his studies indicated that this means of desegregation would hasten white flight.[22] A study conducted by Armor for the school board of Norfolk, Virginia, helped to convince that city's school board to turn away from busing.[23]

Armor predicted that ending white flight would lead to white return to Norfolk schools. Leslie G. Carr and Donald J. Zeigler denied that this return had in fact occurred,[24] a denial in turn rejected by Armor. Despite the controversy over the consequences of ending busing, Armor noted that Carr and Zeigler did not challenge his chief assertion, that forcible desegregation through busing causes white flight.[25] Indeed, Carr and Zeigler did recognize that a large number of studies have found that desegregation plans led to losses in white enrollment.[26] More recently, our own work shows a very strong correlation between the desegregation of Louisiana's two largest urban districts and white flight to urban nonpublic schools and surrounding majority-white suburban school districts.[27]

Almost all researchers have noted the difficulty of distinguishing between white flight as a consequence of desegregation and white movement out of urban areas as a result of the demographic factors identified by Pettigrew and Green early in the debate. Lauren E. McDonald argued in 1997 that the movement of white students out of Boston public schools was largely a product of demographic shifts rather than desegregation efforts.[28] However, Christine H. Rossell, one of the foremost authorities on school desegregation in general and on Boston schools in particular, identified white flight from desegregating schools as a major factor, observing that "fifty percent of the white students who are reassigned to those schools [the desegregating schools] will not show up."[29]

White flight, into public schools outside of school districts with large numbers of minority students or into nonpublic schools, was a clear expression of the potential for self-defeat frequently built into efforts at desegregation. In 1998, when U.S. District Judge Peter J. Messitte ordered an end to busing in Maryland's Prince George's County, public officials declared that the practice had long since become pointless. "When busing started in 1973, what you basically saw was busloads of white and black kids passing each other," observed the school district's transportation director. "Now you see only black kids passing each other. They're going from one predominantly black neighborhood to a school in another predominantly black neighborhood."[30]

So What?

Lauren McDonald raises a fundamental question about declines in white enrollment, although he does so in terms that seem intemperate and intellectually intolerant to us. McDonald voices the "so what" issue when he declares that claims that school districts suffer from a loss of white students are "racist and prejudicial at best."[31] Why should white students be so valuable to a school system that school officials would need to worry about their leaving? The answer to this question returns us to James Coleman's original work on school achievement, and it may offer some answers to the question of why white flight occurs.

Coleman had initially argued that integration is advisable because students are influenced by other students. A substantial body of literature supports Coleman's view that educational outcomes are not produced solely on campuses; they are also heavily influenced by the backgrounds that students bring with them to school.[32] Moreover, researchers have found that students in schools with large black student populations tend to show lower levels of achievement than students in other schools.[33] The reasoning behind these empirical findings is fairly clear: black students in American schools show substantially lower levels of achievement than white students do.[34] The performance of students is affected by the performance of those around them. Therefore, desegregation may indeed be a realistic threat to student performance when desegregation will greatly increase the minority population in a school. White flight may in part, then, be a rational response of parents pursuing the best interests of their own children.[35] To use Coleman's words, "Families use whatever resources they can to get a good education for their children."[36]

Rational Self-Interest

The dynamic of white flight suggested here indicates that researchers and policy analysts may have concentrated too much on opposition to specific means of desegregation, such as busing, and overlooked the fact that the root opposition may be to the consequences of radical desegregation by any means. While, admittedly, sitting on a bus or attending a school out of one's neighborhood may be inconvenient, it is a relatively minor inconvenience. Indeed, as already mentioned, parents will often choose to have their children take buses away from their own neighborhoods to gain access to magnet programs or other special educational benefits. By way of example, one such program for dyslexic children offered at only one Baton Rouge school was so popular with white parents that demand for this program temporarily helped stem white flight from the system.[37]

As uncomfortable as it is, we perhaps need to consider the possibility that middle and upper class "flight"—both white and black—from public

schools may be less a response to the coercion of court-ordered desegregation, or to any specific desegregation strategies such as busing, than it is a
response to the influx of black students from relatively disadvantaged family socioeconomic backgrounds into formerly middle class schools. Parents, it seems, are conscious of a fact that social science has empirically
documented: the peer environment of children has tremendous developmen-
tal influence over many areas of children's lives, including academics.

Gary Orfield, a champion of desegregation, unintentionally provides insight into one of the reasons middle class parents attempt to avoid schools
with large percentages of minority students and, despite a growing black
middle class, there is all too often a strong correlation at the school level
between "middle class" and "white." Orfield reports that "national data
show that most segregated African American and Latino schools are dominated by poor children but . . . 96 percent of white schools have middle class
majorities." Further, Orfield identifies the problems that plague minority-
dominated schools: "low levels of competition and expectation, less qualified teachers who leave as soon as they get seniority, deteriorated schools
in dangerous neighborhoods, more limited curricula, peer pressure against
academic achievement and supportive of crime and substance abuse, high
levels of teen pregnancy, few connections with colleges and employers
who can assist students, little serious academic preparation for college, and
powerless parents who themselves failed in school and do not know how to
evaluate or change schools."[38]

Many of these problems are results of failures of schools to provide
equal educations. Most, however, are results of the influence of student
background on the school environment. High teen pregnancy levels
and peer cultures opposed to achievement are not consequences of school
policies or resources but of the social backgrounds that students bring to
schools. It is hard to keep teachers in schools dominated by an oppositional
culture, so teachers often leave (following their own rational self-interest)
as soon as they have acquired sufficient seniority and experience.

The answer of desegregation to these problems has been essentially
a matter of redistributive justice. By placing minority students in white
schools, it is hoped that they will have access to the social resources of the
majority. There is, though, another perspective. The parents of the 96% of
white schools that have middle class majorities do not have a vested interest in having their children attend schools dominated by minorities. Such

problems as high teen pregnancy levels and peer cultures opposed to academics are situations these parents generally want to avoid.

As we look at how rational self-interest can shape the decisions of parents and lead to white flight, we are not denying the existence of racial prejudice. We are also not suggesting that parents who avoid schools with large numbers of minority group members are necessarily making the correct moral judgement. But moral judgements are often not easy or obvious. Do parents have a greater ethical obligation to make a possible contribution to a more egalitarian society or to promote the opportunities and well-being of their own children? Our experience has been that parents almost universally choose the second option, even when their own conscious beliefs and values would otherwise lead them to the first.

In the following chapters, we take a critical look at Louisiana's school integration experiment. First, using almost thirty-five years of public and nonpublic school population data, we focus on the shifting student racial compositions of three urban and suburban school districts, correlating demographic trends with the implementation of desegregation policy. Without overlooking the uniqueness of the three school districts examined, we argue that they represent three stages through which the effort to desegregate schools tends to lead to the segregation of entire school districts. After looking in depth at these three districts, we take a briefer look at this process around the state. Then, we analyze statewide school academic achievement levels in terms of individual, school, and district-level racial and socioeconomic determinants. Finally, we evaluate Louisiana's desegregation experiment in light of our empirical findings and offer a rational self-interest explanation for the often disappointing results. We conclude with suggestions for long-overdue policy revisions. Though our suggested remedies may be controversial, they may provide a way to help save public education not only in Louisiana, but in other areas of the United States where school desegregation is—and will continue to be—a troubled dream.

Chapter 3

New Orleans

The Beginning and the End of a Process

A few statistics regarding the demographics of New Orleans can help us understand the school situation there at the end of the twentieth century. The city of New Orleans is identical with the parish (county) of Orleans, and with the school district of Orleans. It is bounded on the south and west by Jefferson Parish, on the north just across Lake Pontchartrain by St. Tammany Parish, and on the east by St. Bernard Parish. All of these surrounding parishes are also school districts, and they form a suburban ring around New Orleans (see Figure 3.1).

In 1990, of the 496,938 people in New Orleans, 173,305 (35%) were white and 308,364 (62%) were black.[1] There were 41,222 white family households and 74,955 black family households. Of the white households, 32,546 were married-couple family households, 11,696 of which contained children, and 6,468 were families headed by single females, 2,381 of which contained children. There were 38,851 white nonfamily households. Thus nearly half (48%) of the white households were not families but single individuals, unmarried people living in the same quarters, or individuals in some other living arrangement. Relatively few white households contained children: children were in only 15% of all white households and in only 28% of white families. The overwhelming majority of white families were married-couple families (79%). Only 6% of the white families in the parish and school district were female-headed families with minor children. Over three-quarters (78%) of white children lived in families with two parents present in 1990.

Black households in New Orleans contrasted sharply with those of whites. Of the 103,234 black households, 73% were families. The 31,999 black married-couple families made up only 31% of all black households and less than half (43%) of black families. Thus, a majority of black families in New Orleans were single-parent families, with single-parent families headed by women heavily predominating, since 51% of all black family households were single-parent, female-headed families. While a minority of white families contained minor children, 56% of black households included children under eighteen. These children were most likely to live in single-parent homes: 61% of the black households with minor children were headed by single parents, and 57% of black households with minor children were headed by women. Because single-parent black households tend to have more children than married-couple households, the overwhelming majority (71%) of black New Orleanians under eighteen lived in one-parent families at the time of the 1990 census.

Family structure is an issue that will come up repeatedly in our discussion of the desegregation of schools. Not only does it appear to make a difference whether children come from single-parent homes or two-parent homes, it also appears to make a difference whether they come from homes with only one parent as a consequence of divorce or as a consequence of birth out of wedlock. Here again, we see vast racial differences. According to the 1990 U.S. Census, 51% of the children that had been born to black

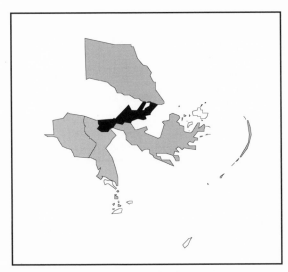

Figure 3.1. Orleans School District and Surrounding White Flight Districts

women aged fifteen to thirty-four in New Orleans were to women who had never been married by the time of the census. Since some women married after giving birth, this is a conservative estimate of out-of-wedlock births. However, it does make it clear that a majority of school-age black children in New Orleans were born to unmarried women and lived in single-parent homes. By contrast, only 6% of the children born to white women aged fifteen to thirty-four in New Orleans were to women who had never been married by the time of the census.[2] It is evident that black and white children in this city found themselves in vastly different family circumstances.

They also found themselves in vastly different economic circumstances. Among the white households, 37,054, or 28%, had incomes below $15,000 per year. This may seem like a large percentage of low-income white households, but it should be kept in mind that almost half were nonfamily households, and most did not contain children. Among the black households, 56,265, or 55%, had incomes below $15,000 per year. Thus, most black households were low-income households. Many were very low-income. Over one-fourth of the black households in the parish (26%) had household incomes below $5,000 per year, compared with only 8% of white households.

There were 18,236 white children of school age (aged five through seventeen years) living in New Orleans and 75,513 black children of school age. Thus 80% of the school-age children in New Orleans were black. As we will see below, though, well over 90% of the city's public school children were black. A clear majority of the black school-age children (40,461, or 54%) were living below the poverty level, while a relatively small percentage of the white school-age children (1,927, or 11%) were living below the poverty level.

Members of the two races differed in educational background as well as family structure and economic standing. Among whites aged twenty-five or older in New Orleans, 37% had at least a bachelor's degree, and 16% held graduate or professional degrees. Only 19% of the whites in the city/parish had not finished high school, and under 10% had less than a ninth-grade education. Among black New Orleanians, 12% had at least a bachelor's degree, and only 4% held graduate or professional degrees. About 42% of black adults had not finished high school, and 16% had finished less than ninth grade.

New Orleans, then, was still a city of enormous socioeconomic disparities along racial lines a quarter of a century after the beginning of the Civil Rights movement. Over 40% of black adults did not have high school educations and therefore possessed limited educational experience to pass on to their children. Most black households were in extremely low-income categories. Most black children lived in families below the poverty line and in single-parent families. This does not mean, of course, that there were no middle class black families. There were black college graduates and professionals in the city. Almost 10% of black households had yearly incomes over $50,000, and just over 1% had yearly incomes over $75,000. At the individual level, then, equating being black with being socioeconomically disadvantaged would be engaging in unfair and unjustifiable stereotyping. At the aggregate level, though, it is entirely legitimate and reasonable to assume that any large group of black children in New Orleans will be heavily made up of children from poor, single-parent families, headed by parents with relatively low levels of formal education. Any parent who wants to avoid placing a child in a school in which children from socially and economically disadvantaged children predominate, then, would quite reasonably avoid schools in New Orleans with large percentages of black children. Given the city's demographics, that essentially means that concerned parents would avoid any New Orleans public school containing anything like a representative sample of the city's population. Our investigation of New Orleans schools has led us to conclude that this is precisely what has happened over the period since initial efforts to desegregate the school system. In order to understand how it has happened, we should look back first at the history of desegregation in New Orleans.

The Desegregation of New Orleans Schools

New Orleans was the first parish in Louisiana to begin school desegregation. With the end of World War II, black Americans, many of whom had risked their lives fighting for the United States, began to demand an end to the Jim Crow system of racial oppression. In New Orleans, one of the earliest expressions of the struggle for equal rights appeared in 1945, when a group of black parents in the city requested that the National Association for the Advancement of Colored People (NAACP) file suit to obtain educational facilities for blacks equal to those provided to whites. Three years later, the NAACP filed such a suit. NAACP leader Daniel Byrd warned the

New Orleans School Board in August of 1949 that if black citizens did not receive schools and resources comparable to those of whites, white schools would be constitutionally compelled to accept black students.[3]

One of the most active and able lawyers of the NAACP was Alexander Pierre Tureaud. Tureaud was a scion of Louisiana's old mixed-race elite that had enjoyed privilege and prestige before the Civil War and that had played a prominent part in governing the state during Reconstruction.[4] Tureaud, who became one of the greatest heroes of Louisiana's Civil Rights movement, filed suit on behalf of Earl Benjamin Bush and other black students on November 5, 1952. Bush's father, Oliver Bush, was president of the Macarty Parent Teacher Association. Macarty Elementary School was one of the most overcrowded and dilapidated black schools in the city. Frustrated by the school board's continued negligence, Oliver Bush and other parents sought to have their children admitted to a white school.[5]

Federal Judge J. Skelly Wright gave his decision in 1956. New Orleans public schools formerly reserved for whites were required to admit black students who lived within the schools' residential boundaries. Opposition to this change was strong, and the New Orleans school board appealed Wright's decision. It was not until 1960, eight years after it was initially filed, that the *Bush v. Orleans Parish School Board* case was resolved and New Orleans' segregated school system was declared unconstitutional.

Initial efforts to integrate New Orleans' public schools met with loud and nationally publicized opposition.[6] Lloyd Rittiner, elected president of the Orleans Parish school board in 1959, sent out a short opinion poll to parents of every child in the public school system. Rittiner asked parents to indicate whether they would rather keep schools open with a small degree of integration or close down the schools instead of accepting any integration at all. The overwhelming majority of white parents (82%) said they would prefer to shut the schools down, and almost all black parents (95%) said that they would prefer to accept some integration. Governor James Houston "Jimmie" Davis did, in fact, attempt to close down the Orleans Parish public school system rather than allow integration.[7]

Although the racial integration of any New Orleans school would have been protested, the school board probably exacerbated the problem by deciding that two relatively low-income white schools would be the first to admit black students in November 1960. William Frantz Elementary and McDonogh 19 Elementary were both located in New Orleans' Ninth Ward, site of black and white housing projects and home to some of the poorest white people in the city. For many of the whites, not being black was one of the few sources of a sense of social self-worth.[8]

The first black student to arrive at William Frantz, six-year-old Ruby Bridges, was met by mobs of white women screaming racial epithets. At McDonogh 19, three other small girls found other angry protestors. New Orleans Police Chief Joseph Giarusso had to send reinforcements to hold back the white crowds.[9] Despite these displays of racism, the wall of separation between black and white in the schools had begun to break down. The following school year, 1961–62, four other New Orleans elementary schools admitted black students, without the horrific scenes that had occurred at William Frantz and McDonogh 19 the year before.

Judge Wright, disturbed by the slow pace of desegregation, in 1962 issued an order that in the 1962–63 school year all elementary school children should attend either the formerly all-black school or the formerly all-white school nearest their homes. In an even more controversial move, Judge Wright forbade the issuing of transfers based on race, making it impossible for white students to transfer from a desegregated school to another one. Wright's appointment as a judge of the Court of Appeals for the District of Columbia and his replacement by Judge Frank B. Ellis slowed the pace of integration briefly, but Ellis proved to be as adamant in enforcing constitutional law as Wright had been. In 1965, Ellis laid out a plan for the desegregation of the schools of Orleans Parish. He ordered the school district to create single-school districts without regard to race on a year-by-year basis for succeeding grades. Schools would be desegregated through the fifth grade in the 1965–66 school year, through the seventh grade in 1966–67, through the ninth grade in 1967–68, through the eleventh grade in 1968–69, and through the twelfth grade by 1969–70.[10] Thus the schools of Orleans Parish would be completely desegregated by the 1970s.

Electoral politics, as well as the judiciary, contributed to remaking the city's educational scene. The Civil Rights movement had ensured the right of black Americans to vote, a right that had been denied many black Louisianians at the end of the nineteenth century. The large black population of New Orleans was in a position to exercise its power at the voting booths. In 1968, even before the schools were completely desegregated, New Orleans elected its first black member of the Orleans Parish school board.

Active desegregation in the *Swann v. Charlotte-Mecklenburg* era, for the most part, proceeded comparatively smoothly and gradually in Orleans Parish. It essentially followed a school-by-school or area-by-area progression, often with the express intention of avoiding direct court intervention. Some tension did accompany this progression. In the 1971–72 school year, for example, there were a number of well-publicized fights between black and white students at Nicholls and Abramson Senior High Schools, and in response, the Orleans Parish school board recommended the formation of a conflict resolution team to help solve the problems at these schools.[11]

Some critics believed that desegregation was proceeding too gradually. A coalition of civil rights groups published a report in May of 1972 that was highly critical of the school board. The report maintained that New Orleans public schools had not pushed to achieve greater racial integration since 1970. Mack J. Spears, the first black school board official and now school board president, found himself in the position of having to defend the slow pace and unevenness of desegregation in the system. He stated, "I do not know that the city of New Orleans will ever achieve an ideal of having a sprinkling of minority students in each neighborhood school. Nor do I feel that it is practical."[12]

The breaking down of exclusively white schools did continue, however. Since black and white neighborhoods in New Orleans tended to be close to each other in most parts of the city,[13] there was little need for busing to achieve racially mixed schools. One of the notable instances of judicial desegregation in New Orleans occurred at the end of 1972, when U.S. District Court Judge Herbert W. Christenberry ordered the merging of elementary schools McDonogh 40, which had no white students, with the adjoining district of Abrams, which had 685 white students and only 3 black students.[14]

In the summer of 1972, the Orleans Parish school board adopted a plan to racially integrate the faculties of all 136 parish public schools.[15] A week later the school board president commented that one reason for the faculty desegregation plan was to avoid further court-ordered desegregation suits and that New Orleans had finally achieved a "unitary system."[16] According to New Orleans public school historians Donald E. DeVore and Joseph Logsdon, the movement of whites out of the Orleans Parish public school system increased greatly after the school board's 1972 decision to use administrative transfers to achieve ratios of sixty black to forty white teachers in all elementary schools and fifty-five black to forty-five white teachers in all secondary schools.[17] It also led to a steady increase in the predominance of Orleans Parish's black faculty, further solidifying the school system's racial identification. Data in the *Annual Financial and Statistical Report* of the Louisiana Department of Education show that the percentage of teachers who were black was fairly constant throughout the late 1960s and early 1970s. In 1972, 58% of teachers were black. Five years later, this had gone up to 68%. By 1980, 72% of teachers were black. The percentage increased very slowly after that, and three-quarters of the district's teachers were black by 1997.

In July 1973, the Orleans Parish school board approved a plan for Lower Algiers elementary schools on New Orleans' West Bank. The preceding May, a group of parents had complained that a previous school board plan had artificially segregated the elementary schools of Algiers. The school board's plan meant busing for 1,950 students. Again, intent of the plan was to avoid going to court, as a court ruling might mandate cross-busing for the entire system.[18]

The involvement of the courts in the desegregation of New Orleans, which had begun with the *Bush* case, came to an end in the late 1970s. Judge Herbert W. Christenberry declared in 1975 that the New Orleans school system was in compliance with the court order resulting from *Bush,* and he suspended the practice of requiring reports on desegregation efforts from the school board twice each year. Judge Christenberry declared that he would completely dissolve the court order in two years if the NAACP filed no new actions. After Judge Christenberry's death, Judge Charles Schwartz finally dissolved the court order in 1978.[19] In the eyes of the law, the Orleans Parish school district was completely desegregated.

There were claims that New Orleans had managed to triumph over the evils of segregation. By 1976, an editorial in the *Times-Picayune,* the major newspaper of New Orleans, observed that Orleans Parish had managed to avoid large-scale court-ordered busing by its gradualist approach. It had also, in the views of the editorialist, not suffered from white flight to the same extent as other major urban areas such as Washington, D.C., and Newark, New Jersey.[20] An editorial in 1978 declared that the long desegregation of New Orleans schools was at last completed.[21]

It was not long, however, before the *Times-Picayune's* sanguine view had changed. In an article in the series "Crisis in the Schools," in April of 1981, staff writer Molly Moore predicted that Orleans Parish schools would be 95% black by the end of the decade if trends continued. This was felt to be problematic, because the disappearance of white students from parish public schools was depriving the school system of its middle class base. She identified New Orleans East, then 65% white, as the last outpost of white students in the Parish.[22] We now look at the data to see the student shifts taking place over thirty-two years of integration and to see whether Moore's concerns about an almost all-black system were justified.

New Orleans: The Trends

Figure 3.2 presents longitudinal data on New Orleans and its metropolitan area for percentage of students who are black in Orleans Parish public schools, percentage of all Orleans white students enrolled in Orleans nonpublic schools, and percentage of all white students in the entire metropoli-

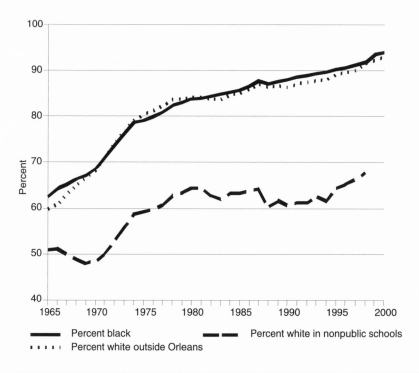

Figure 3.2. Racial Shifts in Orleans Parish, 1965–2000

tan area who are enrolled in schools outside of Orleans Parish. Using archival and historical data, we attempt to interpret the fluctuations of these three variables.

As can be seen in Figure 3.2, even in 1965, when all of Orleans parish schools were still essentially de facto, if not de jure, segregated by race, the parish public school system was already 63% black, with fully 51% of all whites within the parish enrolled in nonpublic schools. Moreover, 60% of all white students in the entire New Orleans metropolitan area were enrolled in schools outside of Orleans Parish. Even by 1968, there were only twenty-five white students enrolled in the city's predominantly black schools.[23]

Orleans Parish public schools grew increasingly black throughout the late 1960s, while an increasing proportion of the white students in the metropolitan area shifted to schools outside Orleans Parish. Until 1970, the percentage of public school students who were black went up at a rate of 1.1% (see Table 3.1). Interestingly, however, within the parish there was a dip in the percentage of white students who were enrolled in New Orleans nonpublic schools (see Table 3.2). The percentage of white students remaining in Orleans Parish who were in nonpublic schools went down by 0.64% per year in the late 1960s. This indicates that while there was a slow but steady movement of white students out of the Orleans school district, those white students who remained in the district tended to move out of private and parochial schools and back into the public school system. This

Table 3.1. Annual Growth in Proportion of African American Students in Orleans Parish Public Schools

Range in Years	Average Annual Growth (%)
1965–1970	1.1
1970–1980	1.5
1981–1990	0.48
1991–2000	0.36

Source: *Annual Financial and Statistical Report* (Baton Rouge, Louisiana Department of Education: 1965–2000).

suggests that the initial resistance by New Orleans whites to de jure integration in 1961 may have diminished, perhaps because they could still attend neighborhood schools where whites were in the vast majority.

However, in the 1970s, the New Orleans school board gradually began the process of more assertively integrating schools in a piecemeal fashion. While the early 1970s do not coincide with a precipitous increase in the percentage of public school students who were black, the black proportion continued to grow. During the 1970s, the percentage of all public school students in Orleans who were black went up by about 1.5% each year (see Table 3.1). When the decade opened, blacks made up over 68% of students in the district. When Judge Christenberry declared in 1975 that Orleans Parish was in compliance with the desegregation court order, 79% of the students in Orleans were black. When the system was finally declared completely desegregated in 1978, over 82% of the students were black. Every year, there were fewer and fewer white students to put into the mix in a system that was now racially mixed by official declaration. In tandem with this trend, the percentage of all whites who attended public schools in the districts outside of New Orleans grew continuously, with the trend slowing somewhat during the 1980s and 1990s (see Table 3.3).

As shown in Figure 3.2, around 1970 there was a sudden spike in the percentage of Orleans whites attending nonpublic schools, a trend which indicates a definite movement of whites out of the Orleans public school system. During the 1970s, the downward trend in white nonpublic school attendance in Orleans reversed, and the proportion of whites in the parish in private and parochial schools went up by 1.5% per year, the same as the rate of growth of the black school population and approximately the same as the rate of movement of public school students away from the metropolitan center. Although most white students inside Orleans Parish were in public schools at the beginning of the 1970s, by the late 1990s nearly 70% of white students in the parish attended nonpublic schools. Additionally, the increase in the proportion of white students in New Orleans suburban schools may provide indirect evidence that as desegregation measures affected the schools they were attending, whites simply decided to leave the district altogether. This process may have had a snowball effect, changing racial balances in neighborhoods to levels where other whites left for reasons that had nothing to do with the schools.

Figure 3.2 shows quite clearly how from the start of court-ordered de-

**Table 3.2. Annual Change in Proportion
of All White Students in Orleans Parish
Enrolled in Nonpublic Schools**

Range in Years	Average Annual Change (%)
1965–1970	–0.64
1970–1980	1.5
1981–1989	0.55
1990–1997	0.73

Source: *Annual Financial and Statistical Report* (Baton
Rouge, Louisiana Department of Education: 1965–1997).

**Table 3.3. Annual Growth in Proportion
of All White Students in Orleans
Metropolitan Area Enrolled in Public
Schools outside of Orleans Parish**

Range in Years	Average Annual Growth (%)
1965–1970	1.8
1970–1980	1.4
1981–1990	0.43
1991–2000	0.51

Source: *Annual Financial and Statistical Report* (Baton
Rouge, Louisiana Department of Education: 1965–2000).

segregation to the mid-1990s, the percentage of public school students who
were black increased in almost perfect tandem with the growing percentage of white students in the metropolitan area who attended school outside
the New Orleans city limits. The lines are virtually mirror images of each
other, and this provides compelling justification for the argument that white
flight from New Orleans is an important cause of the system becoming over

90% African American by the mid-1990s. Though the line is slightly more erratic, there is also a most definite and strong trend over the thirty-year period for those whites who *do* go to schools within the city of New Orleans to opt for nonpublic schools.

After 1980, the apparent movement of white students from Orleans Parish public schools began to slow. From 1980 to 1989, the percentage of New Orleans public school students who were black went up by less than half a percentage point (0.48%) each year, and during the 1990s the trend slowed very slightly to an increase of 0.36% per year, as shown in Table 3.1. The percentage of whites enrolled in private and parochial schools grew by 0.55% per year during the 1980s and by 0.73% per year during the 1990s, as shown in Table 3.2. In the 1980s and 1990s, there was apparently no white movement back to New Orleans schools, but the flood of public school students to districts outside of Orleans slowed to a trickle of 0.43% yearly. This slowdown becomes comprehensible when we look at the graph. By 1980, almost 85% of the public school students in the Orleans district were black. There simply were very few white students left to leave.

Was there any black flight from the New Orleans public school system at this time? Our interviews with black parents in the New Orleans metropolitan area strongly indicate that there was, but black families moved out of the Orleans public school system at a slower rate than white families did, in part because black families were not faced with having their own children become numerical minorities in the schools, in part because the economic situation of black New Orleanians was much more limited than that of whites, and in part because blacks were not subject to the antiblack prejudices that combined with self-interest to encourage the flight of whites. However, there has been a steady trend toward black movement out of the New Orleans public school system, as the public school system became overwhelmingly populated by minority members. As Figure 3.3 shows, over the entire period under consideration, there has been a steadily increasing tendency for black public school students to be enrolled in schools outside of New Orleans, rather than in the metropolitan core.

Until 1973, the percentage of metropolitan area black students enrolled in school districts outside of New Orleans increased at an average rate of 0.15% per year. In 1965, 18.5% of the black public school students in the New Orleans area were enrolled in districts outside of Orleans. By 1973, slightly over 20.2% of black students in the metropolitan area were enrolled outside of Orleans. After 1973, the rate increased to an average of about 0.3% per year. By 1997 over 28% of black public school students were in schools in the surrounding parishes. During this same time, although black students increased as a percentage of all students in New Orleans, their absolute number actually decreased, from 78,165 in 1973 to 75,855 in 1997. This, of course, does not tell us which black students were enrolled in the suburban fringe areas, nor does it tell us whether this was indeed a matter of middle class black flight or simply a matter of more rapid overall population growth outside of Orleans Parish. However, it does suggest that we should give some consideration to the question of why black students, as well as white students, became more and more likely to go to school outside of the minority-dominant schools in Orleans.

The trends in black enrollment in nonpublic schools in New Orleans are less clear. Figure 3.3 shows that after an initial decrease in the nonpublic

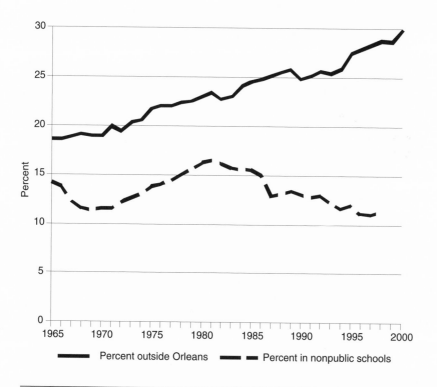

Figure 3.3. Trends in Orleans Parish Black Enrollment, 1965–2000

sector's share of the black student population in the late 1960s, the time that the schools were finally beginning to achieve desegregation under Judge Ellis's plan, black nonpublic enrollments began to go up. From 1971 to 1981, the proportion of Orleans black students in nonpublic rather than public schools increased at a rate of half a percentage point each year. About 1981, however, this trend reversed and the nonpublic share of black students went down by an average of about 0.35% per year through the 1980s and 1990s. The reasons for this reversal are not clear, but it should be noted that throughout the period a relatively small percentage of black students in New Orleans attended nonpublic schools. If we recall the economic statistics at the beginning of this chapter, it would appear that the most likely reason nonpublic schools were not a continuing refuge for black flight was probably the relatively weak economic position of black families in the city.

To sum up the trends, throughout the entire period of school racial integration in the city of New Orleans, the school system went from 63% to 90% black. At the same time, the percentage of all metropolitan area whites attending schools in the suburban districts went from 60% to 90%. Finally, the percentage of all city whites enrolled in nonpublic schools went from 51% to 74%. Taken together, these trends suggest that white flight from the New Orleans public school system was at least partly due to an increasingly African American student body. Along with these clear trends, there is also evidence of an increasing tendency on the part of black families to enroll their children in schools outside of the New Orleans public school system, particularly in the public schools of the surrounding suburban areas. It is difficult, however, to make judgements about causation based on correlations alone. For this reason, we turn now to our own observations of New Orleans public schools and to public perceptions of them.

New Orleans Public Schools: The View from the Ground

In 1994, one of the authors served as a regular substitute teacher in an Orleans Parish high school. It was one of the better schools in the city, located in the midst of a well-kept black suburb on the eastern fringe of the city. In addition to its regular classes, the school contained a magnet component. Fifteen percent of the students were admitted to special magnet classes on the basis of tests and prior grades. These magnet students could come from outside of the school's attendance boundaries. Although close to 75% of the students in the school were black, the overwhelming majority of those in the magnet component of the school were of other races. For the most part, they were not white: there were only a few whites in the entire school. The vast majority of these honors students were Vietnamese, children of refugees who had settled in New Orleans after the end of the Vietnam War.[24]

The principal remarked one day that the pictures of graduating classes on the wall outside of his office showed some of the changes in the makeup of the school.[25] In 1970, the rows of students in rented tuxedos and formal dresses were all white. The clothes changed only slightly over the course of the decades. By the late 1970s, though, about a third of the graduating seniors were black. Half a decade later, about a third were white. By the 1990s, the graduating classes had become virtually all black.

Although most of the students came from nearby suburban homes, the school's boundaries, like those of large public high schools in general, were too expansive to include only a single type of neighborhood. Every non-magnet class contained pupils who came from the impoverished families of public housing projects. Teachers claimed that these students were the source of many of the school's discipline problems. They also maintained, however, that the problems were not limited to the low-income youths.

"They learn from each other," observed a mathematics teacher. "The middle class kids pick things up from the poor kids and it makes them all hard to manage."

The nonmagnet classes were not dangerous places, and the young people, in general, were neither malevolent nor unlikeable. They were, however, hostile to the very idea of academic achievement. Students who made an effort to learn were continually criticized by their peers. In a conversation between classes one conscientious young black woman complained to one of the authors: "I try so hard to do my work. But the way all these people act, I just can't. And they laugh at you and make fun of you if you do what you're supposed to."[26]

"A lot of these kids think its not 'black' to do well in school," said one of the teachers. There were, however, some black students in the mostly Vietnamese magnet classes. One of them, a tall young man with a disarming smile and a pleasant manner, agreed that his fellow students teased him for his dedication to academic activities: "Oh, I don't mind them," he said one day. "They can say or think whatever they like. I intend to be a scientist, and I will work as hard as I have to to reach my goal. Everything else just doesn't matter." Few adolescents, black or white, would have the direction and maturity to react so well to a negative peer environment.

One of the future scientist's closest friends in school was a young white woman. She explained one day how she had ended up in this school. She and her divorced mother had fallen on hard economic times and had moved to east New Orleans to live with an aunt. Despite their difficult financial circumstances, her mother had intended to enroll her at a local Catholic school, but they had missed the registration date. The area public school was the last option.

This young woman said that she was happy in this school. "I've met a lot of friends here and the teachers are good." She also said that being white was "not much of a problem." She explained, "Sometimes people shout 'hey, blondie' at me in the halls, or they say dirty things, but I just don't look at them. I stay with my friends and I feel safe. I don't hang around after school but I go straight home."

Going to this school was clearly endurable, and evidently learning was possible there, especially for those in the magnet program. However, it was not an ideal situation, and many parents would make some effort to avoid it for their children. Our conversations with parents have convinced us that parents do take schools into consideration when making decisions about where to live. One white parent, who moved to the New Orleans area from Houston, decided to settle in St. Tammany Parish, just to the east of Orleans. "I'd have to say that schools were the number one factor in why we bought our house out here," he told one of the authors. "I wish I didn't have to commute all the way across the bridge to go to work every day. But the schools in New Orleans are a nightmare. I couldn't put my kids in one of those places."

A black mother of two children, a social worker who lived in Jefferson Parish, to the west of Orleans, expressed similar views: "I was born in New Orleans. But I want my children to have the best opportunities I can give them. The New Orleans school system . . . I hate to say it, but it's just pitiful."

One of the parents we met who had an unfortunate experience with the public schools of New Orleans was a newly hired professor at one of the city's universities. A committed Marxist, she insisted on placing her two sons in the local public school, against the advice of her colleagues. Before a single semester had ended, she had pulled her children out of public school and enrolled them in a Catholic school. She said that her children were learning nothing and were, as the only white children in the class, threatened on a daily basis by their fellow students. "What else could I do?" she asked.

Some middle class professionals, black and white, do send their children to New Orleans schools. But they agree that the school system has to be approached with extreme caution and some strategy. "There's a few good magnet schools here," said one parent. "I think the school we have our kids in, Lusher, is a good school. But they have a waiting list a mile long and it is hard to get to get in. I don't know what we'll do when they get to high school. We'll try to get them in to Ben Franklin (New Orleans' elite public high school for gifted children). If we can't get them in there, we'll just have to bite the bullet and send them to private school."

Openings in the few magnet schools, especially those with good reputations, have become desperately sought. They have also become a source of some racial resentment within the legally desegregated school system of Orleans Parish. "You can't tell me that there isn't some discrimination for white people in the magnet schools," said one black mother of an elementary school child. "They're all in those good schools, and all we get are the rest. I want my child to go to the good school. I want my child to have the chances they have. I don't want my child to ever have to be stuck with second best, and I think that's what he's getting now."

The constant machination to get children into the "best" public schools has become a concern not only of parents in New Orleans itself, but also in the surrounding districts where the middle class, especially the white middle class, has increasingly settled. A teacher at the elementary school with the highest achievement test scores in nearby Jefferson Parish explained why her class contained over thirty children: "This is the honors class in the best school in the district. All of the parents who can, get their kids transfers to get them into this school, and they all want to get into this class."

One of our critics, an anonymous journal reviewer reading an article based on some of the research in this book, objected to our presentation of white avoidance of black schools as a matter of rational choice. The reviewer objected that we should not assume that parents in general were "sophisticated" enough to make decisions about the schooling of their children based on test scores and school environments. Every discussion that we have had with parents, though, indicates that they are quite sophisticated about the realities of schooling for their own children, frequently more sophisticated than many social scientists. Parents in general seek educational environments that will maximize the opportunities of their own children. There is, then, a competition to move children into the most advantageous school environments and out of the worst school environments. The public schools of New Orleans at the beginning of the twenty-first century are widely seen as among the worst.

We are not claiming that there is no racial prejudice among many of the white parents who choose not to send their children to public schools in New Orleans. Indeed, we did talk to parents who expressed racist feelings. "They just handed New Orleans over to the blacks," said one middle-aged father of two teen-aged children living across the lake from New Orleans in St. Tammany Parish, "and they run it into the ground." Other parents expressed different attitudes, though. "I wouldn't put my children into a school that was mostly minority children," said a mother of elementary school children attending a Catholic school in New Orleans. "I feel kind of guilty about that," she said, "but I have to think about what's best for my children first."

There is racial prejudice, but it does not make a difference in parents' actions. Bigoted parents do not send their children to the majority-black schools of Orleans, and they feel comfortable with the decision. Nonbigoted parents do not send their children to the majority black schools in the district, and they feel uncomfortable. Even the Marxist professor took her children out of the public school system and felt very uncomfortable about it. Regardless of the presence or absence of racial prejudice, they all still made the same decision to remove their children from the city's ailing public schools.

Talking to parents in the New Orleans area has made it clear why the census statistics for 1990 showed so few whites with school-age children living in New Orleans. There are very few positions available in the few magnet schools in the city. White families who cannot compete for these few positions and who cannot afford private or parochial schools live in the suburbs. The fact that whites with school-age children are so dramatically underrepresented in the city offers another piece of evidence that white flight is indeed at least partially promoted by considerations of schooling.

Are the negative perceptions of the New Orleans public school system somehow mistaken? All of the evidence suggests that they are not. Every year, all tenth- and eleventh-grade public high school students in Louisiana are required to take and pass the state's Graduation Exit Examination. Students who have not passed all components (language arts, mathematics, and written composition in the tenth grade; science and social studies in the

Table 3.4. Average Percent Correct on Tenth-Grade Components of 1990, 1994, and 1999 Louisiana Graduation Exit Examination: Orleans Parish and Louisiana

	Math	*Language Arts*	*Written Composition*
1990			
Orleans			
Blacks (N = 4,504)	52.3%	57.5%	69.4%
Whites (N = 301)	75.0%	76.3%	83.2%
Louisiana			
Blacks (N = 19,056)	57.2%	61.0%	73.3%
Whites (N = 25,035)	69.7%	72.2%	83.7%
1994			
Orleans			
Blacks (N = 6,347)	48.6%	62.1%	64.9%
Whites (N = 282)	80.8%	86.2%	84.1%
Louisiana			
Blacks (N = 21,211)	54.7%	67.2%	69.9%
Whites (N = 21,640)	71.4%	80.4%	81.1%
1999			
Orleans			
Blacks (N = 7,100)	45.2%	66.0%	74.6%
Whites (N = 253)	76.5%	86.5%	87.4%
Louisiana			
Blacks (N = 26,996)	50.9%	69.4%	76.4%
Whites (N = 28,493)	67.4%	81.7%	84.4%

eleventh) must retake the test until they pass. Table 3.4 shows the average percentage of correct answers of black and white students in the Orleans district and in Louisiana in 1990, 1994, and 1999. The scores of black students in New Orleans were extremely low throughout the decade: black math and language arts scores were consistently about 20 points lower than those of whites, and written composition scores were at least 13 points lower than whites throughout the decade.

Black scores in Orleans Parish were not only lower than white scores in the district, but they were also somewhat lower than the black averages for the state. As we will discuss in more detail in Chapter 7, we see these dismal test results as a consequence of the segregation of many New Orleans schools, which isolates and concentrates minority members in this district. By contrast, the small number of white public school students in this district displayed better performance than whites in the rest of the state. As we have pointed out, the white families who keep their children in public schools in this district are largely those who can get their children into the magnet programs.

We are not, by any means, suggesting that these test results should be taken as reflections of innate ability. Instead, we see them as consequences of the concentration of socially and economically disadvantaged young people. At the same time, though, the scores do indicate schools with severe academic difficulties, since the African American students who on average did so poorly in all areas make up over nine out of ten students in the system.

The problems of public schools in the city have been well documented and well publicized. In July of 1999, after a succession of school board chiefs, the New Orleans public school system brought in Alphonse Davis, a former Marine Corps colonel, to head Orleans Parish public schools. Unlike his predecessors, Davis had no educational background, but it was hoped that his military training and his personal style of intense dedication could somehow salvage a system in disarray. The desperate condition of New Orleans schools became even clearer a month after the arrival of Davis, when the Louisiana Department of Education published the most recent results of the Louisiana Educational Assessment Progress (LEAP) tests. A reporter for the *Times-Picayune* summed up the statewide standing of New Orleans: "Overall, district students scored far below the state average, as 70 percent of Orleans eighth graders failed math and about 45 percent failed

English, compared with 40 percent and 21 percent statewide. Of the Orleans fourth-graders, 63 percent failed math and 44 percent failed English, compared with 35 percent and 21 percent statewide." Five schools in Orleans, the reporter observed, had more than 90 percent failure rates in math.[27]

The following month, in September of 1999, the Louisiana Department of Education released a ranking of the achievement levels of all of the schools in the state. New Orleans public schools ranked at the very bottom of the state's sixty-seven school districts. New Orleans schools had traditionally scored below the state average on achievement tests. In 1982, for example, New Orleans ranked sixty-fourth among the then sixty-six school systems in the state.[28] By the end of the twentieth century, though, the city's schools were producing the lowest performers in a state with a reputation for poor school systems. Of Louisiana's fifty-seven lowest-achieving schools in 1999, fifty were in the Orleans school district. Explaining these results, a teacher at one of the lowest-ranked schools observed, "We have a lot of poor children and we deal with a lot of neighborhood problems."[29]

Although LEAP scores improved slightly in Orleans in 2000, the parish's scores were still the lowest in the state. Among both fourth and eighth grades, most Orleans Parish students failed the mathematics and social studies portions of the test (55% of fourth graders and 63% of eighth graders failed the mathematics section; 56% of both fourth and eighth graders failed the social studies portion). Nearly half the district's fourth graders (49%) and almost two-thirds (63%) of eighth graders failed the science section of the test. In the section with the least failures, English, 45% of Orleans fourth graders and 37% of Orleans eighth graders failed. By contrast, statewide fourth-grade failures ranged from 20% (science) to 29% (mathematics). Failures among the state's eighth graders ranged from 14% (English) to 33% (mathematics).[30]

New Orleans students, then, continued to show far lower levels of performance than other students in Louisiana. Even among those in Orleans who passed, relatively few were operating at basic grade level. Three out of every four fourth graders and eight out of every ten eighth graders in Orleans scored below basic grade level competence in mathematics on the 2000 test. Nearly 80% of the district's fourth graders and 84% of the district's eighth graders were below basic grade level in science. Close to 80% in both grades were below basic grade level in social studies.[31] Almost 70%

Table 3.5. Performance Categories of Schools in Orleans and Surrounding Districts

	School of Academic Excellence	School of Academic Distinction	School of Academic Excellence	Academically Above Average	Academically Below Average	Academically Unacceptable
Schools in Orleans	None	None	6 (5.8%)	6 (5.8%)	41 (39.8%)	50 (48.5%)
Average percent minority			58%	88%	98%	99%
Minimum			31%	76%	89%	91%
Maximum			89%	100%	100%	100%
Average percent poor			36%	63%	86%	85%
Minimum			25%	36%	72%	61%
Maximum			49%	88%	94%	98%
Schools in Surrounding Districts	None	3 (2.3%)	19 (14.8%)	59 (46.1%)	47 (36.7%)	None
Average percent minority		5%	17%	32%	69%	
Minimum		4%	6%	0%	14%	
Maximum		9%	31%	96%	97%	
Average percent poor		8%	25%	55%	83%	
Minimum		7%	6%	22%	54%	
Maximum		10%	40%	97%	97%	

of fourth graders and over 70% of eighth graders were below basic level in English. These figures mean that unless a student in a public school in Orleans attends one of the few highly selective schools, the student will be in a classroom filled with underachievers. It can also be readily demonstrated that there is a clear connection between schools' racial makeups and their achievement levels.

Table 3.5 shows us the relationships among the racial compositions of schools, the economic level of students in schools, and the academic ranking of schools of the New Orleans area in the 1999 LEAP tests. Before discussing these results, we should note that poverty, minority race, and low test scores are virtually indistinguishable from one another at the school level in this metropolitan area (and, indeed, in the other areas we will examine). The correlation (r, in statistical terms) between the percentage of students who are poor (defined as the percentage participating in free and reduced-price lunch programs) and the percentage of students who are black is 0.83 for New Orleans and its surrounding suburban parishes (not shown in this table). This means that if a parent knows that a school is made up mostly of black children, the assumption that most of those children are poor is not necessarily an irrational product of stereotyping or prejudice. Unless one has some additional piece of information (such as that the school is a magnet school), this is an extremely reasonable and well grounded assumption. Further, parents can reasonably assume that schools in the New Orleans area that are mostly black—which means mostly poor—are schools in which the general level of achievement is extremely low. The correlation between percentage of students who are black and the average school LEAP test score is -0.834, and the correlation between the percentage of students who are poor in schools and the average school LEAP test score is -0.841—very high correlation coefficients indeed.

Table 3.5 shows us these relations in somewhat more concrete and detailed form. The Louisiana Department of Education ranked its schools into five categories. Schools with outstanding overall test scores were said to be "Schools of Academic Excellence" and schools with scores below even minimally acceptable levels were said to be "Academically Unacceptable." There were no Schools of Academic Excellence or Schools of Academic Distinction in the Orleans Parish school district. There were six schools that fell into the third-highest category, Schools of Academic Achievement. All of these were magnet schools, so the element of selectivity must be taken into consideration: these were by definition the best and most selective schools in the district.

A majority of the students in the Orleans school district's top-ranked schools were minority students (58%). In one top-ranked school, 89% were minority students. It is clearly not the case that schools with large numbers of minority students are absolutely condemned to low performance. They can be good schools—as long as they are free to choose among the best students in the district. We should also note that the majority of students in the six Schools of Academic Achievement in Orleans Parish were not classified as poor.

There were also six schools in Orleans Parish classified as Academically Above Average. Thus we can say that according to the measure used by the Louisiana Department of Education, only 12 of the 103 schools in New Orleans showed at least reasonably good levels of performance. It may become clear now why there is such intense demand among middle class parents for entry into the very few valued schools. It is also clear, as we look at this table, that all but a few of the white students in Orleans public schools are in those valued schools. As the parents we interviewed told us again and again, white children would enroll in a private school if they could not get into one of these institutions.

The overwhelming majority of schools in Orleans Parish were either Academically Below Average or Academically Unacceptable. The largest number were Academically Unacceptable—the very lowest category. These were also schools in which all or almost all of the students were black and poor.

In the school districts surrounding New Orleans, by contrast, there were no Academically Unacceptable schools. There were also no schools in the state's highest category, but there were three Schools of Academic Distinction. All of these schools had very small proportions of black students and very few low-income students. There were also more Schools of Academic Achievement, both in number and in proportion, than there were Schools of Academic Achievement and Academically Above Average Schools combined in Orleans Parish. In the Schools of Academic Achievement category, the schools in the supposed white flight districts were both majority white and majority nonpoor. Among the above average schools, there was one school that was almost all black and almost all low-income. This was a small, suburban preschool through fifth grade elementary school. There were also two other schools in the area around New Orleans with majority-black populations that were classified as above average: one with a student population that was 68% black and another with a student population that was 65% black. Of the fifty-nine above average schools outside of New Orleans, then, fifty-six had majority- white student bodies. Among the forty-seven academically below average schools outside of New Orleans, on the other hand, we found only four schools that had majority-white student bodies, and three of these were close to half white and half black.

None of these statistics tell us why the racial composition of schools is so closely related to school performance. We will deal with this issue in Chapter 7, where we discuss the academic consequences of school composition. However, it is clear that if parents in this area want to put their children into schools that show high levels of performance, they will do two things: First, they will attempt to place their children outside of the Orleans Parish public school system. Even among the better schools, there were more highly ranked schools in the surrounding suburbs than in the city. Second, they will place their children in schools that have the smallest possible minority populations: both inside and outside of the city, it is a consistent rule with only rare exceptions that the smaller the minority student body, the higher the performance ranking of the school.

Test results, of course, are not the only school characteristic that parents take into consideration. They are also concerned about the safety and psychological comfort of their children. Few parents who have the opportunity to make choices would choose to put their children in schools in which low-income children from single-parent households make up most of the student body. Indeed, the argument for desegregation offered by Gary Orfield that we discussed in the previous chapter is based on the idea that children who are mostly from low-income, single-parent households should not be placed in schools where children from low-income, single-parent households predominate.

New Orleans schools (and black-dominated schools in general) are widely perceived by white families as not just schools in which the students perform poorly, but as dangerous places, particularly for white children. These families may well exaggerate the threat, but perhaps it is more responsible to exaggerate possible threats to one's children than to minimize them. There is also, moreover, some basis to the fear of black-dominated schools in New Orleans.

The young woman that we mentioned earlier was in one of the better schools in the city. Still, she had to learn to ignore calls and to go home immediately after school. In most of the city's schools, the situation is much worse. In 1986, parents of white children at Gregory Junior High charged that their children were beaten and intimidated by fellow students and that administrators at the school had allowed this. Gregory at that time consisted of 1,100 black students and 26 whites. One of the white parents declared, "Our children are in real danger." Further, she charged, "We don't want to see the children go back to the same type of environment. If necessary we want our kids escorted to classes."[32] Although a federal jury found in 1990 that school board officials were not negligent and civil rights violations had not occurred, no one disputed the parents' claims that their children had been mistreated.[33]

It is not, of course, only white children who suffer in violent schools, nor is violence against children of one race any more tragic or objectionable than violence against children of another race. Black children suffer more serious threats in minority-dominated urban schools because they are too often stuck in the places that whites avoid completely. In March of 1992, for example, Undrell Humbert, a seventeen-year-old student was stabbed by a fellow student at John McDonogh Senior High School. One week later, fifteen-year-old Jomokenyatta Joseph was shot to death at O. Perry Walker High.[34] In the same week that Joseph was stabbed, three gun battles took place in and around Thomy Lafon Elementary, located in the C. J. Peete Housing Development.[35]

Violence can and does strike middle class, suburban schools, as has been widely publicized in several recent dramatic, though isolated cases such as the massacre at Columbine High School in Littleton, Colorado. But the environment of ever-present, chronic danger is much more characteristic of inner city schools. This became clear to psychologist Beverly Howze when she was called to a school in the lower Ninth Ward, the area of the city where conflict over desegregation had erupted long before. Howze was asked to work with five boys in a school that had become, by the 1990s, an all-black, low-income school. The five had been cursing their teacher and making obscene remarks to her. Howze found that five of the six had seen someone shot and that all of them lived in fatherless households. She reported that when the boys were asked, "'[W]hat do men do?' their answers ranged from '[T]hey sleep, beat their wife, drink,' to '[T]hey kill.'"[36] Not only would very few parents want their children to go to a school in which children such as these five predominate, very few parents would want even a sizable minority of children with backgrounds like these sitting next to their children in class.

What Happened in New Orleans?

The desegregation of New Orleans schools was relatively smooth, after the initial racist outbursts. There was little busing, and the racial barriers of schools broke down gradually. Yet whites steadily moved out of the Orleans Parish school system, leaving it an almost completely black district apart from a few magnet schools. What happened? We argue, based on a reconstruction of the history of desegregation in the city, on statistical trends, on examinations of conditions in the schools, and on the testimony of parents regarding their own motivations, that the very rationale for aggressive desegregation was the reason for its failure. A long history of subjection and oppression has meant that blacks have been, in the aggregate, disadvantaged in American history and in American society. Desegregation has aimed at breaking down their isolation from the mainstream of American society.

By moving large numbers of black students into white schools without first solving the problem of black-white inequality in the larger society, however, the process of desegregation undercut itself. Whites in the New Orleans area were and are largely middle class. Blacks were and are mostly poor. It is entirely true that not all blacks are poor, just as not all whites are middle class. Nevertheless, the connection between race and social class is so close at the group level that increasing the proportion of black students in any school means increasing the proportion of low-income students. As the proponents of desegregation have observed, blacks have also been socially isolated as a group and their families, statistically, show much weaker academic backgrounds. Therefore, increasing the proportion of black students has also meant lowering the general level of performance in schools. As we will point out in more detail in our discussion of academic consequences, moreover, performance levels in schools affect all who attend them. Finally, the rapid growth of single-parent families in black communities has meant that any increase in the black student population of a school has meant an increase in students from one-parent families, and the connection between race and family structure has grown stronger over time. There are good reasons for parents to want to avoid having their children go to school with children who are poor, who contribute to an academic environment not conducive to success, and who come from fatherless households. Therefore, as substantial numbers of black children entered New Orleans public schools, white parents—bigots and nonbigots alike—moved out. The few exceptions were the magnet schools, where the selectivity as well as the special programs helped to counterbalance the problems associated with racial composition. In the end, the putatively desegregated school system consisted mostly of schools that were almost completely black and poor, and suffering from the classic problems of inner city poverty.

New Orleans was unlike other places in some respects. Its large black population meant that schools could rapidly become places in which minority students predominated. Its Catholic schools meant that there was already a flourishing nonpublic system even before desegregation began. Nevertheless, we argue that the basic process of desegregation and white movement out of the school system is also taking place elsewhere and is a general pattern in school districts created by continuing racial inequality in the society surrounding schools. To establish this point, we turn now to the capital of Louisiana, Baton Rouge.

Chapter 4

East Baton Rouge

School Desegregation and Unintended Consequences

Baton Rouge, the central city of East Baton Rouge Parish and its associated public school district, is the second largest urban area in Louisiana. We suggest that it provides an excellent example of a desegregation plan causing exactly the opposite of its original intent. Rather than further desegregating an admittedly de facto segregated school system, it arguably reversed a trend of whites leaving the nonpublic schools for East Baton Rouge's public schools and caused the system to go from a majority-white to a majority-black student population. Based on our calculations, if the current rate of white flight continues, East Baton Rouge Parish will be an all-black school system by 2020.

In the previous chapter, we showed how the desegregation experience in the New Orleans public school system evolved over time and how white flight ultimately transformed the system into an almost all–African American school system. In many respects, the situation of Baton Rouge is quite different from that of New Orleans. First, Baton Rouge is not part of Catholic Louisiana,[1] so it does not share the strong historical tradition of parochial schools that we saw in New Orleans. Second, it did not follow the New Orleans pattern of gradual, piecemeal desegregation to avoid judicial mandates. By contrast with New Orleans, Baton Rouge took an approach to school desegregation that involved delay, followed by a drastic effort at coercion.

Demographically, Baton Rouge shows a number of differences from New Orleans.[2] While New Orleans was a majority-black city at the beginning of the 1990s, Baton Rouge still had a majority-white population. The 1990 U.S. Census gave the population of Baton Rouge as 380,105, with

240,961 whites (63%) and 132, 402 blacks (35%). Moreover, while non-family households made up many of the white households in New Orleans, both black and white households in Baton Rouge tended to be largely family households. Of Baton Rouge's 94,254 white households, 63,626 (68%) contained families. Among black households, 74%, or 31,356 out of 42,132, contained families. Thus, Baton Rouge was different from New Orleans, where nonfamily situations made up nearly half of the white living arrangements.

Just under half of the white families in East Baton Rouge Parish (49%) contained minor children. Married-couple families predominated, since 85% of the white families in the parish were of this type. Among the white families with children under age eighteen, 84% were married-couple families and only 13% were headed by single women.

In some important respects, however, the racial demographics of Baton Rouge looked similar to those of New Orleans. Of the 31,356 black family households, 16,013 (51%) were married-couple families, and 15,343 (49%) were single-parent families. Black families in Baton Rouge were more likely to contain children under eighteen than white families, although the difference was not as extreme as in New Orleans. While 49% of white family households contained children, 61% of black households contained children. In black families containing children, single-parent families figured heavily. Half of Baton Rouge's black families with children under eighteen were single-parent families, and 45% were headed by single women. Although slightly below the proportion of single-parent families in New Orleans' black community, then, families with only one adult were extremely common in the black population of Baton Rouge. In 1990, 60% of all blacks under eighteen years of age lived in one-parent families, compared with 18% of whites in that age group. As in New Orleans, also, single-parent households among black families tended to be the result of unmarried motherhood, rather than the result of divorce. Among the births to East Baton Rouge black women aged fifteen to thirty-four at the time of the census, 68% had been to women who were still not married. Among births to white women in this age group, 28% were to women who were still not married.[3]

As in New Orleans, there were also marked racial differences in income level. Among white households in East Baton Rouge, 20% had incomes below $15,000 per year. By contrast, half (slightly over 49%) of the black households had yearly incomes below $15,000. Moreover, more than one out of every five black households (22%) in Baton Rouge had yearly incomes below $5,000. These incomes translated into vastly different economic situations for white and black schoolchildren. Only 7% of white children aged five to seventeen lived below the poverty level in Baton Rouge. However, almost half (46%) of the black school-age children lived in poverty.

Over one-third of black adults (35%) had not finished high school, and 14% of black adults in East Baton Rouge Parish had completed less than ninth grade. Only 12% of white adults had not finished high school and only 4% had not finished the ninth grade.

We can read these statistics as a continuing testimony to the effects of the long history of racial oppression that we discussed in the first chapter. This history has left the black population of Baton Rouge, like that of New Orleans, with high rates of poverty, single-parent families, and limited family educational backgrounds. The effort to overcome the oppressive past and to rectify a present in which racial discrimination has become structurally embedded has lent moral force to the struggle to desegregate the schools of Louisiana's capital. At the same time, though, black social and economic disadvantages have undermined this struggle. As in New Orleans, avoiding schools in which poor children from single-parent families are dominant has meant avoiding schools in which there are large numbers of African American children.

The Desegregation Struggle in Baton Rouge

The constitutionality of Baton Rouge's de jure segregated school system was first challenged in 1956 in the case of *Davis et al. v. East Baton Rouge Parish School Board,* litigation that has been active in the federal court system ever since, making it the longest unsettled desegregation suit in U.S. history. The "freedom of choice" approach to integration was subsequently adopted in the 1960s in East Baton Rouge, ending de jure segregation and allowing black and white students the freedom to attend each others' schools. However, "freedom of choice" rarely resulted in significant desegregation of either schools or school systems.[4]

According to plaintiffs in the original desegregation lawsuit (which included the NAACP), Baton Rouge schools continued to be segregated on a de facto basis throughout the 1970s.[5] In 1981, therefore, Federal District

Court Judge John Parker, who was convinced by the plaintiff's arguments, found that the East Baton Rouge Parish School Board had maintained what he termed a "dual school system" for twenty years. The subsequent desegregation plan for Baton Rouge schools was, therefore, largely Federal District Court Judge Parker's handiwork. Significantly, the Justice Department strenuously opposed Parker's plan from the beginning. The department argued that it was causing whites to flee from the system.[6] The white exodus that ensued probably caught even the Department of Justice by surprise.

In the face of much opposition, Parker ordered fifteen East Baton Rouge schools closed in May 1981 in an effort to achieve racial balance. Under his plan, formerly white and formerly black schools that remained open were to be paired or clustered, and students were to be bused to schools in their "clusters" based on the need to create racial balance.[7] Parker's desegregation orders provoked massive resistance and an immediate hemorrhaging of white students from the public school system. The president of the Central Middle School Parent Teacher Organization, whose daughter would have been transferred to the (largely black) Scotlandville school under the desegregation plan proclaimed at the time, "She will not do that. Private schools are starting up every day."[8] Indeed, by the end of the first year of Judge Parker's plan, private schools in East Baton Rouge Parish were noting that their waiting lists were long and growing longer: so long, in fact, that new schools sprouted up almost overnight to accommodate the sudden demand for nonpublic education. One of the city's largest kindergarten through twelfth-grade nonpublic schools, Parkview Baptist, dates its founding to that first year of forced busing in 1981, and by 1998 it enrolled eight hundred students in its high school alone. Enrollment figures in nonpublic parish schools jumped by approximately two thousand in that first year of busing.[9] Moreover, according to subsequent enrollment trends, those students never returned. Using the same data released annually by the Louisiana Department of Education from 1965 to 2000 that we used to trace trends in the New Orleans area, we now turn to an examination of the demographic trends in East Baton Rouge.

Baton Rouge: What Happened?

In order to answer the question of what actually happened during East Baton Rouge's desegregation efforts, we track and present longitudinal data on the parish and its metropolitan area for three variables: the percentage of all parish public school students who are African American, the percentage of all white students enrolled in Baton Rouge nonpublic schools, and the percentage of all white students in the entire metropolitan area who were enrolled in public schools in parishes immediately outside of Baton Rouge.

For the purposes of this study, we define the Baton Rouge metropolitan area as East Baton Rouge Parish and the two adjacent parishes of Ascension and Livingston (see Figure 4.1). An examination of the population trends quickly reveals that it is in these two parishes that most of the growth in Baton Rouge's metropolitan area is taking place. Indeed, in the mid-1990s, Ascension and Livingston were among the three fastest-growing parishes in Louisiana. (The other was the New Orleans metro white flight parish of St. Tammany.) In 1998, there were an estimated 71,628 residents in Ascension Parish, an increase of 23% over 1990. Twenty-five percent of the people in Ascension Parish were black in 1998 (a decrease of 35% from 1990). Livingston Parish had an estimated population of 88,104 in 1998, also a 25% increase over its 1990 population. Six percent of Livingston's residents were black in 1998, a decrease of fully 41% from 1990.[10]

Thus we see fairly stark contrasts between the demographics of East Baton Rouge Parish and its two fast-growing bedroom communities. While the population of Baton Rouge grew only slightly from 1990 to 1998, the percentage of black residents increased sharply, by 11%. However, while both Ascension and Livingston Parishes grew rapidly during the same eight-year period, the proportion of African Americans in both parishes dropped sharply because settlement in these two suburban areas was largely white.

Focusing on school demographic changes, we can graph the fluctuation of the racial composition of Baton Rouge public and nonpublic schools and the racial composition of the "white flight" parishes over the period since 1965. As can be seen in Figure 4.2 from the line representing the percentage of all East Baton Rouge Parish public school students who are black, a minority (39%) were black in 1965. Moreover, only a small percentage of Baton Rouge's white students were in nonpublic schools in 1965 (24%). Also, the vast majority of the white students in the three-parish Baton Rouge metropolitan area were specifically enrolled in East Baton Rouge Parish schools (74%). Thus, at the beginning of era of desegregation, Baton Rouge's school system differed from that of New Orleans in two major

respects. In Louisiana's capital city, black students were a smaller proportion of the school population than in New Orleans, and nonpublic schools
were much less of a presence.

Following the initial lawsuit to force the integration of Baton Rouge's
schools, the school board allowed schools to desegregate voluntarily during the 1960s, employing the "freedom of choice" approach to desegregation. However, as we pointed out in Chapter 2, "freedom of choice" was
ruled unconstitutional as an integration tool in the 1968 U.S. Supreme Court
case *Green v. County School Board.* Since Baton Rouge's neighborhoods
were largely segregated by race, with most blacks living in the northern
part of the city and most whites living in south Baton Rouge, the city's
public schools remained largely segregated by race until 1981. At that time,
the district was ordered by the federal courts to forcibly integrate. Having
this extended period of voluntary integration, when children in the city attended schools located in their own neighborhoods but were not prohibited
by race from attending any public school, provides an ideal opportunity to
observe trends within the system during the extended period of voluntary
desegregation following the end of de jure segregation in Baton Rouge's
schools.

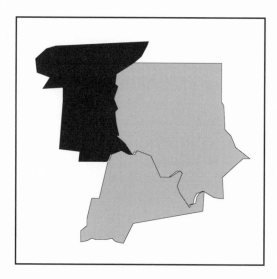

**Figure 4.1. East Baton Rouge Parish
and Principal White Flight Districts**

We can see in Figure 4.2 that from the mid-1960s through 1980, the percentage of public school students who were black remained relatively constant. We calculated that the percentage of the system that was African American was increasing at an average of only 0.22% annually, or roughly only a fifth of a percent per year during this fifteen year period (see Table 4.1).

Also, during the same period, the total percentage of white students in the metropolitan area outside of Baton Rouge increased only slightly. Significantly, within the district there was a noticeable trend for white students to move *out* of the nonpublic schools and *into* Baton Rouge's public schools.

In Table 4.2 we calculated that East Baton Rouge Parish nonpublic schools were actually *losing* enrollment at a rate of about 0.36% per year

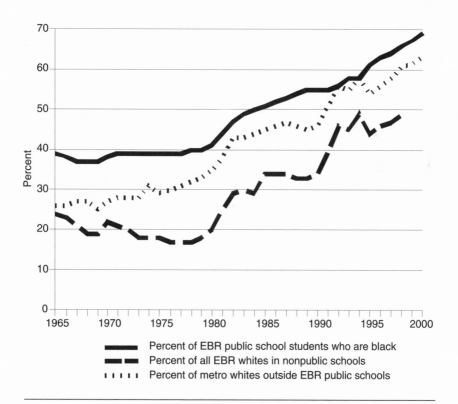

Figure 4.2. Racial Shifts in East Baton Rouge Parish, 1965–2000

Table 4.1. Annual Change in Proportion of African American Students in East Baton Rouge Parish Public School System

Range in Years	Average Annual Change (%)
1965–1980	–0.21
1981–1990	1.1
1991–2000	1.43

Source: *Annual Financial and Statistical Report* (Baton Rouge, Louisiana Department of Education: 1965–2000).

until 1980. Thus, we can surmise that, in general, whites were relatively content with the public school system during this time, even to the extent of leaving nonpublic schools. This is especially noteworthy given that this period coincides with black students attending formerly all-white schools for the first time in the twentieth century. By contrast, in some other areas of the country (e.g., New Orleans) the same scenario resulted in continuous white flight to segregated nonpublic schools. This was decidedly not the case in East Baton Rouge, which suggests that most whites were willing to attend schools with African Americans. The whites did not leave, however, because black students were entering majority-white schools in relatively small numbers. This, though, was the very reason that the court began to pursue a more aggressive desegregation policy.

With the onset of court-ordered, forced desegregation and busing in 1981, the educational situation in the Baton Rouge metro area began to change drastically. As seen in Figure 4.2, there was an immediate and precipitous flight of white students to Baton Rouge's nonpublic schools. The Department of Education data indicate that in the first year of court-ordered busing alone, the East Baton Rouge public school system lost seven thousand nonblack (almost all white) students, or the equivalent of four large public high schools. The percentage of the student body that was African American jumped from 41% in 1980 to 44% in 1981. Since the parish nonpublic school population jumped by almost two thousand students in those same two years, we can be reasonably confident that the massive

Table 4.2. Annual Change in Proportion of All White Students in East Baton Rouge Parish Enrolled in Nonpublic Schools

Range in Years	Average Annual Change (%)
1965–1980	*–0.36*
1981–1989	0.96
1990–1998	–1.36

Source: *Annual Financial and Statistical Report* (Baton Rouge, Louisiana Department of Education: 1965–2000).

decrease in the number of students from the public schools was not due primarily to other demographic factors, such as the "baby bust." Indeed, from the very start, the white flight situation was perceived as so grave a peril to the health of the system that even the U.S. Justice Department, which had early misgivings about the desegregation plan in any case, requested that the court reconsider its earlier position.[11] The Justice Department's pleas fell on deaf ears. By our calculations, the white population of East Baton Rouge's nonpublic school student population increased by 1.4% per year following intensified efforts at forced integration of the public school system (see Table 4.2). When one considers that prior to forced integration whites actually seemed to favor the public schools, as indicated by the steady trickle of students away from the nonpublic schools, the steady increase in nonpublic school enrollment in the years following forced integration seems to be fairly reliable evidence of deep disenchantment with the decision to desegregate the schools through sudden and massive shifts of black and white students.

Figure 4.2 shows that there was a brief period during the late 1980s when white student loss from Baton Rouge's public schools leveled off, before accelerating once again. According to a central office administrator of the East Baton Rouge public school system, the temporary stem in the hemorrhaging of white students was due to a short-lived experiment in which the school board allowed "controlled choice." It was a strategy by the then new superintendent, Dr. Bernard Weiss, to reduce mandatory busing and "regain the trust and participation of families and local agencies who no longer supported the efforts of public education."[12] The school re-design "controlled choice" plan included setting up popular educational programs, such as a dyslexic program, in predominantly black schools and allowing white children from other school districts within the parish to attend these schools. The magnet programs were unavailable anywhere else. As in New Orleans, the disadvantages associated with an increasing black presence in schools could be somewhat counterbalanced by providing special educational opportunities to attract white families. However, after a couple of years of modest success, the board was unable to expand the strategy to additional schools because of funding restrictions as well as a lack of interest among officials of some predominantly white schools who were not (according to our conversations with school officials) particularly happy about having black students bused in.[13]

By October of 2000, a fraction under 70% of the students in Baton Rouge's school system were black. The racial imbalance was even more pronounced in the lower grades than the higher grades, since elementary and middle schools were 72% black at this time, making it clear that there would be fewer and fewer whites in the public schools as older students graduated and younger students moved forward. "The school system is becoming blacker," observed East Baton Rouge Deputy School Superintendent Clayton Wilcox.[14]

As suggestive as they are, the numbers tell only part of the story of the unintended consequences of the sudden, coercive turn in the desegregation of Baton Rouge schools. Our extensive interviews with individuals who experienced the desegregation of this district can give deeper insight into how families responded to these events. We believe their first-hand accounts are fairly representative of the general sentiment of many white parents and citizens toward their city's desegregation experiment. The researchers heard comments about how the shifting school zones, which sometimes sent children from a neighborhood school across from their house on an hour and a half or longer bus ride to another school across town hurt "community ownership" in schools. In one telling example, a student football player who attended a city Catholic high school prior to court-ordered busing shared just how much public school community spirit he observed at a football game against a city public high school (Broadmoor High) in 1977: "When we broke through the banners in the end zone, the stands were filled and there was standing room only." The former student continued that when he returned to watch a game between the same two teams in 1981, after the dismantling of neighborhood schools, "I was in shock. . . . The fan base [at Broadmoor] had gone from standing room only to almost total abandonment. I did feel sorry for the kids on the Broadmoor football team."[15]

A Red Cross volunteer at her children's elementary school in the early 1980s said there was an enormous difference after black children were bused across town to the formerly predominately white school:

I personally saw more kids come to the clinic and often couldn't get in touch with a family member to get the sick children. It seems to me most of the ones coming in there were the students bused in from outside the neighborhood—broken homes, one-parent households, or living with grandparents who could not retrieve them. I often spoke with the teachers I knew, and they all commented about the problems caused by the parents not being from the neighborhood. They just couldn't seem to be involved enough. The teachers couldn't get enough volunteers in the classroom to help for special functions. I also spoke to some of the black mothers, and they were not happy about having their children being bused out of their neighborhoods. It wasn't convenient anymore for them to attend school functions because of the distance and traffic. Very few people were happy with the situation.[16]

As the rising line in Figure 4.2 indicates, with the total collapse of the "school redesign" plan in 1991, white flight from Baton Rouge's public schools continued unabated through the 2000–01 school year, with only one additional slight reprieve in 1994–95. There was a particularly precipitous drop in white student enrollment from 1995–96 to 1996–97, when the white student population declined by more than fifteen hundred—the equivalent of an entire large high school's student population lost from one school year to the next.

The rate at which the district was becoming primarily black at the end of the twentieth century was accelerating. The rate jumped from an average of just 0.22% per year during the freedom of choice period to an average of 1.1% per year from 1981 to 1990 during the first eight years of coercive integration. However, it increased at an even faster rate during the 1990s, accelerating to an average of 1.43% per year. Indeed, from 1995 to 2000, the district lost well over six thousand white students, but gained close to sixteen hundred black students.

As Figure 4.2 shows, whites were not just fleeing to the nonpublic school system but appeared also to be heading toward the suburban parishes of Ascension and Livingston. In the 1996–97 school year, fully 56% of all white students in the tridistrict area were enrolled in these two fast-growing metro parishes. Based on our calculations, the percentage of metropolitan area whites who were in these parishes' suburban public schools rather than in East Baton Rouge schools increased at an average rate of 1.2% per year from 1981 to 1998. This compares with an average rate of increase of only 0.56% per year prior to court-ordered desegregation.

Though there has obviously been out-migration of whites from East Baton Rouge Parish, this was not the primary cause for the initial, disproportionately rapid growth in the proportion of blacks in the parish's public schools. According to estimates from U.S. Census data (1998), the proportion of blacks in the parish increased from only about 29% in 1970 to 37% in 1996. However, during this same twenty-eight-year period, the increase in African American representation in the public schools was much greater, growing from 38% to 65.5%. In other words, the proportion of blacks in Baton Rouge's public schools grew more than three times faster than the black growth rate in the parish overall. Moreover, the overall white population, actually increased in numbers, from 205,528 in 1970, to an estimated 241,271,[17] though these numbers arguably would have been higher, perhaps much higher, had the school system been more attractive to whites than the two suburban systems. In 1999, in the 90% white community of Kennilworth, the local elementary school had only seven whites enrolled. "One can see private school whites waiting outside every morning for their school buses," one local authority reported to us.[18] In the mostly white southeastern part of East Baton Rouge Parish, one of the last battlegrounds of desegregation litigation was at Wedgewood Elementary school in 1999, where the unsettled situation could be the reason for the school population going from 10% to 30% black in a period of five years. Though for the moment the majority of the parish population is white, with almost 50% of all white students in nonpublic schools, sociologist and demographer Charles Tolbert characterized the situation as "very fluid" in a conversation with us in late summer 1999. Tolbert projected that by 2005, 50% of the Baton Rouge school-age population will be black.[19] "Baton Rouge appears to be going the way of New Orleans," Tolbert remarked.[20]

In 1996, the East Baton Rouge superintendent of schools brought in desegregation expert Christine Rossell, who served as the district's principal consultant until 2000, to help draw up a plan that Judge Parker might be willing to approve. The 1996 desegregation plan did away with much (though not all) forced busing. It also created twenty-four separate magnet programs to attract whites to majority-black inner city schools. However, half of the programs failed to attract even ten white students. Moreover, it was not for lack of money that these magnet programs failed to work. Between 1996 and 1999 the school board poured $6.8 million into special programs designed to appeal to white students. Nor was it for lack of creativity that certain programs did not work. For example, even though Louisiana is in the midst of a French language revival and some districts have long waiting lists for certain foreign language programs, a newly created foreign language magnet program in a majority-black Baton Rouge school did not attract even one white student.[21] It appears that a program's ability to attract potentially wary parents and students depends on more than money and course content. Although parents do consider benefits such as magnet programs, the location and the composition of student populations also figure heavily in their decisions.

In summary, the trend toward a majority-black school district in Baton Rouge began almost immediately following the implementation of court-ordered desegregation in 1981. The single best indicator that the white flight was a result of the sudden changes brought about by an aggressive desegregation effort, and not by a tendency toward suburbanization, was the drastic shift of the white student population from public to nonpublic schools that began at this time. Whereas white student enrollment in Baton Rouge nonpublic schools had actually been decreasing prior to forced desegregation, following Judge Parker's court order we see that this trend not only ceased, but actually accelerated markedly in the other direction. In 1965, 24% of East Baton Rouge Parish's white student population was in nonpublic schools. During the next fifteen years, when voluntary racial integration was the official school board policy, the percentage of white students in the city's nonpublic schools decreased to only 20%. However, in the very next year, 1981, when court-ordered busing went into effect, the percentage of whites in Baton Rouge's nonpublic schools jumped to 25%. By 1998, this percentage had climbed to 48%. This strongly suggests that the primary cause of this enormous shift of white students from public to nonpublic schools was a direct result of the dismantling of neighborhood schools and the sudden changes that followed coercive desegregation.

As impressive as the white flight to nonpublic schools was, there appeared to be an equally impressive migration of whites to Baton Rouge's suburban sister parishes during this time as well. And while it is harder to link this population shift to Baton Rouge's judicially mandated effort at desegregation, the coincidence in timing strongly suggests that a link does exist, and that the link may be a strong one indeed. Baton Rouge's bedroom communities of Ascension and Livingston Parishes—two of the three fastest-growing parishes in Louisiana—went from containing only 26% of all white students in the triparish metro area in 1965 to enrolling 56% of the metropolitan area's white student population by 1996. This was during the same time that the overall population of East Baton Rouge was growing rapidly.

A comment by the principal of Denham Springs Junior High, in Livingston Parish's largest city, seems to characterize well the local population's perception of the extraordinary growth in his parish. In an interview the longtime Livingston educator commented to one of the authors that Livingston's growth "is almost exclusively driven by white flight and the initial location of new hires [workers] for industry in EBR who will not live where they work."[22] He believes that avoidance of Baton Rouge's schools is the primary reason for people moving into his parish.

An administrator in the Baton Rouge school system, who wishes to remain anonymous, confided to one of the authors that the white flight from Baton Rouge's public school system is not limited to students but extends to teachers as well. She indicated that the flow of white teachers out of Baton Rouge public schools has been dramatic and that the waiting list of teachers wanting to be hired by the two suburban districts of Ascension and Livingston has been growing even faster than the demand created by the burgeoning white student population. In order to retain teachers in the urban Baton Rouge system, the school board was offering signing bonuses of as much as $3,000 for new teachers willing to join the system.[23] Even so, fully one-third of all teachers at some inner city Baton Rouge public schools are not certified.[24] All of this underscores what one researcher at a recent regional educational conference described as a "complete lack of legitimacy of the Baton Rouge school system."[25] Teacher disenchantment with coercive school desegregation policies is well documented.[26]

All of these statistics have not been lost on an often divided school board that has been struggling to win back the support of white residents. After the school redesign plan of the late 1980s and early 1990s failed, the board proposed in the 1996 plan to rebuild many of the city's crumbling schools, in addition to building several new schools. It was heralded as the most expensive public school expenditure plan in the history of Louisiana, and indeed the entire U.S. The board championed the plan as the last chance to salvage a disintegrating system. In order to fund the $2.2 billion program, the board went to the city's voters with a tax and bond plan. However, Baton Rouge voters defeated the proposal by a margin of two to one. In the city of Baker, in the northern part of the parish, voters were so dissatisfied with the school district that they voted to create a new district because these rural residents "objected to having their children bused up to 30 miles to school."[27] Another constitutional amendment was passed by the voters of Louisiana in October 1999 granting Zachary, another small city in East Baton Rouge Parish, the right to create its own school system.

There is obviously some support for the Baton Rouge public school system, as a much more modest tax hike to improve parishwide education did pass in 1998. However, based simply on the massive, continuous out-flow of white students into both the parish's nonpublic schools and the public schools of the surrounding parishes, it seems that confidence in the school system among whites is steadily eroding. In a 1999 draft of a report on desegregation in Baton Rouge, co-author of the 1996 plan and nationally recognized desegregation expert Christine H. Rossell remarked, "I do not believe I have ever been in a school system where the schools were in such poor condition as a result of taxpayer non-support."[28] Readers should recall the economic statistics that we cited at the beginning of this chapter. In the present state of racial inequality, white taxpayers are the primary potential source of local funding for schools. Future appeals to the voters of East Baton Rouge parish for public school funding are increasingly likely to fall on deaf and uninterested ears, especially of those who have opted to pay the higher costs of nonpublic education and who would resent double payment.

Continuing De Facto Segregation and the Decline of a School System

As already mentioned, a court-approved consent degree in 1996 ended much forced busing in East Baton Rouge Parish. Between 1996 and 1999 the school board pumped $27 million into desegregation efforts, including funding for special accounts, called "equity accounts," for historically black schools. In fact, some majority-black schools were receiving so much funding, including special monies for technology and traditional Title 1 funding for having many students from poor families, that the superintendent was quoted as saying, "The principals are telling me they're finding it difficult to decide what else they need beyond what they've already bought."[29] Meanwhile, none of these financial incentives has stopped the rate of white flight or the increasingly bitter quarreling among school board members, the local NAACP leadership, and the federal judge who initiated the desegregation process. Between 1996, with the new consent degree designed to end white flight, and the opening of schools in 2000, the East Baton Rouge school system went from 63% to just over 69% black. Not only white enrollment but black enrollment as well was significantly lower. On the opening day of school in 1999, the school system registered the smallest number of students in more than two decades. Approximately twenty-three hundred fewer students showed up for the first day of school in 1999 than on the first day of school in 1998.[30]

As a result of the movement of whites out of the public schools in Louisiana's capital city, overall enrollment declined again by 1,321 students from 1999–2000 to 2000–01. This decline meant that the district could lose $3.4 million in state Department of Education funds, in addition to the $2.7 million it had lost the previous year as a result of dropping enrollments. Although enrollments had peaked in 1979, just before Judge Parker had initiated his mandates to achieve desegregation, they had been going steadily downward ever since. Not only was the system losing money, but school officials acknowledged that the changing racial makeup would complicate efforts of administrators to comply with the demands of the court.[31] It seems reasonable to conclude that the judicial program of desegregation had actually pushed the system toward inescapable de facto segregation, at the costs of diminishing revenues and diminishing public support for public education.

While Baton Rouge dropped in enrollment, the neighboring districts were growing. The schools of Livingston Parish, for example, increased by 339 students in 1997, 402 students in 1998, 237 students in 1999, and 259 in 2000, virtually all of them white students. This expansion was occurring in spite of the fact that Livingston had one of the lowest rates of per-pupil spending in the state.[32]

Even as the system was literally disintegrating, the heated rhetoric on both sides seemed to be taking on a quality of the absurd. The local superintendent of education, Dr. Gary Mathews, maintained that the system had demographically arrived at a point where further racial integration was almost physically impossible. This contention was supported by Louisiana State University demographer Charles Tolbert, who projected that if rates of white flight continued, Baton Rouge public schools would be totally African American by 2020.[33] Tolbert has closely studied the movement of blacks and whites into and out of the parish public schools and noted that with virtually each court consent degree or new desegregation plan, the exodus of whites from the system has increased, as whites react to uncertainty in the system by simply leaving it.[34] Superintendent Mathews has pleaded for an end to the longest desegregation lawsuit in history, so that the system would be free to save itself without outside interference. Black parents agree. Larry Galloway, an African American with two children in Baton Rouge public schools has teamed with twenty-five other parents to end the desegregation suit, now more than four decades old. He observed, "I think we're at a point where Baton Rouge probably cannot be fully desegregated."[35] However, a local NAACP leader strenuously took issue with any suggestion that the courts back out, contending, "There is no way we're going to agree to removing judicial involvement in this system as long as we don't feel our children can get a fair shake without it."[36] At the end of 1999, the East Baton Rouge school board voted to meet once again with Judge Parker, with the intention of proposing such measures as reinstating certain magnet/gifted programs targeted specifically at whites and offering to bus white children directly from their homes to these programs.[37] Ironically, similar programs were dismantled only a few years earlier because they created concentrations of whites. Meanwhile, white parents, and increasingly black parents, silently continue to remove their children from a system taking on the inner city characteristics of William Julius Wilson's "truly disadvantaged."[38]

One parent who did not remove her children from Baton Rouge's public schools as a matter of principle—but now wishes she had—is the former head of Louisiana's influential Public Affairs Research Council. Jackie Ducote was a visible, ardent education reformer and public school supporter who felt she could not go before the state legislature and lobby for public schools if she herself did not set an example by keeping her children in

Baton Rouge's public schools. Her children endured the upheaval of the early days of forced busing, and she now admits they were not progressing as well as she would have liked; her sons eventually found themselves in remedial college classes. They never obtained college diplomas. She confesses, "I probably sacrificed Chip and Drew [her sons] for my principles."[39]

The same sentiment was expressed by the quoted Red Cross volunteer earlier who initially left her children in the public schools because "we didn't feel we could afford it [private schools] at the time." However, when she obtained a paying job several years later, she removed her son from the city high school where "he was miserable and became withdrawn" and enrolled him in a private school. She commented that "he loved it. . . . I wished I had taken him out of the public school system sooner. I very strongly feel that the deseg in Baton Rouge was a failed experiment."[40]

But why? Why would changing racial compositions of Baton Rouge schools necessarily equate with inferior education? East Baton Rouge school board member Patrice Niquille is quoted as saying during a board meeting, "I'm concerned because I'm getting the message here tonight that too many black students in our (school system) is bad . . . and I don't think we want to send that message to our community."[41] There is a strong association in the community—not necessarily due to white racism, although racism undoubtedly continues to be part of the problem—between race, socioeconomic status, family composition, and lower levels of achievement.

Simply put, race, class, and education are closely interrelated in Baton Rouge, as they are in much of American society. In 1990, whereas only 9% of all Baton Rouge whites lived in poverty, the rate was 38%, more than four times higher, for blacks, according to 1990 U.S. Census figures. As we pointed out at the beginning of the chapter, there were significant racial gaps in educational attainment as well. Results from Louisiana's Graduation Exit Examination show clear racial differences in achievement levels. From data tapes provided by the Louisiana Department of Education,[42] we calculated that in 1990—a midpoint in the desegregation experiment—East Baton Rouge whites did significantly better than blacks on all three tenth-grade components of the test. As in New Orleans, the black-white gap also continued throughout the decade. Table 4.3 compares black and white test results in East Baton Rouge schools in 1990, 1994, and 1999.

Many of these data were made available to the general public. Indeed, beginning in 1990, the Louisiana Department of Education provided all public school parents in Louisiana with copies of their children's schools' "report cards," which were often published in local newspapers as well. One of the authors, who worked at the Department of Education on the school "report card" project from 1990 to 1992, fielded several phone calls from parents wanting to know which Baton Rouge schools had the highest test scores. In other words, concerned parents have many sources of information on how well Baton Rouge's schools are performing.

The results of the 1999 Louisiana Educational Assessment Program test, which we saw in the previous chapter on New Orleans, were also well publicized. Table 4.4 summarizes some of these results. Baton Rouge schools do not find themselves in the dire situation of New Orleans schools. There was, in fact, one School of Academic Distinction in East Baton Rouge Parish. It was a middle school, located in an upscale suburb of the school district. It also had the second smallest black population of any school in the district, with only 19% African American students.

As we move down the scale of performance among Baton Rouge schools, the black and low-income populations of schools grow steadily larger. Most schools are classified as Academically Below Average. Further, most of the Academically Below Average Schools and all three of the Academi-

Table 4.3. Average Percent Correct on Tenth-Grade Components of 1990, 1994, and 1999 Louisiana Graduation Exit Examination: East Baton Rouge Parish

	Math	Language Arts	Written Composition
1990			
Blacks (N = 1,822)	59.0%	69.4%	74.9%
Whites (N = 1,729)	75.0%	81.9%	85.9%
1994			
Blacks (N = 2,425)	54.6%	67.8%	72.1%
Whites (N = 1,807)	73.9%	82.5%	83.1%
1999			
Blacks (N = 2,566)	54.6%	73.0%	79.9%
Whites (N = 1,611)	72.0%	85.5%	86.8%

Table 4.4. Performance Categories of Schools in East Baton Rouge and Neighboring Districts

	School of Academic Excellence	School of Academic Distinction	School of Academic Excellence	Academically Above Average	Academically Below Average	Academically Unacceptable
Schools in East Baton Rouge	None	1 (1.2%)	4 (4.9%)	27 (33.3%)	46 (56.8%)	3 (3.7%)
Average percent minority		19%	45%	57%	87%	94%
Minimum		19%	13%	19%	28%	86%
Maximum		19%	88%	88%	100%	99%
Average percent poor		19%	41%	47%	64%	70%
Minimum		19%	27%	27%	27%	59%
Maximum		19%	67%	78%	94%	72%
Schools in Neighboring Districts	None	None	8 (17.8%)	34 (75.9%)	3 (6.7%)	None
Average percent minority			4%	14%	90%	
Minimum			1%	0%	85%	
Maximum			9%	47%	95%	
Average percent poor			36%	45%	90%	
Minimum			30%	26%	84%	
Maximum			51%	70%	93%	

cally Unacceptable schools are made up overwhelmingly of black and low-income students.

It begins to become evident why, apart from the inconvenience of busing, white parents in East Baton Rouge would be upset by suggestions of a massive reshuffling of students. There is a great deal of variation in performance levels among schools. Moreover, this variation is closely tied to the racial and socioeconomic makeup of schools. Clearly, parents who are concerned with placing their children in the most advantageous educational circumstances will want their children in schools with few low-income students and few black students. These are the schools the children of white middle class families would normally attend without an official mandate to redistribute students. From 1981 onward, the mothers and fathers of middle class white children were continually faced with the possibility that their children would be taken out of "good" neighborhood schools and moved to low-performing schools.

What are the advantages of settling outside of East Baton Rouge, in the areas generally identified as white flight areas? Although a majority of schools in Baton Rouge are below average, 93% of the schools in the surrounding suburbs are above average or better. The schools in the white flight areas do appear to have a fairly high degree of racial segregation: among the Schools of Academic Achievement, all had very small percentages of black students. The below average schools in the suburban fringe all had student bodies that were almost entirely black. From the point of view of egalitarian ideals of social justice, this is very disturbing. But from the point of view of a parent with a school-age child, the implications for action are both obvious and inconsistent with egalitarianism. Inside the city and outside, the best schools tend to be those with the smallest minority populations. For all the differences between New Orleans and Baton Rouge, the correlations among the percentage of black students, percentage of low-income students, and school scores look very similar in both districts. In the Baton Rouge area, the correlation (r) between percent minority and percent poor is .783, the correlation between percentage of minority students and school test scores is .763, and the correlation between percent poor and school test scores is .716 (not shown in this table). In other words, the more minority students there are in a school, the more low-income students there are in that school. The more low-income and minority students in a school, the lower the school's measured performance.

Our interviews with parents have convinced us that most parents choose what they believe to be the best educational opportunities they can provide for their children. If they believe that transferring their children from relatively high-achieving schools to relatively low-achieving schools could have negative academic consequences for their children, it is only logical to assume that they will opt for a more favorable educational alternative if they are able to provide one. This explains, we believe, the burgeoning nonpublic school population in East Baton Rouge Parish, as well as some of the phenomenal growth in its two fastest-growing suburban parishes.

What can be done to stem the flow of white—and arguably middle class black—students from the Baton Rouge public school system? Our research leads us to believe that desegregation seems to work best where the minority population is in the minority. As minority figures increase beyond a certain percentage, the majority-white population—whether rightly or wrongly—begins to leave the public schools. Perhaps we can learn much from Baton Rouge. We see that after 1965, when schools could not refuse African Americans, yet prior to 1981, when parents were allowed to send their children to their neighborhood public schools, the system's public schools flourished. Nonpublic school enrollment decreased. However, the sudden death of neighborhood schools in 1981 marked the fairly rapid deterioration of Baton Rouge's school system. Had the federal courts never ordered forced desegregation, it seems highly likely the system would still be a healthy one, though it would probably also still have racially identifiable schools. But from a practical perspective, this would still be better than the current plight of the system: it still has racially identifiable schools, but they are now in a crumbling, financially strapped system with virtually no support from the segment of the community with the most resources. In stark contrast to Baton Rouge, the school board of Lafayette Parish (the district we will discuss in the following chapter) opted to keep its neighborhood schools intact during the flurry of desegregation activity in the 1970s—an action that may have stemmed massive white flight.[43]

Though, regrettably, it may be too late to make Baton Rouge's schools once again attractive to large numbers of middle- and upper-middle-income families—regardless of race—we wonder if perhaps a return to the neighborhood school concept is a compromise well worth the tradeoff of having some racially identifiable schools—which Baton Rouge would have regardless—for support from the socioeconomically advantaged segment of the community. Is it possible that this compromise may be the best chance we have of salvaging viable urban public education in many parts of the United States, including Baton Rouge?

In the next chapter, we turn to look at a third Louisiana school system. Lafayette kept its neighborhood school system intact until a recent federal court order forcibly desegregated the system because its neighborhood schools were also racially identifiable schools. The May 2000 court order has plunged the system into chaos, creating a scenario eerily similar to Baton Rouge during the upheaval caused by Judge Parker's ruling of 1981. We now turn our attention to the largest school system in the heart of French Louisiana—a system whose future is very much in the balance.

Chapter 5

School Desegregation and White Flight in Lafayette Parish

In Orleans Parish, the de jure desegregation of schools was followed by the de facto segregation of the school district, in the sense that New Orleans became, for the most part, an all-black school system. For all the differences between New Orleans and Baton Rouge, this process also seemed to be occurring in East Baton Rouge Parish, where the public school system went from a majority-white to a majority-black population, with every appearance of also eventually becoming an all-black system.

Lafayette may provide an example of another stage in this process, the stage of the beginning of the desegregation of schools and white movement out of the district's public schools. Indeed, based on a May 2000 federal court judge's ruling to rezone, bus, and transfer faculty and administrators,[1] Lafayette may be starting on the same path that New Orleans and Baton Rouge took twenty to thirty years ago. This does not mean that the goal of breaking down de facto segregation is new to Lafayette. Desegregation came to this parish only five years after the school battles in New Orleans, when a lawsuit was filed in 1967 challenging the parish's racially segregated school system.

We will look at the Lafayette school system in some detail for two reasons. First, Lafayette is a smaller school district than either of the two major urban districts discussed above, enrolling approximately 29,000 students in the 2000–01 school year. Its smaller size makes it possible to focus on some characteristics of each individual school. Second, Lafayette appears to be beginning the process of desegregation and shift in racial composition that has been completed in New Orleans and that is well under way in Baton Rouge. The third and smallest district, then, gives us an opportunity to examine desegregation and responses to it at an early stage of conflict, controversy—and chaos.

Lafayette Parish provides a particularly interesting case study. It differs from New Orleans, Baton Rouge, and other parts of the state in a number of respects. In some ways, it is also much more unlike other parts of the southern United States than are Louisiana's large metropolitan areas. It is located in the middle of French Louisiana, also known as Acadiana, which is one of the more unusual regions of the South. The majority of the whites who inhabit the area are Catholics of French descent—not Anglo-Saxon Protestant like most of the rest of the former Confederacy. Moreover, in some of the parishes that surround Lafayette, as much as half the population still speaks French at home.[2] Much of the African American population is French-speaking Catholic as well, with a large group of mixed-race "Creoles" who have carved out their own strong identity independent of white and black American culture. The virulent racism associated with white supremacist groups like the Ku Klux Klan, which were anti-Catholic as well as antiblack, never thrived in Acadiana.[3] Consequently, scholars believe that in general, French Louisiana has traditionally been more tolerant of differences than any other area of the South, as evidenced in part by voting data.[4]

Still, there is apparently a strong sense of racial consciousness among the region's inhabitants, as well as enduring racial stereotyping. By way of example, a fair-skinned African American woman from Miami, Florida, who worked in a rural school in neighboring St. Martin Parish shared with one of the authors her shock at having lighter-skinned Creole blacks counsel her upon arriving in Acadiana "not to cut her hair or get too much sun," so she wouldn't be identified with darker-skinned blacks. "I was totally freaked out and thought I was losing my mind!" she exclaimed, especially after a darker-skinned yard worker at the University of Louisiana at Lafayette was surprised that she, a lighter-skinned black, would even speak with him. Her confusion was compounded when she mistook lighter-skinned blacks at the university for whites, who politely pointed out they were African Americans. She had several white male friends and described suffering many subtle and not so subtle slights and insults by others when going out with them in public. "Around here, everyone has their place," she lamented, except her.[5]

Like the rest of the South, between Reconstruction in the 1870s and the Civil Rights movement of the 1960s, racial segregation was the norm in Lafayette, with Jim Crow laws very much in force. Moreover, during the darkest days of de jure segregation, public education for blacks was almost nonexistent, while there were thirty parish white schools in 1910. However, even during the worst days of Jim Crow, Lafayette citizens exhibited moderate racial attitudes for their day, repealing an ordinance one month after its passage that would have created "two separate and distinct communities where all Negroes would have had to reside."[6]

From the viewpoint of school desegregation, Lafayette is unique in yet other ways as well. Like New Orleans, it has a strong tradition of Catholic education, and a sizable parochial school system. However, unlike large cities such as New Orleans, Baton Rouge, and Shreveport, there are no white flight parishes or school districts adjoining Lafayette Parish that would attract disgruntled white or black families attempting to flee central district schools seen as declining. The reasons are essentially economic. Economically, Lafayette Parish is the strongest parish in south-central Louisiana, having a lower average poverty rate (20%) than the state average (24%) and a much greater percentage of households earning $35,000 per year (43%)than the state average (30%), a figure equivalent to the national average in 1990. A higher percentage of parish residents possess a bachelor's degree or higher (23%) than either the state average (16%) or even the national average (20%). Moreover, the percentage of whites living in the parish (76%) is relatively large for a state that is roughly one-third African American.[7]

In contrast to New Orleans, in particular, the Lafayette public school district is not in the urbanized area of a long-established city. Lafayette is a postindustrial, post-automobile district, in which a wide, decentralized, suburban area grew up rapidly from a small town after the 1960s. The Lafayette school district includes schools in fairly urbanized neighborhoods close to the old town center, schools in suburban neighborhoods, and several schools in small towns around the city of Lafayette. These include Duson and Youngsville (schools in rural areas) and Scott, Carencro, Broussard, and Milton (urban fringe schools). In the two rural areas, blacks make up about one-fifth of the student population in Duson and a little over one-tenth of the student population in Youngsville. In the urban fringe, blacks are a small minority (less than one-tenth) of the student population in Milton and about one-quarter of the student population in Broussard. The black-white ratio in the schools of Scott is approximately that of the city of Lafayette. Carencro is a majority-black community, and between two-thirds and three-quarters of its school-age children are black.[8]

This setting has two major implications for school desegregation. First, those families that opt out of the Lafayette Parish public school system are unlikely to move to public schools in one of the surrounding lower socioeconomic status parishes. Those who choose to leave Lafayette's public schools are most likely to send their children to one of the parish's twelve Catholic schools. Lafayette Parish's Catholic schools enrolled 6,200 students during the 2000–01 school year.[9] Another option, which has apparently been chosen by many following the new court order, is to leave Acadiana altogether. A third option, exercised by 390 students as of June 2000, was to opt out of formal schooling altogether and be educated in their homes. It may not be coincidental that whereas there were only 75 renewed applications for home-schooled children from the previous school year, there were 183 new applicants electing to home-school their children for the 2000–01 school year.[10] The second major implication of Lafayette's setting is that residential segregation in Lafayette contributes to racially identifiable schools within the district.

While Lafayette may differ from the major urban areas in some respects, in one it looks very similar to New Orleans and Baton Rouge: the black and white populations are distinct socioeconomic groups. Among white family households containing children under eighteen in 1990, well over 80% were married-couple families. Slightly over 50% of black family households with minor children were married-couple families, and 45% of Lafayette's black family households were headed by single women. Since black single-parent families tend to contain more children than black two-parent families, a majority of Lafayette's black children (58%) lived in homes with only one parent, while only 18% of white children lived in one-parent homes at the time of the 1990 U.S. Census. Again, black single-parent families tended to result from births to unmarried mothers. Over 50% of the children born to black women in Lafayette aged fifteen to thirty-four were born to women who were not married by the time of the 1990 U.S. Census.

Although, as we have noted, Lafayette was in a strong economic position, the economic benefits were largely enjoyed by whites. A clear majority of black households (58%) had yearly incomes below $15,000. One-fourth (24%) of the black households had yearly incomes less than $5,000. As in New Orleans, most black school-age children were living in poverty: 55% of black children aged five through seventeen were classified as below the poverty level. By comparison, only 23% of white households had annual incomes less than $15,000. The white lower-income households, moreover, tended not to contain school-age children. Only 12% of white children aged five to seventeen were below the official poverty level.

As in the other areas we have examined, black adults in Lafayette had limited educational backgrounds that they could draw on for preparing their children for the school environment. Over half (52%) of Lafayette's black population over age twenty-five had not finished high school in 1990. Over one-fourth (27%) of the parish's black adults had not finished ninth grade. In the white population however, over half the adults had attended some college, and 30% had completed degrees.

While the character and pace of desegregation in Lafayette may have differed from the two large metropolitan areas, then, both the rationale for it and the motivations for resisting it are the same. Blacks and whites are two separate socioeconomic groups. The disadvantages of the former make achieving greater equality in education, as in other institutions, an important social goal. But these disadvantages also mean that increasing the proportion of minority children in schools is tantamount to increasing the presence of poor children from single-parent families, children who have received inadequate preparation for the educational environment. Below, we look at some of the indications that white flight is now starting in this relatively prosperous parish—and may be on the point of markedly accelerating. Then, we look at the history of desegregation before considering in detail conditions in Lafayette public schools.

Indications of White Flight

Despite the reported historical racial tolerance and the unique features of Lafayette, there are some indications that white movement out of public schools has begun, and that this movement is related to dissatisfaction resulting from recent efforts at more active desegregation policies than the parish followed in the past. We can find evidence of white public dissatisfaction (white flight)—or conversely, satisfaction—with the public schools by noting changes in the percentage of all white students enrolled in the parish's nonpublic schools over time. If the number and percentage of all white students in nonpublic schools increase in tandem with efforts to integrate the public school system forcibly, especially as white enrollment figures in the public schools drop, it can be surmised that the upward trends most likely reflect white flight. A consequence of white flight is that an increasingly large percentage of the public school population is African American. Therefore, as we did for New Orleans and Baton Rouge, we calculate the percentage of Lafayette Parish's public school population that is black, and we follow the trend over time.

The trends are presented in two line graphs plotted in Figure 5.1, presented in the following section. Using regression analysis, we also calculate the rate at which the system is becoming African American, as well as the rate at which the white student population is shifting into the parish's nonpublic schools. Considering these rates in light of the percentages of the overall population that are white and black, and changes in these figures over time, provides an additional perspective on, and evidence for, white flight. We will look at these indicators of white flight in greater detail below. For the moment, we will note three points of particular interest: First, there has been a general trend toward increases in the percentage of public school students who are black. Second, despite this increase, black students continue to make up a decided minority of the public school students in Lafayette. Third, the white nonpublic school population has gone through periods of growth and decline roughly tied to decades: a period of decline in the late 1960s, a period of growth in the 1970s, another period of decline in the 1980s, and a period of growth in the 1990s. An examination of Lafayette's history of school desegregation may shed some light on these peculiar trends.

De Jure Desegregation and "Freedom of Choice"

Unlike Louisiana districts such as New Orleans, which vigorously resisted desegregation of its public school system, initial efforts to racially integrate Lafayette parish schools were not met with outright hostility by whites, but with an attitude more like resignation to the inevitable.[11] When A. P. Tureaud, the Louisiana NAACP lawyer who championed the cause of desegregation (see Chapter 3), filed a petition in 1953 to desegregate

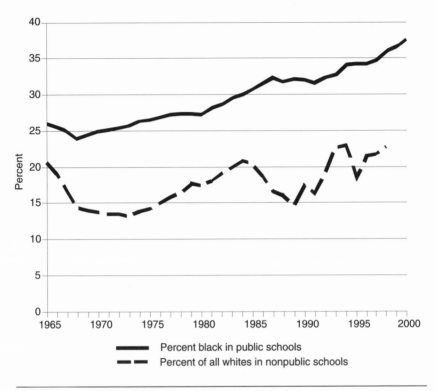

Figure 5.1. Racial Shifts in Lafayette Parish, 1965–2000

Lafayette's school system, the small southwest Louisiana city responded with none of the extremism of its large neighbor to the east. Rather than threaten to close the public school system, the Lafayette Parish school board said that it would take the petition "under advisement." This was a year before the historic *Brown* decision, which declared de jure school racial segregation unconstitutional. Right after the *Brown* decision, in 1954, the Southwestern Louisiana Institute in Lafayette (later the University of Southwestern Louisiana, and now the University of Louisiana at Lafayette) admitted its first black student, without protest from the white community. This is in stark contrast to schools like the University of Alabama, where the governor personally barred the doorway to blacks seeking entrance. Moreover, Southwestern was the first white educational institution at any level in the entire state to admit black students.[12]

Still, the Lafayette school board did not actively try to integrate its schools until more than a decade later, in 1967. The catalyst was a lawsuit filed in March of that year by the NAACP in the Western Division of the U.S. District Court on behalf of Alfreda Trahan and seventeen other black students. Subsequently, the Lafayette Parish school board adopted an incremental "freedom of choice" approach to school integration that initially allowed only twelfth-grade students the choice of attending a school dominated by another race. The plan was extended over the next two years to include students in grades 1, 2, 5, 6, and 11. The approach led to approximately eight hundred to nine hundred blacks enrolling in formerly all-white schools, though no whites chose to enroll in any of the black schools.[13] Not satisfied with the results, Federal District Court Judge Putnam ordered the school system to desegregate more forcibly beginning with the 1967–68 school year. Still, there was no large-scale white public resistance of the kind that tore the Orleans Parish school system apart.

The initial movement of some black students into formerly all-white schools did not result in whites leaving the school system. On the contrary, initial desegregation efforts coincided with a sharp *decrease* in both the number and percentage of all white students in the parish attending Lafayette's extensive nonpublic school system during the late 1960s.

As shown in Table 5.1, between 1965 and 1970 (the year when limited busing was first introduced) the percentage of all parish white students enrolled in Lafayette's nonpublic schools decreased an average of 1.5% per

**Table 5.1. Annual Change in Proportion
of All White Students in Lafayette
Parish Enrolled in Nonpublic Schools**

Range in Years	Average Annual Change (%)
1965–1970	−1.5
1971–1980	0.53
1981–1990	−0.43
1991–2000	0.58

Source: *Annual Financial and Statistical Report* (Baton Rouge, Louisiana Department of Education: 1965–2000).

year. The percentage of the parish's school population that was African American also decreased from 1965 to 1970, by an average of 0.5% per year. These trends suggest that Lafayette did not have the hardened racial attitudes of some other areas of the country, a position supported by research that indicates that French-influenced southwestern Louisiana has traditionally been more tolerant of racial diversity than other areas of the South.[14]

Thus it seems that when children were allowed to attend their neighborhood schools or opt for another school if they so chose, the level of white public contentment with the school system was not diminished, as measured by the percentage of all white students in the public system. Moreover, the admission of eight hundred to nine hundred blacks into formerly all-white schools did not cause a white exodus from Lafayette's public schools. Indeed, the contrary occurred. Under the freedom of choice system, though, only small degrees of racial mixing actually occurred in Lafayette's schools. Whites continued to attend mainly white schools, and blacks continued to attend mainly black schools.

The Supreme Court's decision against "freedom of choice" as an integration tool in the 1968 case of *Green v. County School Board,* affected school systems around the country. This decision led to Louisiana's freedom of choice plans being ruled unconstitutional later in the year. There was resistance on the part of both blacks and whites in Lafayette to abandoning the freedom of choice approach.[15] The end of the 1960s initiated a period of several years of negotiation and experimentation with a variety of racial integration plans. Federal Judge Putnam ordered a modified busing plan that involved busing black students from two areas of Lafayette into predominately white schools. A system of school rezoning was also implemented. However, many other desegregation plans proposed by either the school board itself, outside consultants to the board, or the original plaintiffs in the desegregation lawsuit were rejected. Some were rejected by the board, some were found unacceptable by the federal judge, and others were opposed by the plaintiffs. The early to mid-1970s can best be characterized as a chaotic period of proposals and counterproposals as the community tried to find a desegregation plan acceptable to all.

Finally, during the late 1970s, with strong opposition to all busing of elementary school children, the board adopted a plan to keep neighborhood school zones in tact for kindergarten through fifth-grade schools and to convert a formerly all-black high school (Paul Breaux) into a racially diverse magnet school that could draw students from all over the parish (now Paul Breaux Middle School, which houses the parish's gifted and French immersion programs). This compromise position was accepted by the courts and the plaintiffs in the desegregation lawsuit. The U.S. Justice Department withdrew from the case in 1979 because it deemed the Lafayette Parish school system in compliance with the federal court order.[16]

However, the upheaval and uncertainty of the 1970s were not without some adverse consequences for the school system. In 1969, a year after the implementation of Judge Putnam's court order, the trend of white students moving out of the parochial school system and into the public school system stopped, then reversed itself. Throughout the entire period of debate in the 1970s over how to integrate Lafayette's public schools, an increasing percentage of whites opted for parochial school education for their children in response to growing uncertainty regarding public education. From 1971 through 1980, the percentage of all white students enrolled in the parish's nonpublic schools increased an average of 0.5% per year. Research on public attitudes at the time offers some insights as to why. A survey of sixty-four white Lafayette High School students conducted in 1978 indicated that a majority felt that a return to freedom of choice was the best way to end segregation and that court-ordered desegregation did not enhance the quality of education. The same survey of an admittedly small number of nine black Lafayette High students, however, indicated 67% (six) felt integration had improved their education.[17] These divergent attitudes do, however, roughly follow national trends wherein whites tend to be more disenchanted than blacks with coercive school integration.[18] As can be seen in Figure 5.1, from 1970 through 1980, the proportion of all Lafayette Parish white students enrolled in nonpublic schools increased from 13.7% to 17.4%. Still, it was not the massive exodus of whites from public education that some other systems experienced, most notably those like Baton Rouge, which used a "sledgehammer" approach by comparison, forcing desegregation through busing on a much broader scale.

Even though Lafayette took a gentler approach to school integration, the proportion of parish whites enrolled in Lafayette's nonpublic schools slowly continued to rise, until by 1984 almost 21% of parish whites were opting out of the public school system. Even this relatively high number, however, was much smaller than the 32% of all East Baton Rouge Parish whites who were enrolled in nonpublic schools in the same year, in a parish that was 32% African American in 1980 (in 1980, African Americans constituted 24% of the Lafayette parish population), and in a district without the strong Catholic school tradition of Lafayette.

From 1984 through the early 1990s, the percentage of all parish whites in public schools began to increase once again as the absolute numbers of whites in the parish's nonpublic schools decreased fairly dramatically. This shift to the public schools may have been due not so much to the perceived higher quality of public education as to economic reality: oil prices collapsed, and along with them, so did Lafayette's heavily oil-dependent economy. Unemployment skyrocketed, and it is likely that many who could no longer afford the cost of Catholic schools were forced by economic necessity to send their children local public schools.

Lafayette's racially segregated residential areas helped to maintain de facto segregation in the schools. As in Baton Rouge, most black residents lived on the north side of town, and most white residents lived on the south side. The city grew rapidly in the late 1970s and early 1980s, resulting in rapid growth on the south side, and both racial and economic differences between white and black parts of town became more pronounced.

As oil prices edged upward during the mid- to late 1990s and Lafayette's economy became increasingly diversified, economic good times returned to the parish, with subsequent growth in population. Indeed, the population of Lafayette Parish grew by 12% between 1990 and 1998.[19] As school populations swelled, the school board decided to build four new schools. This necessitated redrawing school attendance boundaries. In order to remain in compliance with the desegregation court order, the school board created a biracial committee to make recommendations to the board regarding rezoning, a process that had to consider school racial concentrations as a criterion in drawing boundary lines.[20] Thus, during the later part of the 1998–99 school year, and in the face of much opposition from some parent groups, the Lafayette Parish school board redrew the attendance zones of several elementary and middle schools. Many were dissatisfied with the new attendance zones. Some (e.g, the NAACP) complained that the new attendance zones were in violation of the desegregation court order, since the racial composition of at least twenty-two of the parish's thirty-nine schools were still "racially identifiable" (either white or black). On the other hand, the changes would have forced some parents who had their children in the highest-performing schools in the parish to send their children to schools with the lowest-performing students in the parish. Moreover, the board decided to move the popular French immersion program from a largely white, high-achieving suburban school in south Lafayette to a school in a black neighborhood in the northern part of the parish with a much higher percentage of African American students.

These two moves prompted angry parents of affected families to pack into standing- room-only school board meetings dedicated to discussing these issues. Several irate parents hired a lawyer and petitioned the school board to restore the original school boundaries, which would have allowed them to keep their children in the high-performing schools. However, under threat from the NAACP and the original plaintiffs in the thirty-year-old desegregation suit, the board decided not to adjust school attendance zones. Affected parents at one board meeting in May 1999 threatened to pull their children out of the system and enroll them in a Catholic school rather than send them to their new school.[21] One white parent told the authors that if school board rezoning would force her daughter to attend a predominately black high school, she would take out a second mortgage on her house to buy land in the predominately white school zone she had been expecting to attend.[22] If she couldn't do that, she said she would "definitely" put her daughter in a Catholic school. She hastened to add, however, that she was not "prejudiced," and even had a black godchild. With the help of their attorney, some of these parents filed a motion with the federal judge overseeing school desegregation asking for a return to the original school zone boundaries. The motion was unsuccessful.

Some parents may have carried out threats to pull their children from the public schools. Official parish enrollment counts for the 1999–2000 school year fell to their lowest level in 5 years, declining by 907 students, 621 of them white. The drastic drop in enrollment caught school officials by surprise.[23] It is true that a winter/spring 1999 downturn in the oil sector forced several companies to scale back operations in the Lafayette area, requiring some families to relocate out of the parish. Significantly, however, Catholic school enrollment increased. Official diocesan figures indicate that enrollment in fall 1999 was up 184 students in Lafayette Parish Catholic schools. The most logical explanation for this increase is that even the egress of families out of Lafayette was not enough to offset the defection of students from public to parochial schools. Our interviews with parents, teachers, and officials in parochial schools indicate that students were indeed moving out of public schools in response to the new desegregation efforts.

However, the most significant impact on the district came when Federal District Court Judge Haik declared in May 2000 that the system was in violation of the 1967 court order to desegregate. He almost immediately ordered the system to close two black schools, bus students from those schools across town to five predominantly white schools, transfer eleven principals based on their race, and adjust faculty racial compositions. The community reaction was immediate as well, and almost eight hundred fewer whites attended the parish's public schools in August 2000. One teacher at a Lafayette Catholic high school, who would speak only on condition of anonymity as she feared being fired by the Catholic diocese if her comments were known, told the authors that "It's no problem with us. Our school benefits whenever the school board tinkers with the system and whites leave the public schools."[24] At least initially, however, the bishop of the Catholic diocese refused to take any white students fleeing the system— an unprecedented action. However, the bishop reversed his order in October 2000. As of November 2000, white enrollment in Lafayette's Catholic schools was up by more than one hundred students from the previous school year.

No Massive Black Flight

It does not appear that there has been any significant black flight from Lafayette's public schools. Indeed, the percentage of black students in the parish's nonpublic schools has decreased steadily from a high of 25% of all blacks in nonpublic schools in 1965 to only 6.5% of all blacks in nonpublic schools in 1997. One long-time resident and educational administration graduate student at the University of Louisiana volunteered that many blacks initially left the black Catholic schools for the predominately white public schools because they believed they would finally get a superior education as they obtained long-awaited access to the resources of the white elite of the community.[25] Still, there is apparently a core of the parish's black middle and upper class who do not enroll their children in the parish's public schools. One Catholic school teacher with whom we spoke claimed that many black students are sent to her Catholic school to avoid having to attend school with "lower income blacks."[26] Nevertheless, for many of the parish's blacks of lower socioeconomic status, attending a school that requires tuition is out of the question. Indeed, though there was a sharp downturn in the number of whites attending Lafayette's public schools in 2000–01, there was an increase of more than two hundred African American students over the previous school year. In short, the black presence in the school system as a whole has increased markedly since recent court intervention ostensibly aimed at desegregating the schools.

Threshold Effect

Based on our examinations of New Orleans, Baton Rouge, and other parts of the state, we believe that Lafayette public schools were at a crossroads at the beginning of the twenty-first century. The proportion of the white population enrolled in the parish's nonpublic schools was close to a forty-year high in 2000, and growing. Moreover, the proportion of the public school population that was African American had never been higher, and was disproportionate to the overall black parish population. In 1970, the parish public school population was only 24% African American. By 1998, the African American portion of the school population had grown to 36%, and by the 2000–01 school year the percentage had increased to 37.5%.

Additionally, the percentage of students who were black was growing at an accelerating rate. Table 5.2 shows the rate of growth in the percentage of the Lafayette Parish public school population that was African American. The percentage of students in the parish's public schools who were black actually decreased during the first five years of "freedom of choice" racial integration, from 1965–1970. However, during the uncertain decade of the 1970s, the percentage of black students in the public schools increased at a rate of about one-third of a percentage point per year. This rate of growth almost doubled to 0.57% per year from 1981 to 1990, and then accelerated yet again from 1991 to 2000, with the average percentage of the public school population African American increasing at a rate of 0.67% per year. Looked at from another perspective, in the school year 2000–01 alone, the white public school student population decreased by 4.5%.

Taking all the trends together, it seems that the growth in the percentage of black students in the public schools is in large part due to whites leaving the system for the parish's nonpublic schools and, more recently,

Table 5.2. Annual Change in Proportion of African American Students in Lafayette Parish Public School System

Range in Years	Average Annual Change (%)
1965–1970	−1.5
1971–1980	0.32
1981–1990	0.57
1991–2000	0.67

Source: *Annual Financial and Statistical Report* (Baton Rouge, Louisiana Department of Education: 1965–2000).

to home schooling as well. If this growth in the African American presence in schools continues at current rates, Lafayette will be a majority-black system in less than twenty years. However, given the "threshold effect," which could result in an acceleration of white flight as the system is viewed, justly or not, as increasingly undesirable whether unjustly or not the rate of racial change could increase markedly.

It is important to note that the growth rate in the percentage of black students in the schools does not correspond with overall parish growth rates. During roughly the same period that Lafayette has been attempting to integrate its schools, the African American population in Lafayette Parish grew only from 22% to 24% of the total population between 1980 and 1990,[27] an increase of less than 0.1% per year. However, the percentage of Lafayette's public schools that is black has been growing more than five times faster than the percentage of the parish's overall population that is black.

Why would black concentration cause white flight? Research and past experience indicate that there is a point beyond which racial concentration tends to lower average school achievement levels. This point has been determined to be approximately 40% minority concentration both in Louisiana and elsewhere.[28] Beyond this point, we can expect an increase in the rate of white flight from public schools as parents, white and middle class black, seek to maximize their children's education elsewhere. Whereas, fortunately, white attitudes nationally toward sending children to schools with

50% or fewer African Americans have been improving, this is not the case with identifiably black schools. Research indicates that historically, a consistently large majority of whites object to putting their children in schools in which large proportions of the students are black.[29]

If Baton Rouge is on the brink of becoming another New Orleans, the medium-sized city of Lafayette is on track to becoming another Baton Rouge. As noted in the previous chapter, white flight from East Baton Rouge Parish between 1965 and 1978, just before the school system reached 40% African American, was marginal.[30] During these years of neighborhood schools, the percentage of black students in the system grew by about 0.1% per year, a figure that was actually less than the overall growth rate of African Americans in the capital city parish.[31] However, when Baton Rouge passed the 40% mark in black representation in the schools, the rate of white flight increased almost tenfold, causing the proportion of black students in the system to increase by more than 1% per year. In a recent report on desegregation in Baton Rouge, a system that has moved well beyond any threshold point, desegregation expert Christine Rossell of Boston University states that "any kind of mandatory reassignment or enrollment caps . . . cause[s] significant white flight and [is] ultimately self-defeating."[32]

Racially Identifiable Schools and School Quality in Lafayette

While Lafayette schools were in danger of approaching the threshold of white tolerance in racial composition at the beginning of the twentieth century, many of the district's schools continued to be racially identifiable. Tables 5.3 and 5.4 show the racial composition of Lafayette schools in 1999. Since Lafayette has fewer schools than New Orleans or Baton Rouge, we are able to present information on all of the schools in the district. In this third and smaller city, then, we can examine the individual schools in more detail than we have in the previous chapters.

Of Lafayette's twenty-three public elementary schools, six were almost entirely black and seven were over 80% white. Over half the district's schools, then, can be said to have been effectively segregated. There is also a close connection between racial composition and socioeconomic composition. The six black schools were overwhelmingly composed of low-income students. In each of the seven white schools, low-income students were in the minority. It is not surprising that racial differences in the schools would be associated with socioeconomic differences, given the statistics that we saw at the beginning of the chapter.

We spoke with a white parent who had moved to Lafayette from another part of Louisiana and confessed that he had intentionally bought a house in a school district with a mostly white student body: "I hate to say it," he said, "but it's true. The schools where the black kids are are bad schools, and the schools where the white kids are are good schools."[33] The

Table 5.3. African American Populations, Academic Rankings, and LEAP Test Scores in Lafayette Parish Elementary Schools, 1999

Percent African American	Percent Low Income	Ranking	Test Scores
99.2	96.8	Below Average	36.4
99.0	81.2	Below Average	63.5
98.8	94.1	Below Average	36.4
97.1	88.9	Below Average	43.6
93.3	92.1	Below Average	45.1
90.6	80.9	Below Average	42.0
63.3	74.7	Below Average	64.2
58.0	67.5	Above Average	89.4
54.2	65.8	Above Average	99.9
39.4	55.4	Above Average	69.9
35.0	64.8	Above Average	69.9
27.5	38.2	School of Academic Achievement	106.0
27.3	45.4	Above Average	96.8
26.3	44.7	Above Average	89.1
25.4	58.7	Above Average	76.3
24.2	64.5	Above Average	73.5
19.8	28.0	School of Academic Achievement	106.0
18.4	25.3	School of Academic Achievement	105.0
18.3	43.9	Above Average	93.2
17.2	17.7	School of Academic Achievement	120.0
16.6	24.6	School of Academic Distinction	127.5
11.4	33.2	Above Average	89.2
6.2	17.9	School of Academic Achievement	100.4

data in Table 5.3 seem to support this observation. Among the seven schools that were over 80% white in 1999, one was a School of Academic Distinction, four were Schools of Academic Achievement, and the remaining two schools were above average. All of the six black schools were ranked as below average. The racially mixed schools generally ranked between these two extremes.

Lafayette's middle schools were not as racially distinctive as the elementary schools, since middle schools have larger student bodies and draw on larger residential areas. Nevertheless, percentages of black students in the district's twelve middle schools were, with one exception, either substantially above or substantially below the percentage of black students in the district as a whole. The exception is a school designed specifically to draw whites. As mentioned earlier, Paul Breaux Middle School is located in the majority-black north part of town and offers magnet classes for honors and gifted students from all over the parish and nonmagnet classes for students in its residential zone. Almost all the students in the magnet classes

Table 5.4. African American Populations, Academic Rankings, and LEAP Test Scores in Lafayette Parish Middle Schools, 1999

Percent African American	Percent Low Income	Ranking	Test Scores
89.2	91.8	Below Average	42.8
67.1	69.6	Below Average	53.3
54.5	59.5	Above Average	77.0
47.9	66.6	Below Average	61.5
34.1[a]	31.9	School of Academic Achievement	119.7
29.8	54.6	Above Average	80.4
28.4	62.7	Above Average	95.5
22.5	38.5	Above Average	85.5
16.7	36.7	Above Average	76.4
16.1	20.5	School of Academic Achievement	106.9
14.0	21.4	School of Academic Achievement	101.1
11.3	31.8	Above Average	90.6

[a]Contains an almost all-white magnet component and an almost all-black component of nonmagnet classes.

are white; almost all the students in the nonmagnet classes are black. Thus, even this school is desegregated on paper only.

Again, there were close connections among racial composition, the economic background of students, and test scores. It may be objected that the apparent relation between racial makeup and school performance is really a matter of poverty and wealth and has nothing to do with race itself. We would accept the argument that the relatively weak performance of majority-black schools is not a consequence of inherent differences between black and white students. As we have pointed out, however, there is such a close connection between race and socioeconomic status in Lafayette, as in other areas, that any school with a black majority would almost necessarily have a majority of poor students, unless that school were extremely small and extremely selective.

Do the high schools differ from the lower grade levels? Since the Louisiana Educational Assessment Program (LEAP) test is only given to elementary and middle-school students, we do not have precisely comparable results for the five high schools in the Lafayette school district. However, we have assembled from the school report cards the racial and socioeconomic compositions of each high school and the percentages of students reported to have passed the language and math components of Louisiana's Graduation Exit Examination in the 1995–96 school year. While these data do not come from the same year as our data on the elementary schools, racial compositions of Lafayette schools remained essentially the same from the mid- through the late 1990s.

Again, since there are fewer schools at the higher grade levels, these schools show greater racial mixing. At the same time, though, even at the high school level, schools were racially identifiable. At one extreme, close to 70% of students were black. At the other extreme, over 80% of students were white. Three of the high schools were majority-white schools, and in only one were blacks and whites represented at close to the ratio of the district as a whole.

While percentages passing tests are admittedly an extremely rough measure of school academic performance, there is evidence here that the school variations seen in the earlier grades tend to be found also in high school. This was particularly noticeable in mathematics, since only 67% of students in the majority-black high school passed this portion of the test (see

Table 5.5. Minority Populations and Percentages Passing the Language and Mathematics Sections of Louisiana's Graduation Exit Examinations in Lafayette High Schools

Percent Minority	Percent Low Income	Percent Passing Language Test	Percent Passing Math Test
68	53	85	67
40	22	86	77
25	26	90	85
22	14	90	89
17	18	90	88

Table 5.5). The general level of school performance appears to be linked to the racial makeup of schools at every grade level.

At the individual level, as well as the school level, there were marked differences between black and white high school students in the Lafayette system. Table 5.6 shows the average scores of black and white students on the Graduation Exit Examinations in 1990, 1994, and 1999. The minority students consistently scored substantially below white students in the district in every test area. This does not mean, of course, that no black students outperformed whites. Among the former in 1990, for example, 28% scored above the white mean in math, 25% scored above the white mean in language arts, and 22% scored above the white mean in written composition. While individual high achievers undoubtedly exist, it remains the case that about three-quarters of black students were below average if we use the standards applied to whites. Further, there were very few high achievers among Lafayette's African American students. Only 10.6% of black students made scores that were in the top quarter by white standards in math, only 4.9% in language arts, and only 5.8% in written composition. Again, we are not suggesting that these test results should be taken as indications of innate ability. Nevertheless, no reasonable observer can escape concluding that, in terms of test performance, most African American students in this district are low performers and that the measurable achievement level of schools is affected by racial composition.

It should be noted that although Lafayette's black students showed lower scores than the white students, the black-white gap in this district was actually slightly smaller than it was in Baton Rouge and much smaller than it was in New Orleans. However, in Lafayette, as elsewhere, there was a close connection between race and measurable school outcomes.

Do better test scores mean better schools? This is a difficult question and one that we will attempt to examine in greater detail in Chapter 7 when we discuss the academic consequences of racial composition. For the moment, however, it should suffice to observe that the general level of school performance is something that parents may reasonably take into consideration when thinking about where they would prefer to have their children. Parents who want to place their children in high-performing schools are likely to attempt to get their children into majority-white schools and keep them there. Those who have children in majority-white schools will be understandably upset by any suggestion of school rezoning. On the other hand, parents (primarily black parents, by definition) whose children are in majority-black schools can legitimately feel that their children are being unfairly denied opportunities by isolation in educational ghettoes. The question of the de facto, as opposed to de jure, segregation of schools, then, seems to us a genuine dilemma between valid, opposing interests. However, whites ultimately have greater ability to pursue the interests of their own families than blacks do, since white families have more opportunities

Table 5.6. Average Percent Correct on Tenth-Grade Components of 1990, 1994, and 1999 Louisiana Graduation Exit Examinations: Lafayette Parish

	Math	*Language Arts*	*Written Composition*
1990			
Blacks (N = 551)	57.9%	60.5%	71.6%
Whites (N = 1,729)	70.3%	71.9%	82.2%
1994			
Blacks (N = 631)	58.1%	68.5%	70.7%
Whites (N = 1,338)	72.4%	80.2%	80.8%
1999			
Blacks (N = 683)	55.9%	71.4%	79.0%
Whites (N = 1,449)	70.9%	82.4%	85.4%

to move out of the public school system if their interests are endangered. We want to make it clear that we are not pointing this out in order to condemn struggling minority schools, nor are we suggesting that there is no hope for the improvement of minority schools. However, it should be evident that parents in Lafayette, like the parents in New Orleans and Baton Rouge, who are concerned about the educational environment of their own children can be realistically concerned about the racial makeup of their children's schools.

The Educational Environments of Lafayette Schools

The black, white, and racially mixed schools of Lafayette differ from one another in more than just socioeconomic composition and test scores. Physical resources are unequally distributed. One mother of a child in the almost exclusively black elementary school reported that her child's school did not have air conditioning in its gymnasium, a serious shortcoming during late spring semester in the hot south Louisiana climate. There are more computers in the white schools, and office equipment such as copiers are more abundant in schools with small minority populations. The classrooms in the white schools have better decorations.

These differences are probably not due to explicit racial discrimination in funding. Indeed, the official per-pupil funding in majority-black schools is somewhat higher than in majority-white schools, since the former receive allocations of federal funds as Title I grants to schools serving low-income students. The variations in resources stem from three factors. First, the majority-white schools are generally located in more recently developed neighborhoods, so the school buildings tend to be of newer construction. Second, government funding is not the only source of money to schools. Candy sales, fairs, and other forms of fund-raising contribute greatly to the equipment and material teaching aids in contemporary public schools. The greater the financial well-being of the families of students, the more money schools are able to raise. Third, parent volunteers play a part in preparing classrooms and schools, with relatively more affluent parents participating to a greater extent.

This last point suggests an important problem of school environments, one that we have discussed in looking at schools in New Orleans and Baton

Rouge but that we can look at in more detail in this smaller school district. Schools with large minority populations do not lack economic resources alone. They also lack social resources, specifically social resources associated with family background.

Table 5.7 gives us some preliminary characteristics of Lafayette public schools related to school environment and family background. Here, we take school suspensions per one hundred students as an indicator of the order or disorder prevailing in schools. This is a very imperfect indicator, but we will look at this question in more detail below.

We distinguish suspensions of students in all schools and suspensions of students in middle schools and high schools alone because behavior is usually a much more serious problem in middle and high schools, and they have higher suspension rates than elementary schools. Among all schools, there was an average of only 8 suspensions per 100 students in the 12 schools with a minority population of 20% or less. This went up to 10 suspensions per 100 students in the 14 schools with a minority population of 20% to 40%. In the 5 schools with 40% to 60% minority students, this shot up to 31 out of every 100 students, a very high suspension rate. In the schools that were almost all black, only 15 per 100 were suspended. However, readers should remember that all but one of the schools that were over 80% minority were elementary schools. When we look at middle and high schools, the suspension rate goes steadily upward as the minority student population rises. Only one middle school had over 80% black enrollment, but in this school there were 53 suspensions for every 100 students in one year, an amazingly high rate. This school also had the lowest test scores of all middle schools and the second lowest test scores of all schools.

It is, of course, entirely possible that suspension rates simply reflect the tendency of administrators to respond more forcefully to black students than to white students. There is, however, another reasonable explanation, one that we will shortly see receives greater support from the reports of those who actually teach in these schools. In the second column of the table, we have included our estimates of the percentage of students in each school from single-parent families.

Readers will recall that experts familiar with the New Orleans school system believe there is a connection between the prevalence of one-parent families in New Orleans and the disorder in that district's schools. Since

Table 5.7. Mean Suspensions, Estimated Single-Parent Families, Student-Teacher Ratios, and Percent of Teachers with Graduate Degrees by Racial Compositions of Schools

	Suspensions per 100 Students	Estimated Single-Parent Families	Mean Students per Teacher	Percent of Teachers with Grad. Degree
≤20% or less minority				
All schools	8	23%	15	39%
Middle and high schools	19		17	45%
20–40% minority				
All schools	10	29%	14	43%
Middle and high schools	21		16	47%
40–60% minority				
All schools	20	36%	15	37%
Middle and high schools	26		17	41%
60–80% minority				
All schools	31	44%	15	41%
Middle and high schools	31		15	41%
≥80% minority				
All schools	15	55%	11	33%
Middle and high schools	53		12	32%

Source: Louisiana State Department of Education, School Profiles, 1995–96.

single-parent families are far more common among black students than among white students, it follows that there is a direct correlation between the proportion of minority students in any school and the proportion of one-parent families in that school. We have calculated that if 58% of school-age blacks and 18% of school-age whites live in families with only one parent, then on average under one-quarter of students in institutions that are 80% or more white and well over half of students in schools that are 80% or more black will live in this type of family. We caution readers that this is an extremely conservative estimate. Since family structure is also related to socioeconomic level, it is probable that the actual rates are higher in the mostly black schools and lower in the mostly white schools.

Although, as we noted, some resources are more limited in majority-black schools than in majority-white schools, the school environments of the former do not appear to be consequences of trained personnel. Student-teacher ratios are, if anything, somewhat more favorable in the schools that are almost entirely black. School administrators and teachers have reported to us that schools with large numbers of minority students do have trouble holding more experienced and more highly trained teachers, since these teachers tend to move on to other institutions. As we see in Table 5.7, however, there seems to be no serious shortage of teachers with advanced degrees in majority-black schools.

Our research in the public schools of Lafayette has strongly suggested to us that the most important factor shaping school environment is not school resources, teacher-student ratios, or qualifications of teachers. The most important factor is the family structure prevailing among the students. In order to look at how family structure can shape school environment, we can turn to the views of the insiders, the teachers of the Lafayette school district.

During the summer of 1996, one of the authors mailed surveys to the 1,432 teachers in the Lafayette school district. Of these teachers, 561 responded. This was a response rate of 38%, a good response rate for a mail survey. Since this response rate was still low enough to raise some question of response bias, however, we compared the demographic characteristics of our respondents, given in the survey, to demographic characteristics of teachers in the parish provided in official reports of the Louisiana Department of Education. The characteristics of our respondents closely matched those of the official reports, so there seems to be no systematic bias as a consequence of nonresponse. The survey gave teacher reports of job satisfaction, student backgrounds in their respective schools, perceived major problems for their schools, and other issues. Teachers were invited to give their own comments on school situations at the end of the survey. This survey, then, provides us with an excellent source of information on teachers' perceptions of conditions in Lafayette public schools.[34]

In response to an open-ended survey item that asked teachers, "What do you see as the most important problem facing our schools?" a clear majority of teachers (52%) plainly identified lack of discipline and a breakdown in order in the schools. Since this included those who gave no answer, fully 57% of those who actually identified a greatest problem said that it was discipline. Because open-ended questions leave respondents the freedom to express their own varying views, instead of choosing among the preconceptions of surveyors, we normally expect substantial variation in answers. Still, we see extensive agreement among these teachers on this issue.

What conditions could be responsible for the lack of discipline teachers see in the schools? Our experiences in New Orleans, Baton Rouge, and in other districts led us to suspect that the family structure of students may be related to orderly or disorderly school environments. In Table 5.8, we present cross-tabulations of teachers' reports of the frequency of discipline problems and teachers' reports of the family backgrounds of students in their schools.

A majority of teachers who said they worked in schools in which almost all or most of the students were in two-parent families also said that they seldom or only occasionally had discipline problems with their students. In contrast, 71% of teachers working in schools in which almost all the students came from one-parent families said that discipline was a constant problem. By checking school characteristics given in survey items (such as size of the school; rural, suburban, or urban location; socioeconomic level of the students; grades taught; etc.), we were able to identify all of the teachers who reported that almost all their students were from

Table 5.8. Lafayette Teachers' Reports of Frequency of Discipline Problems in Schools, by Prevailing Family Structures

	Almost All Students from 2-Parent Families	Most Students from 2-Parent Families	Most Students from 1-Parent Families	Almost All Students from 1-Parent Families
Seldom have problems	33.3%	7.5%	30.6%	1.5%
Occasionally have problems	33.3%	46.9%	20.6%	4.5%
Frequently have problems	20.0%	28.9%	35.8%	22.7%
Discipline a constant problem	13.3%	16.7%	40.0%	71.2%
No. of teachers	15	294	165	66

$\chi^2 = 127.590$, statistically significant at $p < .000$
Source: 1996 Survey of Lafayette Parish Educators, University of Southwestern Louisiana.

two-parent families as being in schools that were over 75% white. All of the teachers who reported that almost all their students were from one-parent families were identified as being in schools that were over 80% black. This should not be surprising, considering the extremely close correlations we have seen between race and family structure.

The phrase "discipline problems" can include behaviors that vary widely in severity. Therefore, to look at the relationship between family background and extremely disruptive behavior, we looked at a survey item that asked teachers about the frequency of violence in their schools. Only two teachers indicated that students in their schools were never safe from violence. Lafayette is, after all, a relatively small city and we should not expect the stabbings and shootings that we saw in some of the worst public schools in New Orleans. Nevertheless, some teachers did answer that their schools were plagued by frequent violence. Again, these problems varied by the kinds of families that produced the student populations. Over half of the teachers who said that almost all their students came from one-parent families also said that violence was a frequent school problem.

The level of discipline maintained in schools tells only part of the story of the educational environments surrounding students. Parental involvement in schools can be an important part of maintaining a healthy school environment. In our survey of Lafayette teachers, the second most commonly mentioned major problem was lack of parental support or involvement. When parents show an active interest in the schoolwork of their children, this encourages the children to develop positive attitudes toward schooling, attitudes that they communicate to fellow students. Parents provide needed help to teachers in preparing classrooms and organizing activities. The problems of discipline and violence that we have just considered can be lessened when there are close connections between parents and teachers. Many of the teachers surveyed explicitly connected parental inactivity as a major source of disorder among students in schools. "Discipline problems in my school stem from the fact that parents just aren't involved," wrote one teacher. We consider this aspect of the school environment by looking at the relationship between parental involvement in schools and the family structures prevailing among students, in Table 5.10.

Teachers in Lafayette schools with students chiefly from two-parent families report high levels of parental involvement. Four out of five teachers who say that almost all of their students are from families with two

Table 5.9. Lafayette Teachers' Reports of Violence in Schools, by Prevailing Family Structures

	Almost All Students from 2-Parent Families	Most Students from 2-Parent Families	Most Students from 1-Parent Families	Almost All Students from 1-Parent Families
No violence	33.3%	25.0%	11.7%	3.0%
Occasional violence	60.0%	66.8%	63.8%	42.4%
Frequent violence	6.7%	7.9%	23.9%	54.5%
Never safe in school[a]	0.0%	0.3%	0.6%	0.0%
N of teachers	15	292	163	66

[a]Only 2 teachers reported that students were never safe in their schools.
$\chi^2 = 97.870$, statistically significant at p < .000
Source: 1996 Survey of Lafayette Parish Educators, University of Southwestern Louisiana.

Table 5.10. Teachers Reports of Parental Involvement

	Almost All Students from 2-Parent Families	Most Students from 2-Parent Families	Most Students from 1-Parent Families	Almost All Students from 1-Parent Families
No involvement	0.0%	3.4%	15.9%	50.0%
Occasionally involved	20.0%	40.1%	63.8%	50.0%
Usually involved	33.3%	32.9%	17.7%	0.0%
Very involved	46.7%	23.6%	3.7%	0.0%
No. of teachers	15	292	164	62

$\chi^2 = 179.62799$, p < .000
Source: 1996 Survey of Lafayette Parish Educators, University of Southwestern Louisiana

parents also say that parents are "usually active" or "very active" in the schools. Over half of the teachers in schools in which most of the students are said to be from two-parent families say that their schools have parents who are "usually active" or "very active." On the other side, nearly four out five teachers who say that most of their students are from one-parent families report that they either have no parental involvement at all or only occasional parental involvement. When almost all students were said to be from single-parent families, teachers reported little or no involvement by parents.

Writing to the editor of the *Lafayette Daily Advertiser* on May 25, 2000, a guidance counselor at one of the district's black middle schools reacted passionately to claims that rezoning schools to achieve desegregation could address the disadvantages of minority students:

> Will this get the minority parents involved in the schools? This is the real problem. I've been in at-risk schools for 23 years. The problem is the same then as it is now. Parental involvement is the real problem. Put the blame where it belongs. Can federal judges drag parents to school and make them become more involved in their child's education? This would be interesting to see. Parent involvement is the main reason for poor test scores and discipline problems. Poor economic conditions, dysfunctional families, and poor family values are the real problems to address.[35]

These statistics can provide some insight into the academic environments of Lafayette's most disadvantaged schools, the schools that serve mostly minority students (for a more statistically sophisticated analysis of this problem, see Appendix A). The statistics also suggest that these disadvantages do not originate in the schools themselves, but in the society outside of the schools. Most minority students come from disadvantaged socioeconomic settings and single-parent families. If concentrating children from one-parent families contributes to an environment that is not conducive to learning, then parents will want to avoid any school with large numbers of children from this family type. Unfortunately, this means avoiding schools with large proportions of minority children. Regarding the efficacy of school facilities, in Lafayette' newest, most high-tech school, opened in 1999, more than 90% of the students were low-income African American children. A faculty survey conducted in the fall of that year indicated that fully 92% of the faculty believed that the school's discipline policies were ineffective, and 68% of the faculty did not even want to be in the school— regardless its high-tech facilities.[36]

Statistics alone can only demonstrate the barest facts of any situation. Let us look now at what the teachers themselves have said about their students and their schools in this small Louisiana city. The teachers in the most disadvantaged schools were not the only ones to identify family structure as a problem for schools. A middle-school teacher who said that she taught mixed-income students in a suburban setting wrote, "The break-down of the family unit has caused so many various problems in my classroom that I must deal [with] before I can ever begin to capture their attention to teach." This was a note sounded far more often, though, by the teachers who described themselves as working in schools with mostly low-income children from single-parent families. Asked to list important problems facing educators, one teacher in an urban elementary school made up almost entirely of low-income students from single-parent homes wrote: "Illiteracy! Teen pregnancy! Single family homes!" Another elementary teacher in a similar school said that the greatest problem facing her as an educator was "trying to discipline students when they have had little discipline at home." A first-grade teacher characterized her students as "disruptive" and wrote, "Teachers in schools such as the one I teach in *cannot* compete with children brought up in homes where both parents are professionals and place education on top."

A fourth-grade teacher who described herself as working in an economically disadvantaged school with racial minority students described the greatest problems facing schools as "class sizes [that] are too large and the breakdown of the family—students do not know right from wrong!" Another teacher in a similar institution complained that her school was plagued by "students that get no help from home. There are many poor parents that don't know how to help their children. I've seen some of these parents curse a principal in front of their child. They have no respect for others or themselves. Many parents take drugs and leave young children alone without food or supervision."

A number of teachers pointed out that all students are affected by being in classes with problem students. "Half the kids in my class have single moms," one teacher wrote; these students "sometimes make it impossible to teach any of them." Another teacher observed: "It is difficult to reach all students when there are 30+ of them in the room, and several are 504 students with discipline problems." Moreover, new facilities are not enough to compensate for student discipline problems. One teacher at the previously mentioned brand-new, technologically advanced, mostly black middle school with a high concentration of students from single-parent families, who is a representative for a local teacher organization, told one of the authors that fully 40% of his faculty had applied for transfers to other schools—in this school's very first year of operation.[37] He blamed out-of-control students for the "very low" teacher morale—in a school that is being showcased as Lafayette Parish's most technologically advanced.

Lafayette Takes the Desegregation Plunge

Lafayette differs in many respects from the major urban areas of New Orleans and Baton Rouge. This smaller city also continues to show a relatively high degree of de facto segregation. Our in-depth examination of Lafayette strongly indicates, however, that the dilemma of desegregation is not limited to large urban centers, nor is it a dilemma posed only when the process is at an advanced stage. The dynamics of the problem are the same. A long history of discrimination and racism has left white Americans and African Americans divided at the aggregate level into two unequal social classes. As long as the latter remain isolated from the mainstream of American society, these two classes tend to be perpetuated. Whenever there are attempts to break down the isolation by even limited efforts at desegregation, though, it threatens the genuine and understandable parental interests of many white parents.

Students make the educational environment of a school. Economically and socially disadvantaged students create disadvantaged academic environments. There are extremely close relationships among race, family economic status, and family educational background. Even more importantly, race is closely connected to family structure in small cities such as Lafayette as well as in the big cities. Every piece of evidence that we can find, including the testimony of teachers, indicates that large proportions of students from one-parent families have serious negative consequences for schools.

The parents whose children were about to be rezoned into majority-black schools said that their objections were not based on racial prejudice. We have no way of peering into their souls to see their true attitudes. But there is no need to do so. The rezoning of their children's schools was not in the interests of their offspring, and as in New Orleans and Baton Rouge, the actions of prejudiced and unprejudiced parents would be essentially the same.

In the spring of 2000, one of Lafayette Parish's nine school board members, David Thibodaux, put forth a proposal to have the board seek unitary status for the Lafayette school system from the federal courts. He contended in a 43-page report that Lafayette Parish had met all 6 of the "Green" factors, and therefore should be released from its 35-year-old desegregation lawsuit.[38] However, his proposal was not warmly received by the superintendent or fellow board members, who claimed it could launch a costly court battle, especially if the Justice Department, the plaintiffs, and/or the NAACP countered that the system was not adequately desegregated. In a hallway after the contentious board meeting, the board's lawyer shared with one of the authors that the judge overseeing the case could indeed demand extensive evidence in order to prove that Lafayette had complied with all the "Green factors."[39] At the same time, board member Thibodaux expressed the opinion that many board members would prefer to "let sleeping dogs lie rather than have the system scrutinized too closely."[40]

However, rather than be allowed to sleep, those dogs were awakened with a vengeance in May 2000, when a scathing report from a Justice Department consultant claimed not only that Lafayette Parish should not be granted unitary status, but that it was operating its school system in violation of the original desegregation court order.[41] Among other violations, the report claimed that the recent zone changes to accommodate the parish's four new schools did not further desegregate the school system. The report also went on to criticize teacher and principal assignment practices, pointing out that there was not a single black principal heading up a predominantly white school in the parish.

This critical report, though challenged both by the school board and in an analysis by one of the book's authors, was used by recently appointed district court Judge Richard Haik to make a momentous decision: in a hearing on May 19, 2000, he declared that "the Lafayette Parish School board operates two separate school systems, one white and one black," and he ordered the board to desegregate the parish's schools more fully.[42] The immediate effect was to throw the city into chaos. "A definite panic is going on! I go to church, shopping, to school, and all parents talk about are getting job transfers, leaving the system, and home schooling!" declared one university instructor.[43] One school board member who attended the decisive court hearings said the Justice Department and NAACP lawyers operated like a "tag team" and basically ganged up on a completely unprepared and unorganized school system that essentially put up no defense to the many accusations made against it. The author's analysis was not even submitted for consideration.[44]

We spoke with the office of the district superintendent of education on May 26, one week after the hearing, and were told that the office had been "deluged" by calls from panicking parents. On the same day, Lafayette's primary newspaper, the *Daily Advertiser,* reported that "private and parochial schools in Lafayette Parish have been overwhelmed with inquiries from parents of public school children about enrollment for next year since an order by U.S. District Judge Richard Haik was handed down one week ago today to rezone public schools."[45]

Although some of the calls to private schools came from black parents who were concerned about the disruptive effects of busing,[46] many black citizens had mixed feelings about the rezoning decision. One black professional told us "a lot of people in the black community feel that this [rezoning] is long overdue." We conducted a survey of African Americans right after Judge Haik's decision and discovered that the perception among many African Americans in Lafayette was that their children had too long received second-class educations and that drastic steps should be taken to create equal opportunities.[47]

Judge Haik's decision, which seemed to echo Judge Parker's earlier decision in Baton Rouge, only increased the similarity between Lafayette and the state's capital city. The racial composition of the schools, the degree of de facto segregation caused by segregated neighborhoods, and the controversial exercises of judicially mandated desegregation made it entirely reasonable to suggest that the Lafayette school system in 2000 was in the same position that the Baton Rouge school system had occupied in 1981.

The similarities between the two systems only seemed to increase following the adoption of a consent decree in late June 2000 worked out between Judge Haik, the school board, the NAACP, and the original plaintiffs. It commanded the school system to close down two predominantly black inner city elementary schools immediately and bus the students affected by the closures to five predominantly white schools on the other side of town. Though the system had just built four new schools, the judge ordered a new, "desegregated" school built. The consent decree went on to order the transfer of eleven black principals from predominantly black schools to predominantly white schools, and eleven white principals from predominantly white schools to predominantly black schools. The decree also ordered the board to assign and reassign faculty on the basis of race in order to ensure that each school's faculty reflect the racial composition of faculty employed on a districtwide basis.[48]

The unsettling effect of so massive a system shakeup showed up almost immediately in the fall 2000 enrollment counts. There were 791 fewer whites in Lafayette's public schools in fall 2000 than a year earlier, a decrease of 4.5%. However, there were eighty-seven more African American students. Moreover, some of the initial positive reactions from the black community seemed to dampen a bit as the reality of the new situation had time to sink in during the fall. Our most recent survey of black reaction to the desegregation order, conducted in early October 2000, showed considerable black disenchantment with having two black neighborhood schools closed and those schools' black children forced to relocated to white schools across town. One typical comment came from a black resident who lives across the street from one of the closed schools. He told us that he had attended that school as a child in the 1950s and 1960s, and he resented the neighborhood children now being bused to schools that would not, in his opinion, emphasize black culture and history.[49]

Given Baton Rouge's experience, it seems likely at the time of this writing that there is going to be even more white flight from Lafayette's public schools not only in the near future, but over the next two decades. In the near term, the archbishop of the diocese of Lafayette is again allowing white students to enroll in the district's schools, after previously having taken the unprecedented action of barring white students from fleeing to the system's Catholic schools. Thus, there are now new options for those wishing to leave the public schools, suggesting that meaningful desegregation will become increasingly difficult as fewer and fewer white students remain in the system. Given current rates of white flight, Lafayette will be another majority-black school district by 2012.

The relatively small city of Lafayette has given us an opportunity to look closely at an unfolding desegregation dilemma that could conceivably drag on for years. Next, we would like to widen the perspective from our three focal points. In Chapter 6, we consider the dilemma of desegregation at the level of the entire state, looking first at the state as a whole and then at specific districts in all regions of Louisiana.

Chapter 6

Louisiana and the Dilemma of Desegregation

Louisiana's black population, especially its school-age black population, was growing steadily as the twentieth century ended. In 1990, the state was 67.3% white and 30.8% black. Significantly higher fertility among the state's black population[1] meant the African American portion would continue to increase. It also meant that the school-age black population was proportionally greater than the black population as a whole. The 1990 census showed that African Americans made up 37.8% of Louisianians aged under eighteen, while whites made up only 60.0% of the state's minors. By 1996, the total black population had grown to 32.0%, and blacks were almost 40% of the school-age population.[2]

Louisiana's black children were becoming a larger part of the state's life, but their families had not overcome the historical disadvantages of the caste system that we discussed in Chapter 1. In terms of income alone, there was a vast gap between the two major races. Per capita income for white Louisianians in 1990 was $12,956, and for blacks it was only $5,687. On average, then, whites' incomes were more than double those of blacks. More than one out of every four black Louisiana households (25.2%) had yearly incomes less than $5,000, and a majority of black households (57.3%) had yearly incomes less than $15,000. By contrast, fewer than one out of every ten white households (7.7%) had incomes less than $5,000, and 71.8% had incomes greater than $15,000.

Black poverty was particularly notable among minors, since a majority of black Louisianians under the age of eighteen (56.5%) were classified as below the poverty level by the 1990 U.S. Census. The poverty rate of white minors in Louisiana, 18.2%, was high compared to the white poverty rate for the nation as a whole, but it was still well below that of the state's black minors. Race, in other words, seems to continue to divide the state into two distinct economic categories. Most black children are poor, and many of them live in extreme poverty. By comparison, most white children appear to be relatively well off.

As in the three districts that we considered in the previous chapters, black children in the state as a whole operate at a distinct disadvantage in family educational background. Nearly half (46.9%) of black Louisianians aged twenty-five and over had not finished high school in 1990. Only one in ten had completed a college degree. We should recognize that this is a great improvement over the educational conditions before desegregation that we described in Chapter 1. Nevertheless, it still represents a substantial racial gap. Among whites, about one-fourth (25.8%) of similarly aged adults had not finished high school, and nearly one out of every five (18.7%) was a college graduate.

We have already seen the implications for schools of these racial gaps in socioeconomic status in our discussions of New Orleans, Baton Rouge, and Lafayette. For the state as a whole, as in these three places, racial inequality means that increases in the minority population of schools are necessarily increases in the proportion of poor children. It means that schools that have more black children will have fewer parents with the educational background to contribute to the academic preparation of their children and that those children will bring weaker academic backgrounds to school to share with one another. From the perspectives of equity and social justice, these are all reasons to seek true desegregation, so that the racial gap can be narrowed and eventually closed. From the perspective of white middle class parents seeking the best possible education for their own children, though, these are good reasons to avoid schools with large minority populations.

Throughout the earlier chapters, we have seen another dimension of the division of the two races into two social classes: the dimension of family structure. When we looked at New Orleans, we saw that the disorder prevailing in many schools is frequently attributed to the predominance of children from single-parent families. We examined this question even more closely in our discussion of the school situation in Lafayette and saw that there is strong evidence that concentrating students from one-parent families can have very serious negative consequences for the educational environment of schools. Indeed, in every district we have examined we have seen that the prevalence of children from single-parent families in schools is closely connected to the schools' racial compositions. This is also true for the state of Louisiana as a whole.

Among white family households in Louisiana, 15.1% of all families and 15.5% of families with minor children were headed by single parents. Among black family households, 51.7% of all families and 54.0% of families with minor children were headed by single parents. The single-parent families clearly contained the majority of black children: 64.1% of black children lived in one-parent homes, while 80.9% of Louisiana's white children lived in homes with two parents. Unmarried mothers, rather than divorced mothers, predominated heavily among Louisiana's black single-parent families—strongly suggesting that children in these families have never lived with their natural fathers. The 1990 U.S. Census figures for Louisiana show that 72% of black women aged fifteen to twenty-four who had given birth were not married by the time of the census, and over 69% of black women aged twenty-five to thirty-four who had given birth were not married by the time of the census. Given the racial differences in family structure as well as socioeconomic status, it is necessarily the case that schools with large minority populations will be schools that bring together poor children from educationally disadvantaged, one-parent backgrounds.

De Facto Segregation in Louisiana Schools

Figure 6.1 gives us a graphic representation of the racial makeup of school districts in the state, derived from the data in the 1999 Louisiana Educational Assessment Program (LEAP) tests administered in all public schools containing elementary and middle-school students. Clearly one of the problems with achieving any kind of meaningful desegregation in the state is that white students and black students are not evenly distributed among the state's sixty-six school districts. In eight of them, over 75% of the student population was black, including two (Orleans and St. Helena) in which well over 90% of students were black (see Table 6.1).

It does appear that twenty-five districts are relatively integrated at the district level, since 25% to 50% of students in these are black, meaning that black and white students are represented in proportions roughly similar to

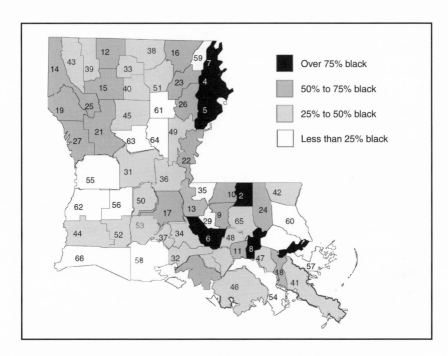

Figure 6.1. Racial Composition of Louisiana School Districts, 1999

those of the state. Another thirteen districts, though, are predominantly white districts, since they contain under 25% black students.

Racial proportions at the district level, however, are not the same as racial proportions at the school level, as we saw in the previous chapter on Lafayette schools. Table 6.1 gives minimum and maximum black student populations in each district in the state. Most of these show a great deal of variation among schools. Even in Orleans, as we saw previously, there was one school that was 69% white. It was one of the six Schools of Academic Achievement in this troubled district. The district of St. Helena Parish is somewhat of an exception in showing little variation: virtually all of the students in its schools are black. Many of the districts, though, show extremes of racial composition, suggesting a fairly high degree of de facto segregation within these districts. St. Landry Parish, for example, has a school that is 100% black and a school that is close to 100% white. By our calculations, nearly two-thirds (66.5%) of Louisiana's black students in schools with elementary and middle-school grades attended racially segre-

Table 6.1. Percentages of Minority Students and Minimum and Maximum Percent Minority Students per School in Louisiana School Districts, 1999

District	Percent Minority	School Minimum	School Maximum	Average LEAP Score
1. Orleans	95.9	31.3	100	37.46
2. St. Helena	93.2	93	93.5	44
3. Monroe City	88	51.3	100	59.31
4. Madison	83	58	100	49.36
5. Tensas	80.7	64.8	94.1	46.7
6. Iberville	80	44.6	92.9	61.57
7. East Carroll	79.2	30	99.8	49.84
8. St. John the Baptist	76.2	43.3	99.4	57.07
9. East Baton Rouge	74.5	12.7	100	63.85
10. East Feliciana	73.2	35	92.5	57.35
11. St. James	70.8	28	100	61.08
12. Claiborne	70.3	37.5	100	63.33
13. Pointe Coupee	69.2	26.7	99.5	52.86
14. Caddo	68	12.5	100	65.83
15. Bienville	66	19.7	95.1	61.95
16. Morehouse	65.3	1.5	98.2	68.13
17. St. Landry	57.7	0.7	100	74.26
18. Jefferson	56.2	1	97.1	65.08
19. De Soto	57.3	13.7	87	64.09
20. St. Mary	55.5	7.6	100	65.75
21. Natchitoches	52.4	24	99.7	69.57
22. Concordia	51.5	3.2	95.3	61.36
23. Richland	51.5	1.3	79.3	63.11
24. Tangipahoa	51.1	5.1	92.6	70.64
25. Red River	50.7	13.3	83	63.63
26. Franklin	50.4	12.2	78.4	57.16
27. Sabine	50.3	13.4	86.6	70.05
28. Bogalusa	50.1	41.6	56	61.99
29. West Baton Rouge	49.5	30	71.4	65.01
30. Assumption	48	0.2	92.4	60.41
31. Rapides	47.4	0.3	99.7	81.8
32. Iberia	47	8.8	97.3	67.71
33. Lincoln	45.2	10.1	79	83.38

Table 6.1 *Continued*

District	Percent Minority	School Minimum	School Maximum	Average LEAP Score
34. St. Martin	45	0	71.1	64.16
35. West Feliciana	44.2	35.1	50.6	81.55
36. Avoyelles	43.9	13.2	58.8	62.22
37. Lafayette	43.2	6.2	99.2	80.65
38. Union	43.2	0	84.6	69.66
39. Webster	42	0.6	100	71.47
40. Jackson	41.4	0.3	99.7	75.51
41. Plaquemines	40.7	18.8	99.3	78.7
42. Washington	40.7	0.4	62.9	63.11
43. Bossier	40.2	8.1	87.8	82.36
44. Calcasieu	40.1	1.6	99.8	82.84
45. Winn	39.7	15.3	48.9	69.54
46. Terrebonne	39.5	7.7	86.3	72.63
47. St. Charles	37.5	13.9	71.2	93.06
48. Ascension	36.1	1	95.2	80.66
49. Catahoula	35.7	1.4	61.8	86.85
50. Evangeline	35.7	2.6	79.1	70.45
51. Ouachita	29.5	0.5	100	82.6
52. Jefferson Davis	28.4	1.2	47.2	88.28
53. Acadia	25	0.5	62.1	72.37
54. Lafourche	23.7	0.6	57	68.09
55. Vernon	23.1	0	53.2	89.62
56. Allen	23	0.8	39.1	78.31
57. St. Bernard	22.3	5.3	72.3	71.36
58. Vermilion	21.2	0	59.6	77.71
59. West Carroll	21	0	52.3	89.26
60. St. Tammany	21	0.4	70.2	95.37
61. Caldwell	20.4	9.6	39.4	75.42
62. Beauregard	16.5	1.2	37	83.01
63. Grant	16.4	0	50.2	67.74
64. Lasalle	12.6	0	27	81.31
65. Livingston	6.5	0	26	91.31
66. Cameron	5.1	0	15.1	89.3

gated schools in 1999.[3] In school districts that were over 60% black, more than 88% of the black students attended racially segregated schools. As we saw in New Orleans, Baton Rouge, and Lafayette, there is strong evidence that desegregation has contributed to white movement out of school districts or out of public schools. There are good reasons for concluding, then, not only that the state's schools remain segregated, but that overly ambitious attempts to desegregate them may ironically help to keep them segregated.

It will be noted that black students made up a majority of the public school students in the 1999 LEAP tests. The tests were administered only to elementary and middle-school students, and therefore the data include only elementary and middle schools and the relatively few schools that contain high school grades in addition to elementary and elementary and middle school grades. In all grades in Louisiana, black students made up a slightly smaller percentage in the late 1990s, about 49% of all students. The fact that black students actually make up a majority (50.9%) of the students in the schools with lower grades is revealing because students in the lower grades represent the future of the system. If we look only at elementary school students, we find that black students made up 52.9% of the total in 1999. This trend toward an increase in the representation of black children in the state's schools has been in existence for a long time. In 1965, 39% of the public school students in Louisiana were black. Five years later, this had grown to over 40%. By 1980, it was over 41%. In 1990, Louisiana public schools were 47% black.

Thus it appears that in the early years of the twenty-first century, Louisiana's public school system is likely to become a majority-black system at all grade levels, in spite of the fact that African Americans will probably not make up more than 40% of the state's total population. There are two reasons for this growth in the black student population. First, higher fertility levels among black Louisianians mean that they tend to be younger than whites, and the school-age black population is therefore proportionately larger than the total black population and growing faster than the school-age white population. Second, as we have sought to document throughout this volume, whites are much more likely than blacks to attend nonpublic schools. During the 1990s, about 22% of white students and less than 5% of black students attended nonpublic schools.

Table 6.2 shows not only that Louisiana public schools vary greatly

Table 6.2. Racial Composition of Louisiana Schools with Elementary and Middle School Students, 1999

Racial Composition	Percent of Schools	Number of Schools	Average School LEAP Score
<10% black	12.8	152	91.29
10–20% black	10.9	130	87.63
20–30% black	10	119	83.01
30–40% black	9.6	114	81.98
40–50% black	8.2	98	75.27
50–60% black	9.6	114	69.96
60–70% black	6.3	75	62.39
70–80% black	6.2	74	60.03
80–90% black	5.6	67	57.36
>90% black	20.6	245	42.07

in racial composition, but that racial composition is closely tied to measured school performance. About 13% of the state's elementary and middle schools are clearly identifiable as almost exclusively white. At the other extreme, 21% of the state's lower- and middle-grade schools are almost exclusively black. Judging by test scores, the all-white or nearly all-white schools do much better than the others, and the all-black or nearly all-black schools do much worse.

If there are black and white schools, it logically follows that black students are concentrated in the former and white students in the latter. Table 6.3 shows how the state's elementary and middle-school students were distributed among the schools in 1999. Nearly one-fourth of white students were in almost all-white schools. A majority of the state's white students in the critical lower grades attended schools in which black students made up under 30%, even though black students were in the majority in these grades in the state as a whole. At the other extreme, four out of ten of Louisiana's black students were in almost all black schools and nearly six out of ten black students were in schools that were over 70% black. Thus, despite a long history of efforts at desegregation, de facto segregation remains the rule in the schools in this state.

Louisiana high schools, as well as elementary and middle schools, showed a fairly high degree of segregation. In fact, evidence from the 1990

Table 6.3. Distribution of Black and White Students in Louisiana Schools with Elementary and Middle School Students, 1999

Racial Composition	Black Number	Black %	White Number	White %
Under 10% black	3,039	1.0	67,130	23.5
10–20% black	9,748	3.3	55,519	19.5
20–30% black	16,200	3.5	48,219	16.9
30–40% black	19,263	6.5	35,191	12.3
40–50% black	21,007	7.1	25,859	9.1
50–60% black	30,002	10.1	25,088	8.8
60–70% black	23,072	7.8	12,601	4.4
70–80% black	28,276	10.0	9,508	3.2
80–90% black	25,086	8.5	4,029	1.4
>90% black	120,244	40.6	2,548	0.9
Total	295,937	100.0	285,242	100.0

and 1999 Graduation Exit Examinations, taken by all of the state's tenth and eleventh graders, indicates that there were more segregated high schools by the end of the 1990s than there were at the beginning. Table 6.4 shows that in 1990 black students made up less than 10% of the students in one out of every five high schools. By 1999, however, black students made up less than 10% of the students in more than one out of every four Louisiana high schools, even though the black proportion of the public school population had increased.

At the other end, the percentage of high schools that were all or almost all black (90% or over) increased from 13.3% to 16.4% during the 1990s. Using the National School Boards Association definition of a segregated school as one that is 60% minority or greater, segregated schools increased from 22.2% of schools to 29.3% in this time period. In the face of a growing black public student population, the proportion of schools in which over 80% of students were white increased from 33.1% to 36.4%.

More predominantly white schools and predominantly black schools meant that at the end of the decade black students were more likely to attend school chiefly with other black students, and white students were more likely to attend school primarily with other white students. Table 6.5 shows that in 1990, 17% of white tenth and eleventh graders were in schools that

Table 6.4. Racial Composition of Louisiana High Schools, 1990 and 1999

Racial Composition	1990 (% of schools)	1999 (% of schools)
<10% black	19.9	25.7
10–20% black	13.3	10.8
20–30% black	14.4	11
30–40% black	13.8	11.5
40–50% black	7.8	7.3
50–60% black	8.6	4.4
60–70% black	3.5	5.4
70–80% black	3.5	3.2
80–90% black	2	4.4
>90% black	13.3	16.4

Source: Louisiana Department of Education, Graduation Exit Examinations, 1990 and 1999.

Table 6.5. Percentages of Black and White High School Students in Louisiana Schools, 1990 and 1999, by Racial Composition of Schools

Racial Composition	1990 Black	1990 White	1999 Black	1999 White
<10% black	1.1	17.1	1.5	22.8
10–20% black	5.2	21.7	4.5	21.6
20–30% black	7.7	17.3	7	16.7
30–40% black	13.8	20.2	11.5	17.5
40–50% black	8.7	8.5	8.9	9
50–60% black	14.2	9.6	10.1	6.2
60–70% black	6.8	3.1	8.4	3.6
70–80% black	4.6	1.2	6.4	1.8
80–90% black	3.3	0.5	4.6	0.5
>90% black	34.7	0.8	37.0	0.4

Source: Louisiana Department of Education, Graduation Exit Examinations, 1990 and 1999.

were over 90% white. Nine years later, 23% of white Louisiana tenth and eleventh graders were in schools that were virtually exclusively white. At the other end, black students in schools that were almost all black increased from under 35% to 37%.

Racial change in the composition of Louisiana schools appeared to move only in one direction. Our examination of the data on students taking the Graduation Exit Examination shows that one-third (33.2%) of the schools that contained tenth and eleventh graders in both 1990 and 1999 had changed from majority-white schools to majority-black schools. No schools that were majority-black schools in 1990 had become majority-white by the end of the decade.

One possible response to the continuing and even increasing de facto segregation of Louisiana schools is to conclude that desegregation has not been aggressively pursued and that greater federal coercion is required to enforce racial redistribution. The three examples that we have considered above, however, suggest that majority-black and majority-white schools are not simply results of an insufficiently committed federal government. Instead, shifting racial compositions are produced by families in racial groups with different levels of social and economic resources attempting to pursue the best interests of their own children. Indeed, federal intervention seems only to have aggravated the situation, furthering segregation.

The racial composition of Louisiana public schools, then, is an issue that continues to deserve close attention and will arguably become an even more important issue as the minority student population grows. We have attempted to achieve some understanding of the consequences of changes in racial composition by looking at desegregation issues in three districts in the state—one that has become an almost entirely minority district, one in which minority students have recently become the majority, and one in which schools are still largely segregated and white students remain in the majority (though federal intervention may hasten the creation of a majority-black school district). However, desegregation has been a basis of struggle and controversy throughout the state. While the process has varied somewhat from place to place, the underlying dynamics of attempts at desegregation and resistance to those attempts have been fundamentally the same. To illustrate this point, we turn now to a brief discussion of desegregation struggles throughout the state.

Desegregation Struggles around the State

Jefferson: White Movement from and within a Suburb

As we saw in Chapter 2, the term "white flight" is frequently used to refer to white movement from urban to suburban neighborhoods. Those who argue that desegregation or particular means of desegregation, such as busing, do not cause white flight often claim that white movement to suburbs is a consequence of residential shifts unrelated to changes in the racial composition of schools. We see white flight as more complicated than simply movement from cities to suburbs. It also involves movement out of public school systems into private schools. Beyond this, however, the evidence suggests that families move from one suburb to another in response to racial changes in schools. The automobile has given members of the middle class, who are unfortunately still largely white, a great deal of flexibility in choosing where they will live, and school districts have become a major consideration in choice of place of residence. Since, as we have seen repeatedly, there is such a close correlation between racial composition and publicly recognized, measurable school quality, the search for good schools leads to white flight from one suburb to another. Further, even within a school district, middle-class families frequently attempt to place their children in the best possible school environments, doing whatever is necessary to get into the "best" schools. We saw, in looking at New Orleans, that a decline in good schools can not only produce white, middle class settlement outside of a district, it can also intensify the urgency for placing children in the few good schools within the district. Turning to New Orleans' neighboring parish, Jefferson, we can see these same dynamics at work in a suburb.

Jefferson Parish was the first of the suburban parishes that ring New Orleans to become home to large numbers of people in the greater New Orleans area. Jefferson consists of two halves, East Jefferson and West Jefferson, separated by the Mississippi River. From the 1950s until approximately the late 1970s, Jefferson grew rapidly. This growth occurred in tandem with that of New Orleans until the 1960s; then Jefferson began to outpace the urban core as the population of the region began to settle in the suburbs. From the 1970s through 2000, population growth in New Orleans first slowed, then significantly regressed, as other, newer suburbs in St. Tammany and St. Charles Parishes rapidly increased in population.

The public school population of Jefferson also grew steadily until 1976, when it reached a peak of 72,300 students, over 20,000 more students than had been in the district a decade earlier. After 1976, however, the student population began a steady decline, falling to 50,335 by 2000–01. As Figure 6.2 shows, this decrease in students was due entirely to a decrease in white students in the Jefferson Parish public school system. The number of black students grew continually over the entire three decades.

Where were the white students if not in Jefferson Parish? Figure 6.3 indicates that changing racial proportions in the district were due primarily to a tendency of whites to locate in suburban areas other than Jefferson. The top, broken line in this figure shows the percentage of students in the suburban ring around New Orleans who were located in St. Bernard, St. Tammany, or St. Charles Parish rather than in Jefferson. We include St.

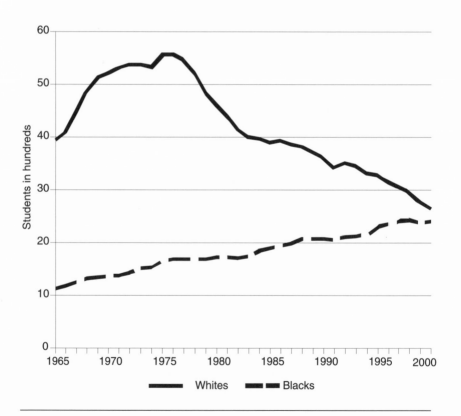

Figure 6.2. Black and White Students in Jefferson Parish, 1965–2000

Bernard here because it is part of the suburban ring of New Orleans, even though it has not experienced the growth of St. Tammany and St. Charles. During the same period when the white student population was decreasing in Jefferson, white students grew increasingly more likely to attend school in other suburbs. The lower, unbroken line in Figure 6.3 represents the growth in the percentage of public school students within Jefferson who were black. As in New Orleans, the movement of white students into other school systems is almost identical with the increase of black students in Jefferson's school system. By themselves, these strikingly similar trends are not proof that whites were leaving in response to an increasing black school population. However, given the dynamics of white flight that we have seen so far, the lines in this figure are highly suggestive.

The white student population was decreasing because whites were in-

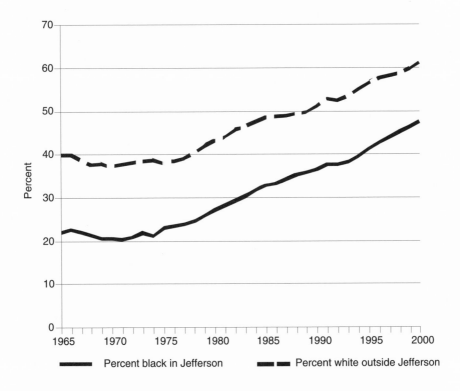

Figure 6.3. Racial Shifts in Jefferson Parish, 1965–2000

creasingly settling in areas other than Jefferson. Part of this, of course, was due to new housing development in other suburban areas within driving distance of New Orleans. Newer homes are frequently seen as more desirable by many home buyers. However, the majority of jobs are still located in New Orleans, and neither St. Tammany nor St. Charles Parish is as convenient as the northern parts of Jefferson for commuting. The commute from many of the neighborhoods in St. Tammany involves a daily, tedious drive across Lake Pontchartrain on the Causeway toll bridge, which is more than twenty miles long, is often buffeted by high winds or shrouded in fog, and requires the commuter to drive through a portion of Jefferson Parish in order to get to New Orleans. Even those who live in Slidell, at the southwestern corner of St. Tammany Parish nearest New Orleans (see Figure 6.1), have to cross a bridge to enter Orleans Parish, drive across much of New Orleans, and go over another bridge at the Industrial Canal (a notorious local traffic bottleneck) to reach the urban core. This is a half-hour drive when traffic is flowing freely; however daily traffic jams are the rule at rush hour. Those living in St. Charles Parish must commute all the way through Jefferson Parish to get to New Orleans. While it is true that there are jobs outside of central New Orleans, few of these jobs are actually located in St. Charles or St. Tammany Parish, which remain chiefly bedroom communities.

Why would people settle in more distant and less convenient suburbs? When we spoke with those who chose to live in the newer suburbs, they never failed to mention schools as a primary motivation. "I hate driving across that bridge every day," said a businessman who lives in St. Tammany, "but the schools are a lot better than they are on the South Shore [New Orleans and Jefferson]." A housewife in St. Charles Parish who grew up in Jefferson said that she and her family had purchased a home in St. Charles "definitely because of the school system."

Table 6.6 indicates that these perceptions of school systems were fairly accurate. Among the four suburban districts around New Orleans, Jefferson had the lowest average achievement test score in 1999, although it was better than the score of the urban core. St. Tammany and St. Charles, the preferred places of middle class settlement, did quite well on the test.

Table 6.6 suggests an important point about white flight that is often overlooked. Even if parents do not see any connection between the racial makeup of schools and the academic quality of schools, the search for good

Table 6.6. Selected Characteristics of Elementary and Middle Schools in the Jefferson, St. Bernard, St. Tammany, and St. Charles Districts, 1999

	Jefferson	*St. Bernard*	*St. Tammany*	*St. Charles*
Percent minority	56.2	22.3	21	37.5
Percent low income	74.6	59.5	37.6	48.8
Average LEAP score	65.1	71.4	95.4	93.1
Below-average schools (%)	42 (58.3)	6 (46.2)	2 (5.0)	3 (18.8)
Above-average schools (%)	30 (41.7)	7 (53.8)	23 (57.5)	6 (37.5)
Schools of Academic Achievement (%)	0	0	12 (30.0)	7 (43.8)
Schools of Academic Distinction (%)	0	0	3 (7.5)	0

schools leads families toward majority-white schools and away from majority-black schools. However one explains the connection between minority representation and school performance, there is a very clear connection. Among the New Orleans suburbs considered here, the top schools, the schools that parents say are a primary consideration in the selection of place of residence, are generally schools with small African American populations. In the St. Tammany district, the black student population in the twelve Schools of Academic Achievement ranged from 6% to 18%. In St. Tammany's three Schools of Academic Distinction, the top-ranked schools in the entire metropolitan area, blacks made up only 4%, 5%, and 9% of students in each school. St. Charles showed somewhat greater minority representation in its best schools: in the two with the largest minority student bodies, black students made up 31% in each school. Still, this means that all of the top-ranked schools in the region are readily identifiable as majority-white schools, and in the very best schools whites make up over nine out of every ten students.

Averages can be misleading. The fact that schools in a district on average score badly does not necessarily mean that all schools show uniformly poor performance. However, low averages frequently mean that good schools are scarce commodities. When commodities are scarce in a market, it can lead to attempts to find them in other markets where they may be more abundant, such as in the rapidly growing suburban areas of

St. Tammany and St. Charles. Scarcity also leads to intense competition within markets. In Chapter 3, we saw both of these processes occurring in New Orleans. The tight market in acceptable schools meant that middle class families (disproportionately white) looked for homes outside of New Orleans. It also meant that within New Orleans there was intense competition for the relatively few good schools. In Jefferson, the oldest suburb of New Orleans, the trend toward white movement out of the district was also accompanied by increasing competition to get children into the best public schools within the district.

A teacher at the elementary school that received a top ranking in the 1999 LEAP scores explained to one of the authors, in the fall of 1999, why her class held more students (over thirty) than other classes in the district. "This is the honors class in a school that's seen as a really good school," she said. "All the parents try to get transfers to get their kids into this school and into these classes." Although the school was nearly 45% minority, there were fewer than a half dozen black children in this honors class.

In February of 2000, we visited the Special Services Office of the Jefferson Parish school system. The secretary at the office handling school transfers confirmed that parents in the district had been watching the test scores very carefully and that this influenced the demand for certain schools. "Ever since the scores came out," she said, "we've been flooded with requests" for the top-ranked middle school in the district. Even though transfer requests were not yet officially available in the schools, parents were going to the Special Services Office to request transfers to the most highly ranked schools. The same month that we visited this office, we spoke with a grandmother (who did not want to be identified by name) rearing a grandson currently attending fifth grade at one of the top schools in Jefferson on a transfer. She expressed concern that she would not be able to get her grandson into a good school because there was so much demand for transfers out of the school zone of her residence and into the better school zones. Because they were Jewish, she said that attending Catholic school was not an option for them. "It's really important to get into a good school," she said.

Tracking inside of schools masks the association between school performance and racial composition. Nevertheless, the association still appears quite clearly, so that it is evident that the search for good schools tends to create white flight even within districts. Table 6.7 gives the ranking of elementary and middle schools in Jefferson by racial composition in 1999. There was one anomalous school that was over 80% minority with students who placed the school in the highest-performing quartile. This was a small elementary school (249 students) containing kindergarten through the eighth grade. Of course, we are not suggesting that all majority-black schools are low-performing schools, any more than we are suggesting that all black students are low-performing individuals. Just as individuals may overcome situations that put them at risk as students, schools with all types of students can be excellent schools. But exceptions do not establish trends. All but four of the thirty-three schools with over 60% minority populations were ranked in the bottom two quartiles in the district. All but one of the nineteen schools with less than 40% minority students were ranked in the top two quartiles. The one minority-dominant school in the top quartile was very much an outlier. None of the other schools in the top quartile were more than 45% minority.

Parents who want to put their children in the best public schools will either tend to settle in districts with relatively small numbers of minority students or they will attempt to avoid minority-dominant schools within their districts. Busing, the destruction of neighborhood schools, and loss of parental control over local schools may all alienate white middle class parents from desegregation. These may well be side issues, however. Since there is such a close association between school quality and school racial makeup, the quest for good schools by white middle class parents can be the most fundamental and inexorable source of white flight.

As in most other districts, the racial composition of schools is not af-

Table 6.7. Ranking of Elementary and Middle Schools in Jefferson into Quartiles, by Racial Composition

	<20% Black	*20–40% Black*	*40–60% Black*	*60–80% Black*	*≥80% Black*
Highest quartile	3 (50%)	5 (38.5%)	6 (30.0%)	0	1 (7.7%)
Second quartile	2 (33.3%)	8 (61.5%)	8 (40.0%	3 (15.0%)	0
Third quartile	1 (16.7%)	0	3 (15.0%)	9 (45%)	4 (30.8%)
Lowest quartile	0	0	3 (15.0%)	8 (40%)	8 (61.5%)
N	6	13	20	20	13

fected just by demographic characteristics of neighborhoods in Jefferson, but also by a long effort at desegregation aimed at overcoming racial inequalities. A 1965 lawsuit for the desegregation of Jefferson Parish schools, *Dandridge et al.,* was the legal basis of desegregation activities in the district. This became active policy in August of 1971, when Judge Herbert W. Christenberry ordered the busing of students to achieve greater racial integration. Judge Christenberry took this step because about 13,000 of Jefferson's 68,000 students (just under 20%) were attending one-race or predominantly one-race schools. The school board and a group of parents appealed the desegregation plan, but these appeals were rejected by the Supreme Court in 1972.[4]

The 1971 plan affected efforts in the following years to desegregate the schools. In September 1974, the school board closed two elementary schools in Jefferson Parish to contribute to desegregation. Ten years later, students were still being bused in efforts to achieve more favorable racial mixes. When Woodmere Elementary School was opened on the West Bank of Jefferson Parish in predominantly white Harvey in September 1984, black students were bused in to create a racial balance that would comply with the 1971 court order. That same semester, sixty-six black students who had been bused from the West Bank community of Marrero were transferred once again to another school when it was found that Woodmere was excessively overcrowded and did not need them to balance its racial books. The previous year, these sixty-six children had been bused to George Cox Elementary in Gretna. Leaving Woodmere did not put them back in the school closest their home, however, because this school, Lincoln Elementary, was judged already to have its black quota.[5]

How much desegregation was achieved through all the years of racial juggling? We have already seen that the white student population declined following the mid-1970s, so we should expect that this would lead to fewer predominately white schools. The chief goal of desegregation, though, was to create fewer predominately black schools. In 1971, Judge Christenberry had ordered the desegregation of Jefferson Parish schools because just under 20% of students attended predominantly one-race schools. After three decades of segregation, as Table 6.7 shows, there were still thirteen middle and elementary schools in Jefferson that were over 80% black. These schools contained over 22% of the district's black children. Of these thirteen schools, six were 90% black or more and held over 10% of the district's black students (not shown in this table). Nearly two-thirds of the black elementary and middle school students at the end of the twentieth century were attending schools that were over 60% minority in composition.

This does not include figures for high schools, which, since they are larger and draw from wider geographic areas, do tend to be more balanced in racial composition. Still, these figures indicate very limited success for a thirty-year period of desegregation. Moreover, if the trend that has been steady for a quarter of a century continues, this district will be a majority-black district by 2004 and will be over 60% black by 2014 or 2015, making it very difficult to avoid predominately black schools at all grade levels.

We turn now from efforts at desegregation in a suburban school district to a school district that is more rural in character. As we see in the following section on the St. John the Baptist school district, the quality-equality dilemma posed by school segregation is not limited to metropolitan regions. Here, too, the struggle to achieve greater equality through the school system was threatened by racial inequalities outside of the desegregating system.

St. John the Baptist: Desegregation and White Flight from a Rural Area

St. John the Baptist Parish and its school district offer a particularly interesting case study. Although the Louisiana Department of Education classifies it as an "urban fringe" district because it is considered part of the metropolitan area of New Orleans, St. John is largely rural, with some small towns and modest suburban areas. It is also far enough from New Orleans not to be considered as desirable a place to live as closer-in parishes, since one must cross Jefferson and St. Charles Parishes to reach St. John from New Orleans.

As we saw in Chapter 2, critics of the concept of white flight often claim that white movement out of minority school districts is a result of white shifts out of urban and into suburban neighborhoods for reasons that have little to do with the racial composition of schools. If this is true, we would expect to see little white flight from schools in rural regions. The recent history of the St. John the Baptist school district offers strong evidence that white flight from nonurban places does occur, and that it occurs as a direct consequence of aggressive desegregation.

In the census year of 1990, 36.5% of the people in this parish were black, making it similar to the state in its racial composition. As in other areas of the state, economic inequality between the two races was marked. Median per capita income for whites was $12,726. For blacks, the median per capita income was half that, at only $6,533. Over three-fourths of persons below the poverty level in St. John were black, and 37% of blacks in the parish were classified as poor. Among children, economic disparities were even greater. Black children constituted 82% of the minors below the poverty level, and nearly half (47.4%) of black children were poor, compared with only 8% of white children.[6]

During the summer of 1969, a federal judge ordered the St. John the Baptist school district to desegregate its schools. For the rest of the century, school boards in St. John would struggle to come up with a desegregation plan that would satisfy the U.S. Justice Department. One of the chief problems, as in many other communities, was that neighborhoods were segregated. On the "East Bank" of the Mississippi River, the areas north of Airline Highway, which runs parallel to the Mississippi River and connects New Orleans to Baton Rouge, were mostly white, whereas the areas south of Airline Highway were mostly black. Moreover, most of the parish population on the "West Bank" of the Mississippi was black as well. This problem was compounded by the fact that many people in the district wanted neighborhood schools, and several school board members had committed themselves to maintaining neighborhood schools. Since the neighborhoods were segregated, the schools could not be effectively integrated.

The school board also faced another problem: racial compositions kept shifting. When black students were moved into a primarily white school or whites were moved into a primarily black school, whites would enroll in other schools. In September 1988, the school board held a meeting to discuss the problem of "boundary jumpers," families that lived in one school attendance zone but enrolled their children in another. Principals reported that parents were giving false addresses. One parent who admitted to "boundary jumping" declared, "I want my daughter out [of her assigned school] and if I have to lie, I'll do it."[7]

Despite efforts to stop this movement out of attendance zones, white parents seeking to avoid sending their children to schools with large black populations continued to evade compliance by almost any means possible.

According to then School Board Superintendent Gerald Keller, "Parents have moved their house trailers, changed their post office addresses, and changed the addresses on their drivers licenses and voter registration cards to send their children to different schools. Some parents have even transferred custody of their children."[8]

One school board member cited the case of Woodland Elementary School to illustrate the difficulties created by these evasive parental maneuvers. Woodland, built as a school for black students in the 1950s, was scheduled by the school board's desegregation plan to hold 278 students in the 1989–90 school year. Black students were to be 55% of the student body, and 45% were to be white. By January 1990, though, there were only 191 students in Woodland, and 93% were black.[9] Nearly all the whites who were supposed to attend Woodland had either found ways to get their children in other schools or had left the public school system.

Still, throughout the 1980s, the proportion of whites to blacks in St. John's public school system remained remarkably stable. In the 1980–81 school year, 43% of all students in the public schools were white. At the close of the decade, in the 1989–90 school year, whites (with a very few Hispanics and Asians) still composed 43% of the parish's public school population. One of the authors (Caldas) taught at the parish's largest high school, East St. John High School, from 1982 through 1987. The high school's racial population closely mirrored the parish public school population at large, with about a 55:45, black-white ratio. During the 1980s, neither the board nor the Justice Department tampered with school racial compositions.

The high school's racial composition remained very stable while the coauthor was there, and he recalls no parents, white or black, ever being anxious about shifting racial balance. Race relations within and without the schools were good. Indeed, during the 1984 two-month-long districtwide public school teacher strike—the longest in Louisiana history at that time—black and white teachers remained unified throughout the disputatious work action, though there was some talk that the school board was trying to divide the strikers along racial lines. If that was the board's strategy, it did not work, and after the end of the strike, during which teachers wrested concessions from the board, it was not race that was the issue, but whether or not one supported the strike. The author recalls a very strong sense of solidarity and purpose among the parish's teacher corps, with the two most visible leaders in the local teacher union being a white and a black, who were close friends as well as colleagues.

However, things had changed by the spring of 1990, as the St. John school board decided to adjust its attendance zones in order to avoid intervention by the U.S. Justice Department. Some of the district's black citizens had filed a $10 million class-action suit alleging discrimination, and board members favoring change had filed complaints with the Justice Department alleging racial imbalance in the schools. In addition to changing attendance zones, the school board also decided to close Woodland Elementary, which had proved so difficult to desegregate, and to move Woodland's students to other areas. Although some parents of Woodland students felt that this could lead to better educational opportunities for their children, others in the surrounding community objected to the closing. Retired Woodland principal Emily Watkins gave voice to the opposition when she exclaimed, "The whole community revolves around Woodland school. Why are they so particular not to close the neighborhood schools in the white areas and they're so quick to close the schools in the black areas?"[10]

Discriminatory decision making might be part of the answer to Ms. Watkins' apposite question. A large part of the answer might be, though, that there was much greater opposition to radical desegregation efforts in the white neighborhoods. For black families, the closing of schools mixed harm and benefit. They would lose community centers, the parents would have fewer ties to schools, and children would have to be bused to other locations. But there was also the possibility that their children might receive better educational opportunities. White families stood to receive no benefit from desegregation. The best they could expect from changes would be schools that would be no worse than the schools they already had.

Early in the following school year (1990–91), St. John's school board accepted a plan to create magnet schools for students from all over the district. This incentive would complement the unpopular closing of schools and continual redrawing of districts. Officials hoped that this would make desegregation more palatable. The board was especially concerned to avoid setting up any standards or courses that might exclude black students, since this would defeat the purpose of creating the magnet schools.

In 1991, a new U.S. District Court order was imposed on the district. Under this order, St. John was required to make even more efforts toward desegregation. The school board could not draw attendance zones, build schools, or make substantive changes in curricula without the approval of the federal Justice Department. A new plan in the spring of 1991, aiming at satisfying the Justice Department, called for reopening and revamping the newly closed Woodland Elementary, changing attendance boundaries once again, and increased busing. By the fall of 1991, the proportion of whites in the public school system had fallen 1% from the previous year, to 42%.

One of the most controversial aspects of the 1991 plan was a proposal to move grades six, seven, and eight from the kindergarten through eighth-grade Glade Elementary. Glade had been developed as a neighborhood school, with the intention of maximizing parental involvement and student and family attachment to the school by keeping students in the same school throughout the elementary years. During the two years previous to the new desegregation plan, parents at Glade had raised over $10,000 to buy equipment and resources for the school. Many of these parents were now faced with the possibility that their children would not be able to use the resources the families had worked to provide, and all were faced with the possibility that their children would not receive the long-term benefits anticipated. "When it was built," explained Glade Parent Teacher Organization president Randy Noel, "we were to take the Glade and make it a model school. A child would study in the same school for nine years."[11]

Woodland remained closed, and Glade continued to be a kindergarten through eighth-grade school. However, Glade was affected by the moving of student populations around the district. Over the course of the 1990s, moreover, all the evidence indicates that the schools of St. John Parish became more segregated, rather than less segregated, and an increasing minority representation made true desegregation difficult to achieve. By the 2000–01 school year, the proportion of whites in the parish's public schools had fallen to a low of only 23%.

Figure 6.4 tracks the numbers of black and white students in St. John Parish schools over the period from the 1965–66 school year, before St. John was ordered to desegregate its system, through the 2000–01 school year. For most of this period, numbers of black and white students remained relatively stable. White students in the district even increased over the course of the 1980s. As desegregation efforts intensified at the end of the 1980s and beginning of the 1990s, though, white representation in the district's public schools began a precipitous drop.

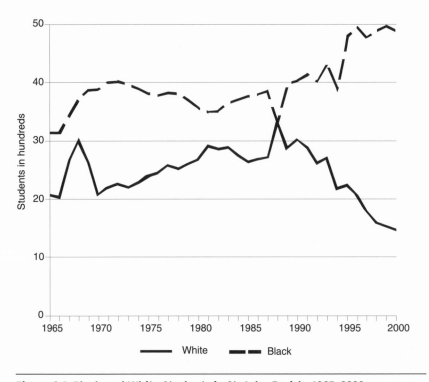

Figure 6.4. Black and White Students in St. John Parish, 1965–2000

Table 6.8 shows the racial compositions of the elementary and junior high schools in St. John Parish in the school years 1989–90 and 1998–99. These were not, strictly speaking, precisely the same schools because there were so many changes in pursuit of successful desegregation during the intervening decade. Fifth Ward Elementary and the St. John Child Development Center were added to the schools during this time. Also, as a consequence of the magnet-school plan, John L. Ory and Garyville Elementary became, respectively, the John L. Ory Communications Magnet Elementary and the Garyville–Mt. Airy Math and Science Magnet School.

In a few schools, the black-white ratios had changed in the direction of greater desegregation. Garyville and Leon Godchaux both had proportionately more whites in majority-black schools. In John L. Ory, the black-white proportion remained roughly the same, with the proportion of black students slightly lower. Since Garyville and John L. Ory were the centerpieces of the magnet-school portion of the desegregation plan, it appears

Table 6.8. Percentages of Black Students in Elementary and Middle Schools in St. John Parish, 1989–1990 and 1998–1999

	1989–1990	*1998–1999*
Glade Elementary and Junior	31.8 (420)	79.0 (836)
LaPlace Elementary	21.5 (173)	70.5 (324)
Woodland Elementary	88.7 (173)	closed
Godchaux Grammar	87.2 (340)	closed
Reserve Elementary	81.7 (223)	closed
John L. Ory	46.6 (279)	43.3 (145)
Garyville Elementary	84.6 (171)	69.4 (401)
Sixth Ward Elementary	79.1 (174)	100.0 (405)
Fifth Ward Elementary	not yet opened	92.6 (441)
St. John Child Development Center	not yet opened	95.0 (191)
Leon Godchaux Junior High	81.8 (444)	73.0 (232)

Sources: St. John Parish School Board, May 1990; Louisiana Department of Education, 1999.

that there may have been some very limited success in drawing or holding white students in these two schools.

Overall, though, the elementary and junior high schools went from 53% black in 1989–90 to 76% only nine years later. (Black students made up only a slightly greater proportion in school board statistics that include high schools.) By 1999 all of the schools in the district had become racially segregated by the definition of the National School Boards Association except John L. Ory Communications Magnet Elementary. In the earlier year, there were 4,523 students in kindergarten through ninth grade, of whom 2,126 were white. By the end of the decade, there were only 939 white students in these grades. The total elementary and middle-school population had dropped to 3,914 because the white student population had decreased by more than half.

We do not have precise information on where the white students went. However, we have strong evidence to suggest that many whites transferred to the highly regarded parish Catholic schools. In 1989–90, there were only 1,862 whites in St. John's Catholic schools. However by 1998–99, the white Catholic school population had burgeoned to 2,597. This is an increase of 735 whites (one very large elementary school) over the same time frame that the white population of the parish's public schools decreased by 1,082 (one large high school).[12] Moreover, given the maneuvers of parents that we have seen, it seems plausible that some may have managed to put their children into schools in neighboring parishes, perhaps without actually moving to those parishes. However, it is evident that they were no longer in St. John's public school system. One could, of course, argue that it is theoretically possible that the desegregation of schools was not the cause of white movement out of public institutions. Such a line of argument would be highly implausible, however, precisely because of all of the earlier efforts of white parents to avoid majority-black schools and because of the controversy and disruption clearly caused by continuing desegregation efforts.

By 1999, all but two of the lower-level schools in St. John were classified as Academically Below Average. Garyville–Mt. Airy Math and Science Magnet School had the dubious distinction of being the only magnet school in the state, as far as we are aware, to be classified as Academically Below Average. Normally, magnet schools are above average by definition, since they are based on selectivity. The magnet schools of St. John could not be very selective, though, because they had to be as racially inclusive as possible. La Place Elementary scored in the lower range of the Academically Above Average category. Only John L. Ory, which contained over one-third of all the white students left in the district, was in the middle of the Academically Above Average category.

Revolt in Rapides

One of the state's most widely publicized controversies over desegregation unfolded in the Rapides Parish school district. Rapides contains the mid-sized city of Alexandria, as well as both suburban and rural areas. In 1990, blacks constituted 28% of Rapides' population. As in other areas of Louisiana, there are great socioeconomic differences between black and white school children. In 1990, most (58%) of blacks below age eighteen in Rapides lived below the poverty level, compared with just under 16% of white children. As in the rest of the state, also, single-parent families predominated in black households. Over half (54%) of the black families with minor children in Rapides in 1990 had only one parent in 1990.

Court intervention in the schools of Rapides dates back to the early 1960s, when an Alexandria attorney filed suit against the district school board, accusing the board of maintaining a dual system. The desegregation struggle in this district began in earnest in 1980, when U.S. District Judge Nauman Scott issued a desegregation plan that required massive busing of students and the closing of two elementary schools, the 92.9% black Lincoln Williams Elementary in Cheneyville and the 91.7% white Forest Hill Elementary in the mainly rural community of Forest Hill. Under Judge Scott's plan, children would be bused up to forty miles per day in order to achieve racial mixing.

Reactions to the judicial mandate were dramatic and prolonged. Following the order to close Forest Hill, parents took over the school building and held classes there in defiance of the law until Judge Scott ordered federal marshals to evict them. The clash between the local population and the judiciary had broad community implications, since the school served as a social and recreational center for Forest Hill. After the parents' revolt, Judge Scott issued an additional order, forbidding the use of the school buildings for any purpose, depriving the people of their primary location for public activities.

To the people of Forest Hill, the judge's exercises of power seemed repressive and dictatorial. One side effect of the controversy was that Clyde Holloway, a local nurseryman and previously unsuccessful political candidate, rose to statewide prominence as a result of his leadership of the Forest Hill protests. In 1981, Holloway was elected to the U.S. House of Representatives.

When the 1981–82 school year opened, the people of Forest Hill held a symbolic protest at the site of their closed school. Two former students placed a wreath on the school door, and two others raised an upside-down American flag on the flagpole. In 1983, a group of Forest Hill parents known as the Concerned Citizens of Forest Hill built a private school near their old closed institution.

In the meantime, the fight against Judge Scott's plan entered the appeals courts. A 1981 decision by the Fifth U.S. Circuit Court of Appeals affirmed Judge Scott's decision but required him to reconsider it in the light of the opposition it had provoked. When Judge Scott did not change his mind after reconsideration, the case went back to the Court of Appeals. This time, one of the three appellate judges dissented from the decision upholding the desegregation plan. The dissenting judge said that Judge Scott had not given sufficient weight to the consequences for neighborhoods and the negative effects of busing. The two judges who affirmed the plan admitted that it had serious drawbacks but believed that it was the best way to achieve a desegregated school system.

The town of Buckeye was the site of a second widely publicized reaction to Judge Scott's plan. The redrawing of school zone boundaries and busing removed some white students from the nearly all-white district of Buckeye and required them to attend a nearly all-black inner city school in Alexandria. In an effort to keep their children in Buckeye, the parents of three girls gave up legal custody of their children to others living inside the new school boundaries of Buckeye. The "Buckeye Three" captured the attention of all Louisiana. Judge Scott declared that the transfer of custody was a sham and ordered the three girls to attend the school where he had placed them. Instead, the parents of the girls made the financial sacrifice to enroll them in Hickory Grove Academy, a private school established in response to the desegregation plan.

In 1981 alone, according to school board estimates, the cost of complying with the federal judge's orders came to nearly $600,000. Judge Scott continued trying to force the schools of Rapides to desegregate until his retirement in 1997. A group of black parents formed the Concerned Citizens for Rapides Parish in 1995 to try to persuade the federal government to change further plans for redistricting and busing, objecting that it would place too much of a burden on their younger children.

From 1979, the year before the desegregation controversy became so heated, to 1998, the year of Judge Scott's retirement, white public school enrollment in Rapides Parish decreased by over 20%, from 17,595 to 13,299. During that same period, black public school enrollment increased slightly, from 9,526 to 10,024. Thus, an increase in the percentage of black public school students was due largely to the loss of whites from the system. Many whites did remain in the system, though. Despite the publicity given to desegregation in Rapides, the district did not go the way of New Orleans.

As shown in Figure 6.5, the increase in the minority portion of the student population occurred primarily in the early 1980s. Moreover, the rise in white students attending nonpublic schools was also limited to the early 1980s. From 1979 to 1982, white nonpublic school enrollment increased by 40%, from 2,595 to 3,622. Throughout the later part of the 1980s and the 1990s, though, white students in the nonpublic system declined sharply.

Does this mean that we should see these trends as white families gradually accustoming themselves to a *fait accompli* and accepting successfully desegregated schools? The evidence suggests that, on the contrary, after decades of bitterness and expense, desegregation had achieved little in Rapides.

The 1999 LEAP test results published by the Louisiana Department of Education can give us some insight into the extent of desegregation in Rapides. As shown in Table 6.9, over one-fourth of the white elementary and primary school students in the district attended the six schools that were over 90% white, and nearly one-fourth of the black students attended the six schools that were over 90% black. Moreover, three-quarters of the whites were in schools in which whites made up at least 60% of the student body, and over half of the black students were in schools in which blacks

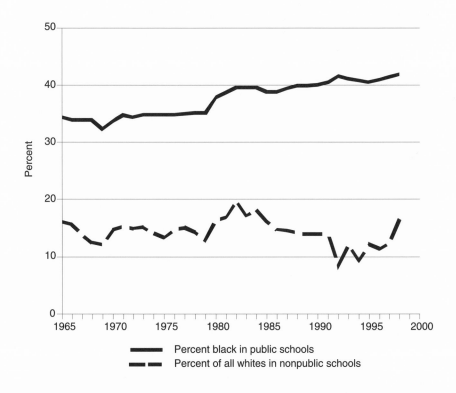

Figure 6.5. Racial Shifts in Rapides Parish, 1965–2000

made up at least 60% of the student body. Evading desegregation was no longer a motivation for white students to enroll in nonpublic schools because the schools in Rapides were still largely segregated. Buckeye High School, site of the controversy over the "Buckeye Three," was still 98.2% white in 1999.

The continued existence of segregated schools in this district raises serious questions about the wisdom of forcible desegregation during this entire period. The two judges who had upheld Judge Scott's plan in 1983 acknowledged that the closing of schools and the busing of children could be damaging to schools and painful to communities, but they justified it as the best way to achieve the desired end. The end, however, was not achieved.

Table 6.9 also offers some insight into the motivation on the part of white families for resisting desegregation, and it is consistent with findings that we have seen again and again in this book. Based on test scores, the best schools were those that had the smallest minority enrollments, and the worst schools were those that had the largest minority enrollments. We want to repeat that this does not reflect on the innate ability of minority students. We believe that it does reflect social and economic backgrounds that in

Table 6.9. Racial Distributions and LEAP Scores in Rapides Parish, 1999

Racial Composition	All Students % (N)	LEAP Score (School Average)	Black %	White %
<10% black	13.6 (6)	91.29	0.5	27.6
10–20% black	0.0 (0)	87.63	0	0
20–30% black	22.7 (10)	83.01	14.2	32.2
30–40% black	11.4 (5)	81.98	9.4	13.8
40–50% black	6.8 (3)	75.27	9.1	8.2
50–60% black	13.6 (6)	69.96	16.4	10.3
60–70% black	4.5 (2)	62.39	6.3	2.3
70–80% black	11.4 (5)	60.03	17.5	4.5
80–90% black	2.3 (1)	57.36	3.5	0.4
≥90% black and over	13.6 (6)	42.07	23.2	0.4
Total	100.0 (44)	81.8	100.0 (7,783)	100.0 (9,945)

general prepare minority students poorly for school. But parents who want their children to be in environments of academic excellence will understandably avoid sending their children to majority-black schools. This pursuit of rational self-interest is necessarily intensified when desegregation means taking children out of community schools to which families feel a strong attachment in order to send the children to schools that parents have good reason to believe are low-achieving institutions.

Table 6.9 indicates that educational opportunities continue to be unequally distributed in Rapides, and black families and political activists may justifiably see this as unfair. Black students are most likely to be found in the lowest-ranked schools of the district. We would question, though, whether this is a result of the inequalities among the schools or a reflection of the social and economic inequalities that continue to exist outside of the schools.

Caddo-Bossier: De Facto Segregation in the Northwest

Caddo Parish and Bossier Parish lie in the far northwest of the state of Louisiana (see Figure 6.1). The cities of Shreveport and Bossier City make up a single urban area that overlaps these two parishes. Shreveport by itself is the third largest city in Louisiana, with an estimated population of 192,945 in 1995 (198,034 in 1990). Bossier City constituted the smaller half of the Shreveport-Bossier concentration, with an estimated 1995 population of 55,035 (52,721 in 1990). Despite their proximity, the two parishes, which are also two separate school districts, have distinctive demographic and socioeconomic differences. According U.S. Bureau of the Census estimates, Caddo was 42.3% black and 56.9% white in 1996. Whites in Caddo tended to be older than blacks, and black children made up just over half of the parish's school-age population. Bossier Parish was 76.5% white in 1995 and 21.7% black, although just over one-fourth of Bossier's school-age children were black. Eighty percent of Caddo's 1990 248,253 people lived in Shreveport. Shreveport's minority population was only slightly larger, proportionately, than that of the parish as a whole, since blacks made up 44.8% of those in Caddo's central city.

In 1993, just over one-fourth of the people in Caddo (25.3%) lived below the poverty line, compared with only 16.3% of the people in Bossier. The 1993 median household income of Caddo was $26,274, compared with a median household income of $30,610 in Bossier. Caddo, then, had a much larger minority population than its neighboring parish and school district, and Caddo was generally the poorer of the two.

Not all of the people in Caddo were poor. In the 1990 census, more than one out of every five white households had incomes over $50,000, and over half of the white households had incomes over $35,000. On the other side of the racial divide, over 58% of black households had yearly incomes less than $15,000, and nearly one out of every four black households in the parish had yearly incomes amounting to less than $5,000.

In Caddo, black children were mostly poor, and most poor children were black. The 1990 census showed that 57% of blacks below the age of eighteen were below the poverty level. Further, black children made up 86% of all the poor children in the district. Bossier also showed racial disparities in poverty statistics. A majority of Bossier Parish's black children (51%) lived below the poverty level at the beginning of the 1990s, compared with only 12% of the white children. Even with Bossier's overwhelmingly white population, poor children tended to be black children. Almost two-thirds of the minors in Bossier (62%) who were classified as below the poverty level in the 1990 census were black. Clearly, throughout this area, going to school with black children has meant going to school with poor children, but the chances of not attending school with low-income black children are in general much better in Bossier than in Caddo.

Shreveport in particular showed many of the social problems associated with concentrated economic disadvantage, and situations in the schools reflected these problems. In 1991, for example, a debate over sex education in Caddo's public schools erupted. This debate was particularly pointed because Shreveport had the fourth highest student pregnancy rate among the nation's 120 largest cities.[13] The National Center for Educational Statistics (NCES) classified 15% of Caddo's school-age children in 1990 as "at risk," compared with just under 14% of all Louisiana and less than 7% of Bossier's children. Caddo's percentage of at-risk children was much smaller than that of New Orleans, where over 25% were classified as at risk, though it should also be recalled that the overwhelming majority of children in New Orleans were low-income minority members. Caddo's racially stratified society contained both black children, who were mostly poor, and white children, who were mostly middle class.

Single-parent family structure is closely related to race and economic disadvantage in this northwestern corner of the state, as it is elsewhere. Single parents headed 58% of the black households with children in Caddo Parish and 47% of the households in Bossier Parish in 1990. Although only one out of every five families with children in Bossier were black, they constituted over 44% of the single-parent families in the parish. In Caddo, black families accounted for 73% of the single-parent families.

Like other parts of the state, the Caddo-Bossier region has a long history of judicially imposed desegregation. This has been much more of an issue in Caddo because of its much larger black student population. Caddo began to desegregate its schools at the beginning of the 1970s, at approximately the same time that other districts around the state and the nation began this process. In 1977, Judge Nauman Scott declared that Caddo was desegregated. However, the U.S. Justice Department disagreed with Judge Scott's decision, saying that the district had too many one-race schools. In early May of 1981, U.S. District Judge Tom Stagg approved a desegregation plan that closed three elementary schools and one junior high school and imposed busing. This plan met with strong opposition from whites and from school officials. Caddo school board official Steve Jordan predicted that the new plan would "result in the loss of students to private schools."[14]

In reality, the loss of students to private schools appears to have happened much earlier, at the time of initial desegregation. During the 33-year period 1965 to 1998, the population of public school students in Caddo Parish declined from 56, 949 to 47,234. This pattern of declining enrollment has been the trend since 1969, when the total public school population reached its apogee of 61,217. As Figure 6.6 illustrates, this has been specifically the result of a decline in the enrollment of white students. Caddo's black student population remained fairly stable throughout the 1970s, began to increase in absolute numbers in the 1980s, and grew rapidly in the late 1980s and early 1990s. Over these three decades, the numbers of black students in Caddo increased by nearly five thousand.

The late 1960s and early 1970s, the time of initial desegregation, were also the years in which white enrollment in nonpublic schools soared. From 1968 to 1973, the number of white students in Caddo Parish in nonpublic schools increased from 2,276 to 8,473. By 1973, approximately 16% of white students were in nonpublic schools, compared with a negligible percentage of black students. After this, the proportion of white students outside of the public school system did not continue to increase, although it also never returned to the low of 6% of 1968. Instead, the absolute numbers of white students in Caddo Parish went down steadily. Throughout the 1990s, about 17% of Caddo white students and about 2% of Caddo black students were in nonpublic schools.

During this three-decade period, numbers of both white and black students increased in neighboring Bossier Parish. In 1997, there were about one thousand more white students than in 1965 and about seven hundred more black students than in 1965. The far northwestern region of Caddo-Bossier, then, has seen an overall dramatic decline in white public school pupils and a substantial overall growth in black public school pupils, mainly in Caddo. Whites during this period became increasingly likely to settle in the comparatively affluent, majority-white district of Bossier, rather than in Caddo. White movement to the much smaller neighbor, however, cannot account for the loss in the white school-age population of Caddo.

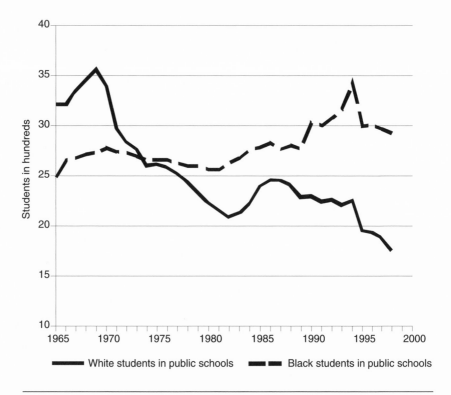

Figure 6.6. White and Black Students in Caddo Parish, 1965–2000

As Figure 6.7 shows, the black proportion of Caddo's student population increased steadily through the entire time period. The percentage of whites located in Bossier Parish rather than in Caddo, though, peaked at the time of the 1981 desegregation plan and remained relatively stable after that. This may create some questions about whether desegregation resulted in white flight out of Caddo Parish public schools. The answer is that white movement out of the schools was limited because desegregation was largely ineffective. In 1999, 78% of black children in Caddo's elementary and middle schools were in majority-black schools, and 78% of white children in these grade levels were in majority-white schools. Three-quarters of white students were concentrated in the sixteen of Caddo's fifty-six schools that were over 60% white.

If we keep in mind the patterns we have seen in other Louisiana schools, it becomes evident that many of the white families living in the Caddo-

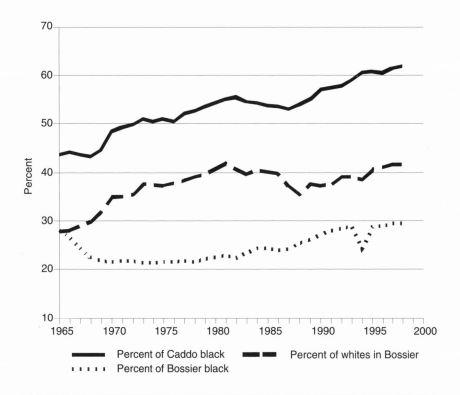

Figure 6.7. Racial Shifts in Caddo and Bossier Parishes, 1965–2000

Bossier area had open to them all three of the major options we have seen in other districts. They could attempt to get into a relatively small number of academically desirable schools in Caddo, they could attend private schools, or they could settle in nearby Bossier Parish. All three of these options tended to place white students in majority-white schools and, *ipso facto,* black students in majority-black schools. Table 6.10 reflects these tendencies.

There was one school in the Caddo-Bossier area that received the state's highest designation—indeed it was the only school in the entire state designated as such based on student test performance—as a School of Academic Excellence. It was a magnet elementary school in Shreveport, open to all students in the district on a competitive basis. The opportunity to place a child in this school provided strong motivation to settle in Shreveport or to stay there. The school did have a substantial minority population (38%), but the selective nature of the school meant that they were drawn heavily from the district's small black middle class. In a school district in which 57% of the majority-black minor population lived below the poverty level, only 12.5% of students in this school were classified as low income.

Caddo also contained two schools with the second highest rank, Schools of Academic Distinction. One was an elementary school and another was a magnet middle school, both located in Shreveport. Both of these held majority-white student bodies (56.2 % white and 63.9% white, respectively) and small percentages of low-income students (21.6% and 17.9%, respectively).

While Caddo did have some excellent schools, though, most of its schools were not highly ranked at all, and these were the schools attended by most of the district's black students. Of the fifty-six elementary and middle schools in Caddo, thirty-seven were classified as below average, and these schools contained 78% of the black students in the district. Just under half (twenty-four) of the middle and elementary schools in the district were over 90% minority, and twelve were 98% to 100% minority. Despite substantial racial mixing at the parish's few elite schools, then, most black students in the district attended heavily segregated schools because the whites were concentrated in the few elite schools.

Bossier, as a much smaller district, had fewer public schools, meaning fewer available slots for parents seeking schools for their children through magnet programs, transfer permits, or relocation. Bossier also did not have

Table 6.10. Ranking of Schools and Racial Distribution of Students in Caddo and Bossier Parishes, 1999 LEAP Tests

	Caddo	*Bossier*
Academic Excellence	1 school	0
Percent minority	37.8	
Percent of district whites	2.5 (303)	
Percent of district blacks	0.9 (184)	
Academic Distinction	2 schools	1 school
Percent minority	39.8	8
Percent of district whites	8.4 (1,016)	5.7 (515)
Percent of district blacks	3.1 (631)	1.0 (45)
Academic Achievement	8 schools	4 schools
Percent minority	39.1	14.8
Percent of district whites	24.7 (2,982)	22.7 (2,040)
Percent of district blacks	8.1 (1,688)	7.6 (353)
Above Average	8 schools	12 schools
Percent minority	36.3	28.6
Percent of district whites	30.7 (3,699)	63.2 (5,680)
Percent of district blacks	10.0 (2,093)	57.6 (2,675)
Below Average	37 schools	6 schools
Percent minority	83.5	67.5
Percent of district whites	33.6 (4,056)	8.4 (755)
Percent of district blacks	78.0 (16,331)	33.8 (1,568)
Total number of schools	56	23

the top school in the region, and it had only one School of Academic Distinction, compared with Caddo's two. These are reasons that Caddo has managed to hold on to a majority of the white students in the area, even though its white student population has been falling steadily. Bossier does have its attractions, though. Both black and white students, but especially white students, were much less likely to be in below average schools in Bossier than in Caddo.

If families are shopping for public schools, then, there are reasons for them to consider both Caddo and Bossier. Caddo has one of the state's most acclaimed schools, but most of its schools receive extremely low rankings. How serious are parents about getting their child accepted into the state's highest-scoring school? An educator from Shreveport told one of the authors that parents have their children on the school's waiting list as soon as the mother knows she is pregnant.[15] As in New Orleans, the existence of magnet schools does appear to hold some whites in a majority-black school district, but this also tends to concentrate the white students in a relatively small number of schools. At the same time, the plummeting number of whites in Caddo public schools indicates that school officials cannot, realistically, simply reallocate whites. Since, as everywhere else, whites are much more likely than blacks to leave the public school district (or not to enter it to begin with), school officials must take special care to create policies and programs that appeal to white families. Although Bossier's school system continues to be much smaller than that of its adjoining district, it has been growing and, given the addition of funds from new settlers, could continue to grow. We should also note that the majority-white district of Bossier provides greater opportunities for meaningful racial mixing than Caddo does. While 78% of black students in Caddo attend schools that are over 80% black, only one-third of black students in Bossier attend majority-black schools.

Do parents of public school students really shop for schools? In our discussions of the three focal parishes, we provided evidence that middle class parents do. Here, it's worth quoting the *Shreveport Times'* Web site, which offers online information for those seeking to relocate in the Caddo-Bossier area: "We know how important schools are when deciding where to buy a house, so we profiled each public and private school in Caddo and Bossier parish. Our profiles include information on fees, curriculum, sports, magnet admission, and activities. We also have state and local administrative information and 1991–1997 LEAP (Louisiana Educational Assessment Program) scores for our public schools."[16] All of the information made available online by the newspaper for those "deciding where to buy a house" is also readily available by calling the paper or the school board. Most of it can also be easily obtained by consulting parents or teachers already residing in the area. The *Shreveport Times* does not publish the racial compositions of schools or the socioeconomic characteristics of the students. However, as we have seen repeatedly, parents looking for magnet schools, schools with high parental involvement, and schools with high test scores will inevitably be drawn away from minority-dominated schools.

Monroe and Ouachita: The District within a District

Monroe, with a 1990 population of 54,909, is one of the largest cities in north central Louisiana. The Ouachita River divides it from its sister city, West Monroe, which is less urban and more suburban in character than Monroe itself. Although Monroe is the seat of Ouachita Parish, it is one of only two cities in Louisiana to have its own school district (the other is Bogalusa, in Washington Parish).

Monroe and the rest of Ouachita Parish are demographically distinct areas. In the 1990 U.S. Census, the city had a majority-black population (55.4%), while just over 80% of those in Ouachita outside the parish seat were white. Among children enrolled in school, three-quarters (74.35%) in the city of Monroe district were black in 1990, compared with only 21% of Ouachita school children outside of Monroe. Thus, the parish of Ouachita contained one predominantly black school district and one primarily white school district. As we will see, this was part of a trend of de facto segregation that continued after the census year.

The districts differed in socioeconomic level, as well as in racial composition. The median household income of Monroe in 1990 was only $16,223, compared with $23,959 in the rest of the parish, $21,949 in Louisiana as a whole, and $30,050 in the United States in general. More than one out of every three people in Monroe (35.04%) lived below the poverty level. In the rest of the parish, the poverty rate was 16.65%, which was higher than the rate for the United States (12.76%), but substantially lower than that of Louisiana (22.91%). The differences in socioeconomic levels, of course, meant differences in the well-being of school children. According to NCES, 27.5% of Monroe's children were considered "at risk," compared with 7.4% of the children in the Ouachita district. Over half of all the school children in Monroe (52%) were below the poverty level, compared with only 17% of the children in the Ouachita district.

In Ouachita Parish as a whole, including Monroe, most black children were poor and most poor children were black. The 1990 census recorded that 64% of the black families with minor children were poor and that 84% of all poor families with children were black. In addition, most black children were in single-parent families and most of the single-parent families were black. Of the black families with children in the parish, 62% were headed by single parents, and 64% of all single-parent families with children were black.

The existence of these two districts poses clear problems for desegregation. The more urban district is mostly black and poor. Around it is a majority-white district with comparatively low poverty rates and fewer apparent risks for children.

Efforts to desegregate the schools of Ouachita and Monroe began in 1965, when black plaintiffs filed a lawsuit alleging that school attendance in the city of Monroe was racially discriminatory. A 1970 attendance system addressed the suit by allowing children in south Monroe to attend one school through the sixth grade and then change schools in the seventh and tenth grades. Children in north Monroe also attended one school through the sixth grade, but they then had to change schools every year through the eleventh grade in order to maintain a racial balance throughout the schools. In 1978, parents in north Monroe who were disturbed by this complicated system of yearly moves from school to school filed a motion requesting that their children be allowed to stay in the same school in grades seven through nine and grades ten through twelve. However, the Justice Department intervened to deny the motion, saying that this stability of attendance would lead to racially imbalanced schools.

The two school systems posed a problem that the strategies in Monroe did not address. Under a 1973 desegregation plan approved by U.S. District Judge Ben Dawkins, some students lived in overlapping zones and could choose whether they would attend a city school or a parish school. By 1980, about 2,400 Monroe children were enrolled in Ouachita schools. A lawsuit challenging the 1973 plan led U.S. District Judge Tom Stagg to issue an order in the Spring of 1980 abolishing the overlapping attendance zones.[17]

By the 1980s, however, the desegregation of Monroe schools was becoming a moot point. As happened in New Orleans, the loss of white students meant that by this time there were simply too few white students in the Monroe district to achieve any kind of meaningful desegregation. Figure 6.8 shows that in 1965, when the initial lawsuit was filed, there were slightly more whites than blacks in Monroe schools. Through most of the 1960s, the numbers of whites climbed while numbers of black students remained relatively stable.

In the 1970s, the Monroe school system began to lose white students at a rate of 240 students each year. This slowed to a loss of eighty white students each year during the 1980s and to a loss of only fifty-four students

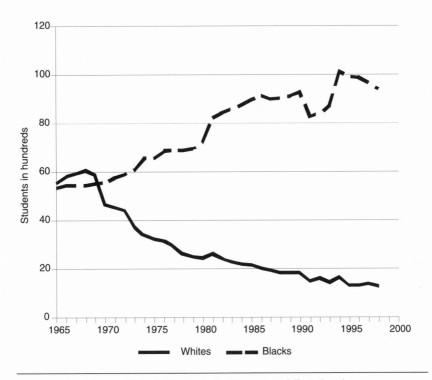

Figure 6.8. White and Black Students in Monroe Public Schools, 1965–2000

each year during the 1990s. As fewer whites are left in any school system, there are fewer to leave, and those who remain tend to be those with the least options to attend school elsewhere. Over the course of these same decades, black students enrolled in the Monroe system increased from 5,333 in 1965 to around 10,000 in the late 1990s. A true desegregation of schools requires the presence of both blacks and whites in adequate quantities. The Monroe system obviously does not lack black students. Its chief obstacle to desegregation seems to be the attraction and retention of whites.

The Department of Education's *Annual Financial and Statistical Report* does not indicate private school enrollment in Monroe for most of the years under consideration, so we cannot say whether Monroe's private schools grew during this time. In 1990, however, 1,238 of the white students in the city were in private schools, compared with 2,057 in public schools. More than one out of every three whites in the city, then, were outside of the public school system, in an area of the state that is heavily Protestant and does not have the tradition of Catholic schools that we saw in New Orleans, Lafayette, and St. John Parish. Fewer than 2% of Monroe's black students were in nonpublic schools.

At the same time that Monroe was hemorrhaging white students, the surrounding Ouachita school district was growing slowly in both black and white students, though continuing to be a predominantly white system. The local consensus among school officials and the general public has been that white flight is the primary cause of the movement of white students out of Monroe city's public schools and into predominantly white Ouachita Parish schools.[18] The numbers bear this out. From the academic year beginning in 1972 to the year beginning 1973, for example, the Monroe system lost 646 white students, and the Ouachita system gained 888 white students. It is very unlikely that these types of sudden decreases and increases could be due to a sudden drop in white birth rates on one side of the Ouachita River and a sudden jump on the other side five to six years earlier. However, the numbers of white students enrolled in Ouachita did not, in the long run, increase at a rate approximating the rate of loss in Monroe. There were 12,919 whites in Ouachita schools in 1965 and only 13,321 in 1997. Readers should recall, though, that white flight can be thought of as whites deciding not to settle in an area, and not just as moving out of that area into another. Increasingly, the whites who were in Ouachita Parish were living in the attendance zones of the parish rather than in the attendance zones of Monroe.

Figure 6.9 shows the proportional distribution of white and black students in Ouachita and Monroe over the course of the thirty-three-year period. As the percentage of students who were black in the city of Monroe district increased from just under half to nearly 90%, the percentage of Ouachita-Monroe white students who were in parish schools rather than city schools grew from just under 70% to over 90%. Essentially, the city lost all but a handful of its whites, since white families either moved out of city school attendance zones or did not settle in the city at all. This cannot, moreover, be attributed to expanding suburbs: numbers of white students in Ouachita grew only modestly over these three decades, peaking at 16,372 in 1976 and then gradually decreasing to 13,321 in 1997. In other words, Ouachita's share of the white students grew even when the entire region was going through a demographic slump. If we note that the gap between the percentage of white school-age children and black school-age children in Monroe was much greater than the gap between the percentages of all city blacks and whites, it becomes evident that the city was specifically losing white families with children.

In contrast to Monroe, virtually all of Ouachita's students were in public schools, even though the income level outside of the city was higher. In 1990, only 11% of white children and 4% of black children living in Ouachita attendance zones were enrolled in nonpublic institutions. As we can see from Figure 6.9, the white proportion of the parish public school system actually increased during some of the years that whites were quickly leaving the city system. Throughout the 1960s, Ouachita public schools were consistently 73% white. In the 1970s, this gradually increased and reached just over 80% in 1981.

Given the socioeconomic and demographic differences between the two

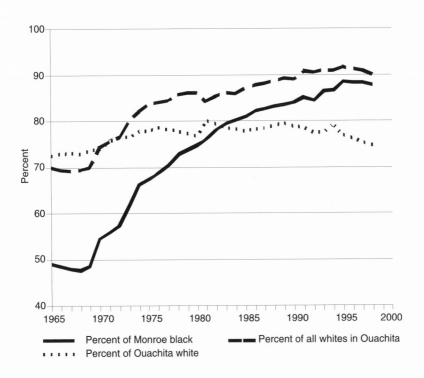

Figure 6.9. Racial Shifts in Ouachita and Monroe Districts, 1965–2000

racial groups, the exodus of whites from Monroe necessarily meant that most of the children in the city's schools would be poor and from single-parent families. As we have seen elsewhere, middle class families (unfortunately disproportionately and overwhelmingly white) try to avoid schools in which the economically disadvantaged predominate. This, in turn, leaves minority-dominated schools increasingly isolated and even more undesirable for those who have other options.

As Table 6.11 shows, middle and elementary school students in 1999 were not evenly distributed according to race in either Monroe or Ouachita, and the academic ranking of schools was closely related to racial composition in both districts. In Monroe, the majority of schools were below average and almost entirely black. Moreover, almost three-quarters of the district's black students attended these schools. Desegregation had clearly had little success.

Almost all of Monroe's few remaining white students were in the five better schools of the city, where they were heavily overrepresented. Even these schools, though, were racially identifiable. All but one were over 60% minority, and all had majorities of low-income students.

Judging from test scores, Ouachita offered better educational opportunities to families with children deliberating about where to settle in the Monroe-Ouachita area. The five Schools of Academic Achievement in the parish could accommodate more students than the single school of that rank in Monroe. White students benefitted disproportionately from attending these schools, since one-third of them could be found in these top-ranked institutions. Nearly half of Ouachita's black elementary and middle-school students, on the other hand, were in the district's seven below average schools. Among these seven schools, one contained 100% minority students, one 97.9% minority students, one 76.4% minority students, one 70.1% minority students, one 61.6%, one 38.9%, and one 27.6%. In other words, minority students were vastly overrepresented in almost all of the parish's worst schools.

Nearly three and a half decades after the first desegregation lawsuit, then, Monroe and Ouachita schools were largely segregated at both the school and the district levels. They were segregated at the school level because both whites and blacks were disproportionately represented in different schools, with most of the whites in the better schools and most of the blacks in the worse schools. They were segregated at the district level be-

Table 6.11. Ranking of Schools and Racial Distribution of Students in Monroe and Ouachita School Districts, 1999 LEAP Tests

	Monroe	*Ouachita*
Academic Achievement	1 school	5 schools
Percent minority	67.2	5.7
Percent of district whites	18.0 (169)	32.3 (3,094)
Percent of district blacks	5.2 (332)	5.5 (203)
Above Average	4 schools	15 schools
Percent minority	67.9	20.4
Percent of district whites	78.5 (706)	58.3 (5,599)
Percent of district blacks	22.2 (1,417)	47.6 (1,749)
Below Average	9 schools	7 schools
Percent minority	99.3	67.5
Percent of district whites	3.4 (31)	8.1 (777)
Percent of district blacks	72.6 (4,630)	46.0 (1,691)
Academically Unacceptable	0	1 school[a]
Percent minority		19.5
Percent of district whites		1.5 (140)
Percent of district blacks		0.9 (34)
Total number of schools	14	28

[a]This is an "alternative school" for behaviorally disordered and otherwise troubled students.

cause the Monroe district was nearly 90% black, and the Ouachita district was about 78% white. There is good reason to believe, moreover, that efforts at desegregation at the school level in Monroe simply contributed to the racial segregation of the districts, since whites were increasingly to be found in the majority-white district. The observer is left wondering what desegregation efforts accomplished in Monroe, aside from moving students from school to school on a yearly basis, while causing whites to relocate to nonpublic schools, move out of the city, or avoid Monroe schools altogether. The black students, on the other hand, suffered the heaviest consequences of a policy implemented ostensibly to help them.

Chapter 7

The Academic Consequences of Desegregation and Resegregation

Revisiting the Harm and Benefit Thesis

One of the most compelling and influential arguments for school desegregation is the view that racially integrated schools result in greater academic achievement among minority students. This theory arose from the "harm and benefit thesis," which was developed by social scientists as early as the 1940s, and submitted to the U.S. Supreme Court as part of the Brown deliberations in the early 1950s.[1] In short, the harm and benefit thesis originally posited that official de jure racial segregation caused psychological, social, and academic difficulties for children—both black *and* white. The high court adopted the rationale of the harm thesis in its ruling in the famous 1954 *Brown et al. v. Board of Education of Topeka* case, stating that "Segregation of white and colored children in public schools has a detrimental effect upon the colored children."

The social science theory, as it was first formulated, was not intended to apply to de facto racial segregation. In other words, the thesis was strictly developed with regard to the forced legal separation of the races extant prior to 1954. The application of the thesis to all racial segregation came much later, in the late 1960s and 1970s, when the courts turned their attention to desegregating northern schools that had no history of legal, government-sanctioned school segregation, but that nevertheless had extensive de facto school racial segregation.

The harm and benefit thesis posited that legal racial segregation impacted four general areas: "academic achievement, self concept and aspirations, race relations and prejudice, and long-term educational and vocational attainment."[2] However, the claim that racial segregation was the root cause of the black-white achievement gap has been the most powerful component of the harm and benefit thesis, and has, justifiably or not, driven much subsequent school desegregation policy. A central implication of the harm and benefit thesis was that desegregated schools should benefit blacks academically, while not detracting from the academics of white students, and could perhaps even enhance white academic achievement. The reasons for this argument were several. However, at the core of the achievement-benefit thesis, as it has come to be called, was the assertion that there is a causal link between white prejudice on one hand and black-white inequality in educational outcomes on the other.[3]

Early on, it was argued that one way in which white prejudice, as manifested in the legally sanctioned separation of the races, might negatively affect black educational achievement was through lowered black self-esteem. Through their enforced isolation, black children would become painfully aware of the inferiority with which whites in power held them and would tend to internalize the negative stereotype of their oppressors. After all, black children might reason, society has set us at arm's length and relegated us to an inferior status. Therefore, we must be inferior. There was some empirical justification for the self-esteem hypothesis, provided by doll studies in the late 1930s. These showed that black children tended to ascribe negative characteristics to black dolls and positive characteristics to white dolls.[4] Lowered black self-esteem could produce lowered educational expectations, and as a consequence, diminished academic performance.

However, during the 1960s and 1970s, well after the end of de jure segregation following the Brown decision, two major reviews of three dozen studies on black self-esteem found that the majority of research indicated that black student self-esteem was either equal to or greater than white self-esteem.[5] Indeed, in two additional, separate reviews of research that specifically focused on black self-esteem in both segregated and desegregated schools, seventeen studies concluded that black self-esteem was actually higher in racially segregated schools, while only six studies found that black self-esteem was higher in racially integrated schools.[6] In other words, it seemed that attending racially desegregated schools not only did not enhance the self-esteem of black students, but may actually have hurt black self-esteem. More recently, a review of 140 studies on African American student motivation found that, overall, black students have high expectations and enjoy positive self-regard.[7]

Thus, one of the pillars of the harm and benefit thesis was undermined, damaging a key initial justification for racially integrating schools. More recently, ethnographers have suggested that it is not so much self-esteem as it is an African American peer culture that enforces norms opposed to academic excellence—in part as a result of racial segregation—that has had a powerful negative influence on students in predominantly minority schools. Indeed, blacks achieving well in school are often derisively accused of "acting white" by other blacks.[8]

Of course, assuming that black self-esteem was suffering in the first place—a questionable assumption given the preponderance of research to the contrary—the reason for attempting to raise black self-esteem was the belief that black test scores would rise as well. It was well established that black academic achievement was lower than white achievement on many measures. The findings of the now famous Coleman report,[9] when most schools were still racially segregated, provided documented evidence that there was indeed a very large achievement gap between whites and blacks. However, Coleman et al. extended understanding of *why* there was a black-white achievement gap by providing a compelling overarching theory to explain it. Coleman et al.'s theory continues to provide the major justification for American school racial integration into the third millennium.

Their research indicated that the most readily measurable outcome of schools—academic achievement—was least influenced by school resources, was only somewhat influenced by teacher qualifications and experience, but was substantially affected by the student's family socioeconomic status (SES). Indeed, more than a quarter of a century after Coleman's controversial report, Hanushek arrived at essentially the same conclusion after reviewing four hundred studies of educational achievement.[10] However, others have argued that many previous studies were misspecified and biased and that more recent research suggests that additional school resources translate into modest—though not spectacular—gains in test scores.[11] Even so, very recent studies have found that math and science students with uncertified teachers faired no worse academically than those students with standard teaching credentials—a finding consistent with Coleman's theory.[12]

Coleman went on to discover that educational achievement was affected not only by a student's own SES but also by the peer environment created by the combined SES backgrounds of his fellow students. Coleman et al. contended that students brought social resources from families to schools, where those resources were pooled and magnified. These social resources included familiarity with middle class norms, reading habits, and high educational expectations. Given that blacks had significantly lower overall SES than whites, and that this socioeconomic disadvantage was magnified in segregated black schools, one would expect lowered educational outcomes from black children, regardless of their "self esteem." Indeed, Coleman et al.'s 1966 study found evidence that black self-concept was lower in predominantly white schools.

The Coleman SES theory was much more compelling and complete than the previous self-esteem or isolation theories of the black-white achievement gap, and indeed, subsumed them quite handily. It shifted the debate from the psychological consequences to the social and economic consequences of segregation. However, the report was issued in the early days of racial desegregation, and the verdict was in a sense "still out" on whether the major social experiment the United States was about to embark upon would produce the intended results: raising black academic achievement levels while not lowering the achievement levels of whites.

More recent research has found long-term evidence to support the notion that a desegregated educational experience for inner city African American students who are educated in predominantly white suburban schools not only have higher achievement test scores than their disadvantaged counterparts, but are also more likely to go on to higher education. This research credits the success of these black students in part to the system of networking available to them in the predominantly white schools— an advantage of being surrounded by white middle class peers. Indeed, this review of twenty-one studies on the long-term effects of desegregation on black students concluded that interracial contact in elementary and secondary schools tended to break the cycle of "perpetual segregation" and open up access to higher-status universities and more upwardly mobile occupational paths for African Americans.[13] Interestingly, one of the same co-authors of this study found in another study that there was essentially no relationship between white student achievement and school racial mix, and actually found a negative relationship between black student achievement and the percentage of the student body that was white.[14]

In any event, it became widely accepted by many researchers that segregated minority schools, even those with the best physical resources and the best-trained teachers, could not completely overcome the damaging *socioeconomic* consequences of isolation from the majority population. Active desegregation, then, came to be seen as redistributive in character—a means of not just equalizing schools, but of redistributing the social resources students brought from their homes to the schools.[15] Lower-SES blacks attending predominantly white schools might be expected to perform better academically by being exposed to a school climate dominated by middle class norms and expectations. The positive effects would somehow "rub off" in interactions between lower-status blacks and higher-status whites. Our own research has tended to validate the strong relationship between the SES of one's school peers and school academic outcomes for both blacks and whites.[16]

Following this logic, Coleman was one of the original proponents of busing and other forms of active desegregation, if it would bring lower-status blacks and middle class whites together. With the social-scientific justification firmly in place, the catalyst that triggered massive busing and other coercive forms of school desegregation was provided in 1968 when the U.S. Supreme Court ruled in *Green v. Board of Education* that "freedom of choice" as an integration tool was unconstitutional since it often did not lead to significant school integration.[17] Thus, it was during the 1970s that the most extensive period of school racial desegregation in the United States took place, finally providing the hard data necessary to determine the effectiveness of widespread school desegregation as a remedy for reducing the black-white achievement gap. Ironically, busing also seemed to cause massive white flight from some public school systems, resulting in Coleman changing his position and calling for an end to forced busing.[18]

Regarding the central question of whether desegregated schools raised black academic achievement levels, perhaps the most extensive and rigorous review of studies examining this relationship took place in 1984 as a project of the National Institute of Education (NIE). A panel of desegregation experts was assembled and assigned the task of ferreting through the mountain of research then available on this important question. The panel set rigorous methodological standards that studies had to meet even to be considered for review. Only nineteen studies that had examined desegregation and black achievement were ultimately selected. The renowned research methodologist Thomas Cook, lead author of the influential work

Quasi-Experimentation, was selected as a referee of the entire process. The final results of the extensive review on whether school desegregation was related to enhanced black academic achievement were inconclusive at best. Cook summarized the overall findings of the nineteen studies as follows: "Desegregation did not cause any decrease in black achievement. On the average, desegregation did not cause an increase in achievement in mathematics. Desegregation increased mean reading levels. . . . [T]he *median* gains were almost always greater than zero but were lower than the means and did not reliably differ from zero."

Regarding the most positive findings for black reading achievement, Cook continued that these studies were characterized as having "small sample sizes . . . two or more years of desegregation, desegregated children who outperformed their segregated counterparts even before desegregation began, and desegregation that occurred earlier in time, involved younger students, was voluntary, had larger percentages of whites per school, and was associated with enrichment programs."

In conclusion, Cook contended that due to methodological shortcomings, "little confidence should be placed in any of the mean results presented."[19]

Thus, the harm and benefit thesis was further weakened as a justification for school racial desegregation when the empirical studies on the black-white achievement gap examined in the 1984 NIE study were in general found to be far from conclusive in crediting integrated schools with raising black achievement levels. However, the NIE study looked at relatively short-term effects of desegregated schooling, since many school districts had not begun actively desegregating until after 1970. It is important to note that other positive, long-term outcomes for African Americans have been attributed to school desegregation, including higher graduation rates, more years of college, increased likelihood of having white social contacts as adults, fewer problems with police, less perceived racial discrimination, and greater likelihood of living in desegregated housing.[20]

An important extraneous factor that complicates efforts to measure the effect of school desegregation on academic achievement is in-school segregation as a result of tracking. Thus, a school that looks desegregated on paper may indeed be segregated at the classroom level. One study found that blacks and Hispanics tend to be disproportionately segregated in low-ability classes in the name of tracking—a practice that can have negative consequences for minority achievement, since these students' opportunities for advancement are limited.[21] Still, in a series of studies done in Louisiana, school-level racial concentration was determined to have a significant relationship with individual student achievement—both black and white. It is to these studies that we now turn.

Academic Consequences of Desegregation in Louisiana

To examine the validity of the harm and benefit thesis in Louisiana and answer the question of whether school desegregation academically benefitted black Louisiana students, while not detracting from the academics of whites, we extensively examined score results of blacks and whites on the 1990 administration of Louisiana's Graduation Exit Examination (GEE).[22] Using 1990 data for approximately 43,000 tenth graders allowed us to look at one of the first cohorts of students who began school during the early 1980s. This was after the disruption normally associated with the first years of aggressive desegregation,[23] but before much of the white flight and resegregation that took place during the 1990s. In other words, this cohort of students attended schools that were as desegregated as Louisiana schools have ever been.

We examined scores of black and white students on the 1990 GEE in an effort first to document differences by race, and then to attempt to account for those differences in terms of many factors, including the central variable of interest, school racial composition, and many of the student background factors originally included in Coleman et al.'s 1966 study. Many of these sociodemographic/economic variables were not included on subsequent state-level exams in Louisiana. Using these data enabled us to address the central question of whether desegregation has made a significant, measurable difference in academic achievement, while controlling for important extraneous factors.

In 1990 there was indeed a sizable gap between blacks and whites on the three tenth-grade components (English language arts, mathematics, and written composition) of the Louisiana GEE. We calculated that whites had an average score of 79% correct on the three components, compared to only 67% correct for blacks—a 12% gap. Moreover, we see that scores for both whites and blacks vary depending upon the racial composition of

**Table 7.1. Average Percent Correct on Three Tenth-Grade Components
of 1990 Louisiana Graduation Exit Exam by School Racial Composition**

Percent African American Concentration in Schools	Blacks	Whites
< 25%	72% correct	80% correct
26–50%	70% correct	79% correct
51–75%	67% correct	76% correct
>75%	66% correct	74% correct

schools. As can be seen in Table 7.1, in schools that had less than 25%
black students, blacks scored an average of 72% correct, whereas whites
scored an average of 80% correct.

In schools with 26% to 50% black students, the scores went down to
70% correct for blacks and 79% correct for whites. Schools with 51% to
75% black students showed average correct scores of 67% for blacks and
76% correct for whites. Schools with over 75% black students had average
scores of 66% correct for blacks and 74% correct scores for whites. This
downward trend is strong, linear, and statistically significant. Figure 7.1
graphs the average GEE scores of both whites and blacks over the spectrum of school racial concentrations from 0% African American to 100%
African American. As can be seen, the covarying lines indicate that racial
concentration affects both white and black scores in much the same way.
As the percent African American student population increases, both white
and black average scores on the GEE decrease in unison.

Could it be that both blacks and whites do worse in increasingly black
schools as a result of being surrounded by poor peers? After all, the poverty rate among African Americans in Louisiana is much higher than among
whites. Whereas the poverty rate for the total population in Louisiana was
24% in 1990, the poverty rate for Louisiana whites was only 13%, but the
poverty rate for blacks stood at 46%.[24] However, when we look at the population of students who took the 1990 tenth-grade GEE, though we see similar rates of poverty for whites, we see much higher rates of poverty among
black students. Among whites who took the GEE, 13% qualified for free
lunch. Among blacks, however, 64% qualified for the federally subsidized

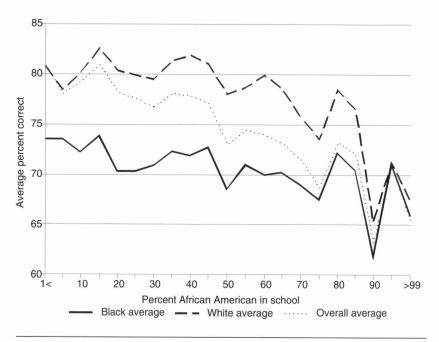

Figure 7.1. Average Percent Correct on GEE

meal. Overall, then, almost half (49%) of all Louisiana public school tenth graders in 1990 came from impoverished backgrounds, but blacks were five times more likely than whites to be poor as defined by eligibility for the federal free/reduced-price lunch program.

In Table 7.2, we do indeed see that both whites and blacks score better in schools with fewer students from poverty backgrounds. In fact, the average percentage correct of both blacks and whites in each category of school poverty level very closely correspond to the average scores of whites and blacks by category of racial concentration seen in Table 7.1. A simple measure of statistical correlation between percentage in poverty and percentage black verifies the very high correlation between these two measures ($r = .792$, p <.0000). In other words, black students also tend to be low-income students.

Thus, our work confirms Coleman's hypotheses that an individual's SES is associated with academic achievement and that the average SES of an individual's school also affects his or her individual academic performance. However, unlike both the harm and benefit thesis and Coleman et al.'s

Table 7.2. Average Percent Correct on Three Tenth-Grade Components of 1990 Louisiana Graduation Exit Exam by School Poverty

Percent of Students on Free/ Reduced Lunch	*Blacks*	*Whites*
< 25%	73% correct	80% correct
26–50%	70% correct	79% correct
51–75%	69% correct	77% correct
>75%	64% correct	75% correct

(1966) seminal work, we found that racial concentration continued to have an *independent* negative association with both white and black achievement, even after controlling for important SES factors.

We decided to look deeper into the relationship between racial concentration and the achievement of both black and white students, to see if there might be another important, overlooked explanatory factor. Our interest was drawn to student family structure. The research literature is replete with evidence suggesting that family structure can have a strong direct effect on school performance, independent of socioeconomic status,[25] and on behavior and attitudes relevant to school performance.[26] As we have pointed out, black students are much more likely than whites—both nationally and in Louisiana—to come from single-parent families. In 1994, fully 70% of all births to nonwhite mothers in Louisiana were out of wedlock, compared with only 21% of births to white mothers.[27] Since 94% of all nonwhites in Louisiana were African Americans,[28] we can safely state that a black child was approximately 3.5 times more likely to be born into a single-parent family than a white child.

We therefore set out to answer two questions: (1) does coming from a single-parent family hurt test scores, and (2) does concentrating children from single-parent families in one school hurt individuals' test scores, apart from their own family status? Fortunately, information on student family backgrounds was gathered during the 1990 administration of the GEE, and from these data we were able to determine which students lived in single-parent family settings. Of the 42,054 tenth graders for whom we were able determine family status, 26% resided in single-parent families. However,

Table 7.3. Student Family Structure of Black and White Tenth Graders Taking 1990 Louisiana GEE

	Blacks	*Whites*
Two-parent families	56% (N = 10,682)	85% (N = 20,128)
Single-parent families	44% (N = 7,632)	15% (N = 3,612)

as can be seen in Table 7.3, only 15% of all tenth-grade whites were from single-parent families, whereas three times as many blacks (44%) lived in this type of family.

Turning our attention back to the 1990 GEE test scores, we did indeed discover that among both blacks and whites in Louisiana, being from a single-parent family was significantly—and negatively—related to lower test scores. As can be seen in Table 7.4, white tenth-grade test-takers from two-parent families scored an average of 81% correct on the 1990 GEE, whereas white test-takers from one-parent families scored much lower, achieving an average of only 68% correct.

The results for black tenth-grade test-takers, while lower, followed the same trend: those from two-parent families on average answered 71% of the test items correctly, while those from one-parent families answered only 61% correctly. There was still clearly a racial gap—but there was also a large family structure gap as well. But could it be that coming from a single-parent family was simply synonymous with coming from both a poor family and a family with lower parental educational levels, so that socio-economic status—not family structure—was depressing test scores? We discovered that the answers are "yes" and "no." Yes, there is a correlation between single-parent family status and poverty. In Louisiana in 1990, whereas only 20% of all families lived in poverty, fully half of all female-headed families were poor, and 73% of all single-parent families with children under five years old were living below the poverty level.[29] In our sample of tenth graders, 72% of all students from single-parent families qualified for the free/reduced price federal lunch program, while only 22% of students from two-parent families did. However, we found that even after statistically controlling for family SES—poverty and parental educational level—there was still a negative association between coming from a

Table 7.4. Average Percent Correct on Three Tenth-Grade Components of Louisiana Graduation Exit Exam by Student Family Structure

	Average Black Percent Correct	*Average White Percent Correct*
Two-parent families	71% correct	81% correct
Single-parent families	61% correct	68% correct

single-parent family and average test scores of both students and schools on the GEE.[30] In other words, there is something else associated with coming from a single-parent family that hurts a student's level of academic achievement independent of family SES. We also found that the negative relationship between student family structure and test scores still remained after controlling for other important factors, such as the racial composition and SES status of schools (as will be shown subsequently).

Having determined that an individual's own family structure had an independent effect on his or her performance on the 1990 GEE, we focused on answering the second question—does clustering students from single-parent families together in the same schools hurt black and white student academic achievement? This is an especially salient question with regard to school segregation, since black students are much more likely to come from single-parent families, and blacks also tend to go to racially segregated schools. As can be seen in Table 7.5, blacks scored an average of 72% correct on the GEE, and whites an average of 80% correct, in schools where less than 25% of tenth graders lived in single-parent families. However, at the other end of the spectrum, we found that blacks scored an average of only 45% correct, and whites an average of only 50% correct, in schools where more than 75% of tenth graders lived in single-parent families. Thus, we see that the family structure of the school appears to have a much stronger relationship with outcomes on the GEE than either the racial composition or poverty status of the school student population. We confirmed the powerful independent effect of school family structure—even when taking into account a student's own family structure and SES—using sophisticated multilevel modeling, which controlled for an array of important individual and school-level effects (see Appendix B, Table B.6). We found that the percentage of students from female-headed families has an even stronger effect on individual achievement than a student's own family structure—though both factors are the best predictors of achievement in our multilevel model.

We discovered that the negative effect on an individual's test scores of going to school where there was a high percentage of students from single-parent families is stronger than the negative influence on scores of coming from a single-parent family onself. Indeed, the effect of school family structure is stronger than all the district-level inputs we examined combined. In short, attending a school dominated by students from single-parent families hurts an individual's academic achievement, regardless of that student's own background, the SES and racial composition of the school, and an entire array of district-level input and process factor effects.

The Concentration of Disadvantage

Overall, our findings are particularly important with regard to blacks attending predominantly black schools in Louisiana. But it is not because of racial segregation per se. It is because we see that segregated black schools concentrate poor students, students from families with less education, and students from single-parent families. Since students from both low-SES backgrounds and students from single-parent families are at an academic disadvantage, concentrating these students together in schools magnifies these disadvantages and consequently tends to impact the entire learning environment negatively for all students. White students, on the other hand, are much more likely to attend schools where the disadvantages asso-

Table 7.5. Average Percent Correct on Three Tenth-Grade Components of Louisiana Graduation Exit Exam by School Family Structure

	Average Black Percent Correct	*Average White Percent Correct*
< 25%	72% correct	80% correct
26–50%	67% correct	76% correct
51–75%	63% correct	71% correct
>75%	45% correct	50% correct

ciated with low SES and single-parent family structure are minimized and distract less from the school's academic agenda. School district support does not seem to mitigate these negative environmental factors, at least in Louisiana.

Thus, the mechanism by which racially segregated schools hurt academic achievement may have little to do with such justifications given for school integration as lowered black self-esteem. Indeed, a recent national study found that black students had a higher degree of overall satisfaction with themselves than any other ethnic or racial group.[31] We do find justification for one of the early pillars of school desegregation theory, family SES: both blacks and whites score better in schools with lower rates of poverty and higher parental education, regardless of their own family backgrounds. Thus Coleman's original justification for placing blacks in predominately white schools, at least with regards to Louisiana students, remains a sound one, and one we have in theory sided with: blacks do better in schools with lower concentrations of African Americans. However, unlike the popular belief of the "Colemanites" in the 1960s, we see that the academic performance of whites does suffer with an increasing concentration of blacks in school. Ironically, this outcome can actually be explained in terms of Coleman's theory—white students are affected by their schools' environments in much the same way as black students.

We have found that one of the greatest negative influences on the academic performance of both whites and blacks is the prevailing student family structure of schools—something never given much play in Coleman et al.'s influential study, or almost any other study for that matter. Indeed, we find that being surrounded by students from single-parent families has an even more powerful negative influence on students' GEE scores than does a student's *own* family background, poverty status, or parental educational level. This fact may be the key to accounting for much black underachievement. In 1965, Senator Daniel Patrick Moynihan referred to the "tangle of pathologies" associated with the disintegrating black family,[32] at a time when 70% of black families were still headed by two parents. Some of Moynihan's critics denounced his views as racist; others claimed that his concerns embodied patriarchal and antifeminist assumptions about the superiority of male-headed households. In the ensuing years, the conventional wisdom purveyed by sociology textbooks has consistently pointed to the Moynihan report as an example of the "culture of poverty theory," which is identified as a reactionary line of thought that "blames the victim" of social injustice by claiming that socially disadvantaged statuses are products of inferior cultures.

In retrospect, Moynihan has perhaps been dealt with too harshly and may deserve credit as one of the more fair-minded and prophetic modern social critics. As William Julius Wilson has acknowledged in the insightful volume *When Work Disappears,* Moynihan did recognize that the unstable black family was the consequence of the American socioeconomic structure.[33] Moynihan simply maintained that, having been produced by an unequal and discriminatory economy, one-parent families yielded unfortunate results of their own. Of course, discrimination against blacks and black families is as old as the institution of slavery, when extremely stressful and precarious circumstances (to put it mildly) made stable "nuclear" family life almost impossible.[34] What many scholars, including Moynihan, Wilson, and Coleman, did not consider, however, were the negative consequences of *concentrating* and *magnifying* the disadvantages ("pathologies" is a bit loaded) associated with the precarious family structure of the black community.

The research is clear: children from two-parent families do better academically than do children living in single-parent families.[35] The large majority of one-parent families are headed by mothers, and modern research now substantiates the importance a father plays in a child's social competence and cognitive development.[36] Moreover, a father's involvement (or lack of it) in his children's lives has elsewhere been associated with differences in academic achievement between groups.[37]

Since the publication of the Moynihan report, there has been a remarkable increase in one-parent families among Americans in general, and among black Americans in particular. This is as true in Louisiana as it is anywhere else in the country. However, in Louisiana, families of all stripes simply tend to be poorer. Researchers have accumulated substantial social-scientific information on single-parent families that indicates that this family form *can* indeed contribute to an educationally disadvantaged environment. Though it is hard to determine an individual's motives, if Moynihan's thinking about black family structure had shortcomings, they were more likely to lay in an underestimation of the problem rather than in any alleged racism, sexism, or cultural bias. Moynihan was not able to foresee in 1965 just how complex and extensive the interrelated problems of single-parent families and racial inequality would become.

Our own research suggests that those concerned about the growth of the single-parent family have missed some of the most serious difficulties created by change in family structure. Families do not influence only their own children, nor are children socialized only by their own families. Children bring influences from their families to their peer groups and, in peer groups, share the influences of their backgrounds with one another. Children's school achievement, then, is not simply affected by the composition of their own families; it is influenced by the family compositions of all those around them, as we have shown with our GEE data. The undesirable consequences of one-parent families, poverty, and low SES then, are not additive, but exponential when those from this type of home setting are concentrated in a social environment. This concept has implications for those who would stress, and perhaps overemphasize, the importance of physical resources such as school buildings and supplies, on raising academic achievement. They are important, but apparently not nearly as important as the social environment created by the students.

Nationally, a majority of black students now come from single-parent families. There is a plethora of research that suggests children from one-parent families are more likely than others to show behavioral and emotional patterns that interfere with schoolwork.[38] For individuals, coming from a one-parent family is associated with only a slight lowering of test results. When individuals from one-parent families are concentrated, though, the result appears to be a disruptive school environment that lessens educational opportunities for all students. Our analyses of achievement test data indicate that the type of family structure prevailing in a school is a powerful predictor of individual test scores. Moreover, the comparatively poor performance of students in majority-black schools seems to disappear when we control for the percentages of students from single-parent families in those schools. As pointed out earlier in our chapter on Lafayette Parish, survey results show that teachers in schools with high percentages of students from one-parent families are more likely than other teachers to report discipline problems and violence.[39] At the national level, an important study involving over 22,000 students found that those students from two-parent families had the lowest reported levels of misbehavior and highest test scores, while those from single-parent/guardian families had the highest levels of misbehavior and lowest test scores.[40]

We find that there is strong evidence that the rise of single-parent family structure in the minority community has been one of the factors undermining the effectiveness school desegregation. Some white parents may have left majority-black school districts out of racial prejudice, out of resentment at judicial coercion in forced desegregation, or out of feelings of a loss of local control over urban school systems. However, many have also realistically seen majority-black schools as undesirable social environments where students generally achieve less than elsewhere.

Conclusions

Overall, we do see that in Louisiana schools, there is a strong correlation between racially segregated schools and academic outcomes. Both white and black scores on the GEE are lower in schools with higher concentrations of African Americans. This trend holds true both in 1990, when schools were as close to being desegregated as they have ever been, and in 1999, after a decade of slow resegregation. Moreover, we see that white and black scores tend to be lower in schools with higher concentrations of students from poor backgrounds.

However, on closer examination, we see that it is not racial concentration per se that causes lowered academic outcomes (as reported by others),[41] but the association between racial concentration and single-parent family structure. Among students who took the 1990 Louisiana high school exit examination, blacks were far more likely than whites to come from single-parent families. Since the percentage of black students in hypersegregated schools increased dramatically from 1990 to 1999, the negative academic consequences of school racial segregation for black students is on the increase.

Using multilevel statistical modeling techniques, we have found that school racial composition has no relation to school achievement after we take the percentage of students from single-parent families into consideration. In other words, the problem is not racially segregated schools per se. Further, the percentage of students from single parent-families is a more powerful predictor of individual test scores than an individual's own family structure or SES background. We must conclude, then, that, at least based on our Louisiana data, the radically different educational outcomes between racially segregated schools are largely a result of the differing predominant family structures found in racially segregated schools. Since there is research that suggests that there are unique benefits to blacks only to be found in attending segregated schools,[42] we would suggest that those benefits may be offset if these schools are dominated by students from single parent-families.

What do our findings imply with regard to the harm and benefit thesis? Overall, our research tends to support the notion that, at least in Louisiana, there *is* academic harm associated with attending racially segregated schools. Moreover, the SES of students and schools explains part, though not all, of this disadvantage. However, white academic achievement also tends to suffer in schools with higher concentrations of blacks. This was not a consequence anticipated by the harm and benefit thesis, and is a finding in direct opposition to some earlier research,[43] as well as to a recently published statement by the senior attorney of the Legal Defense Fund, the group that originally brought the 1954 *Brown* case before the U.S. Supreme Court.[44] Moreover, a major mechanism through which segregation seems to hurt academic achievement is through the family structure of students—something not foreseen when the harm and benefit thesis was first put forth more than half a century ago. Neither could it be foreseen at a time when two-parent African American families were much more the norm than they are today.

Something else not anticipated was the very strong influence on the peer environment created by concentrating children from single-parent families—or conversely, children from two-parent families. Moreover, SES cannot explain all of this concentration effect. A good example that makes this point is the Vietnamese community in Louisiana, which was initially a very low-SES community—but with a high proportion of intact two-parent families. Louisiana eventually received a disproportionately large share of poor Vietnamese boat people fleeing Vietnam following the Communist takeover in 1975. In research on the academic performance of the Vietnamese in New Orleans, we found that low-SES Vietnamese outperformed both blacks and whites on standardized tests.[45] These immigrants, in general, tended to come from intact, very tightly knit families, which together with other tightly knit Vietnamese families created community institutions that provided the necessary family support for academic and business success.[46] Within just a few years of this newest ethnic group's arrival to south Louisiana, the Vietnamese—for whom English was a foreign language—were disproportionately represented in the top-achieving students in high schools throughout the state.

Thus, family seems to matter—and matter a great deal with regard to academic outcomes. And how might we apply what we know about racial desegregation, family structure, and educational outcomes to school organization in Louisiana, and elsewhere? First, we should at least be aware of the cause of some of the racial inequalities in academic achievement. Since parents seek to optimize the educational outcomes of their children, and schools that concentrate children from one-parent families may create environments that are detrimental to high academic performance, then it is not unreasonable to expect that many parents will avoid placing their children in these schools. Thus, we face a Catch-22 of sorts: on one hand, school desegregation is a tool by which districts can reduce the concentration of children from one-parent families. On the other hand, we now know that beyond a certain threshold percentage of African American (which statistics show translates to a high concentration of children from single-parent, poor families) both whites and blacks with the financial means are likely to pull their children from such schools. Thus, there remains a strong incentive to racially integrate schools, at least if raising test scores remains a high priority. However, the challenge will be to do so in a manner that does not surpass a threshold that will trigger white flight—and higher-SES black flight. In many urban schools in Louisiana, achieving such a school balance is now numerically impossible, as white flight has already rendered districts such as New Orleans, Baton Rouge, Shreveport, and Monroe predominantly black districts with high concentrations of poor students from single-parent families. The future challenge may be to make these schools once again attractive to a large enough number of children from two-parent families—whatever their race—and hopefully help reestablish stable learning environments that will benefit all students.

Chapter 8

Recommendations

Louisiana no longer has the legally mandated segregated schools of the first half of the twentieth century. The era of two separate school systems is now fortunately behind us. Still, de facto racial segregation in the schools remains a reality. Despite all governmental efforts to undo it, racially identifiable schools continue to be common. Indeed, they are on the increase. The struggles to balance schools racially, as we have seen, have required continual coercion from the federal government—coercion that has largely resulted in failure and has often made a bad situation intolerably worse. If whites no longer resist with the vulgar, racist displays of some of the citizens of New Orleans forty years ago, they still do so in more subtle ways. Moreover, so do many African Americans who increasingly have the financial means to escape low-performing, minority-dominated schools. Throughout this book, we have seen whites leaving heavily black school districts for majority-white districts. We have seen white families abandoning public school systems for private schools. We have seen white parents strategically placing their children in the schools that have smaller black student populations than other district schools. While all of these strategies have optimized the educational opportunities for those with the financial means, it has left poor African Americans in increasingly desperate schools and school systems.

There is a real dilemma in school desegregation, one that scholars and policy makers too often try to ignore or refuse to recognize. The justification for striving for racial balance is the view that minority schools exist in a state of systematic social disadvantage. Students in today's majority-black schools do not receive the outdated second-hand books given to their grandparents. Too often, though, they are isolated in institutions where most of the other children are poor, where many of the other children do not have role models who promote success, where the habits and means of self-presentation conducive to upward mobility seem unfamiliar and out of place.

A major goal of desegregation has been to give minority children access to a middle class that is still dominated by whites. Academic environments, however, are created by all of the students in a school from the backgrounds that all of the students bring with them. The dilemma of desegregation is that increasing the proportion of minority children in a school can, in some ways, present genuine problems for both black and white children. Poverty, jobless neighborhoods, parents with limited educations, and single-parent families are all widely acknowledged to put children at risk for academic failure. The more children there are in a school who are at risk, the worse the academic environment of the school. As we have seen repeatedly, all of the factors that place children at risk are so strongly correlated with race that the racial composition of schools is one of the most accurate predictors of the performance levels in schools. Moreover, parents with the means who are seeking the best educational opportunities for their children sense this and avoid placing their children in majority-black schools.

In the long run, a more racially egalitarian society is in the interest of all Americans, not only black and white. Most parents, though, would not sacrifice benefits to their own children for the distant and uncertain goals of racial equality. One of the reasons that desegregation has required judicial coercion over many decades is that the families who generally have the greatest control over the education of their children—white, middle class families—would not desegregate voluntarily. While prejudice may be part of the explanation for this reluctance, we cannot understand the resistance and the avoidance fully without seeing that these families have little to gain from desegregating schools. Although there are unquestionably disadvantaged white children, for the most part, whites already have good schools. Desegregation can at best mean no loss, and the close correlations that we have seen between racial composition and academic ranking suggest that loss is a real possibility. Offering people a deal in which they can at best hope to break even is not the best way to ensure eager participation.

Coming up with policy plans to deal fairly and constructively with the dilemma of desegregation will be very difficult precisely because desegregation can so easily undermine its own goals. Although coercive strategies for achieving desegregated schools have undoubtedly contributed to white avoidance and resistance, the strategies have not been the ultimate problem. Busing and redistricting are frequently unpopular, but parents are often willing to have their children take fairly long bus rides or go to schools away from their own neighborhoods if these inconveniences mean that their children will enjoy improved educational opportunities. The avoidance of schools with large minority student bodies is less a response to the means of desegregation than it is a response to the consequences. The continuing existence of racial stratification *outside* of the classrooms means that desegregation can frequently be self-defeating because increasing the representation of minority children in schools brings the problems associated with racial inequality *into* the classrooms. In addition, the role of family structure in producing the academic environment of schools suggests that overcoming the racial gap in school performance, at the individual and aggregate levels, may well require far more than just the enhancement of educational opportunities for minority group members.

While we believe that the challenges of achieving both excellence and racial equality in education are daunting, we do not think that daunting challenges should provide excuses for defeatism. A permanent division of American society into quasi castes would be a serious threat to the health of the nation, and educational institutions must be part of the effort to meet this threat. At the same time, effective policies must be based on realistic assessments, not on wishful thinking. We would like to conclude this book with a few policy suggestions that we think are solidly grounded in our findings and that may provide broad outlines for ameliorating the problem of race in American education.

Neighborhood Schools

There is evidence of strong support for neighborhood schools in many parts of the United States. In the September 1999 issue of *Governing* magazine, Rob Gurwitt observed that "'Neighborhood schools' are no longer the rallying cry of a disaffected or prejudiced white minority. City after city, tired of busing, has seen support for educating children close to home become the political norm, the preference of families of every race, the simple inclination of the streets."[1] In Baton Rouge, desegregation authority Christine Rossell found backing for neighborhood schools among both black and white families. Discussing a 1993 survey of the opinions of Baton Rouge parents, Rossell found that neither white nor black parents supported controlled-choice desegregation plans. Rossell observed that "the most popular alternative plan for white parents is returning to neighborhood schools with 96% supporting this. Returning to neighborhood schools is the second most popular option for black parents (after voluntary magnet programs) with 84 percent supporting this."[2] More recently, in our own research on the ongoing desegregation drama in Lafayette, we found strong resentment in the black community against the closing of two black neighborhood schools and the busing of those children across town to "further desegregate" the system.[3]

Although neighborhood schools are popular, many academic authorities and policymakers are skeptical of a return to schools with close ties to an immediate residential basis. In an overview of recent changes in school desegregation, Jeanne Weiler writes:

> Despite this belief in the value of neighborhood schools, the reality is that many urban students return to schools that are segregated and inferior. Often new funding for upgrading school facilities and educational programs is promised but not delivered. However, as is the case with many large urban schools, even an infusion of extra funds is often not enough to transform a school, as schools must struggle with the profound and increasing poverty and joblessness in their local communities. Moreover, in cities that previously used busing measures to desegregate their schools, costs to create new schools and classrooms that had been underutilized for years can run as high as hundreds of millions of dollars.[4]

The dangers that concern Weiler are real, and neighborhood schools do allow some de facto segregation, since blacks and whites continue to live in largely separate neighborhoods. While we acknowledge these dangers, we still think that neighborhood schools can be an important part of reaching constructive compromise solutions. One argument in favor of the neighborhood concept is precisely that it does receive such wide popular support. Educational policy cannot be made by plebiscite, but public schools are, after all, public institutions. They are established and maintained by an elected representative government that should be responsive to the desires of the electorate. Any time there is a clear policy preference among the constituents of a democratic society, this should weigh heavily with public officials—especially when the alternative has proven so destructive.

This brings us to a central theme of this book, that the abandonment of neighborhood schools has not really led to true desegregation. If true desegregation is the bringing together of black and white students, then, as a precondition, we must have adequate numbers of both races. The fact that neighborhood schools seem to be particularly popular with white—and increasingly black—families should be seen as a point in favor of this type of arrangement. Whites are clearly the ones who have the greatest power to shop around for school districts and school zones and to make choices between public and private schools. In the various districts of Louisiana that we considered, we saw no difficulty in keeping adequate numbers of black students. Throughout the state, but especially in the urban areas, we saw a trend toward black predominance in public schools, in large part because the poor have no other options. Neighborhood schools can help maintain critical white participation and white support—financial and otherwise. Thus, this arrangement, contrary to a popular misconception, does not benefit just "well-to-do" whites. The whole system benefits when middle- and upper-middle-income families remain planted in both the community and its public schools, not only maintaining a healthier tax base, but actually tapping into that base by passing taxes that fund the entire educational enterprise.

If those in overly white districts want locally based schools, they should be willing to give in order to receive. Increased spending on minority schools must be part of any neighborhood schools program. We should assume that any parent will only support a school plan that gives a satisfactory answer to the question "What will my child get out of this?" The central difficulty with desegregation as it has generally been practiced in Louisiana and other states for the past thirty or so years is that it has essentially demanded that white families make sacrifices in the education of their children. They have not been willing to do this, and there is no logical reason to expect that this behavior will change in the future. The same is true of black families. Blacks, on average, may have less power than whites to leave school systems that do not satisfy them, but neither group is entirely powerless. Collective action and lawsuits are legitimate and reasonable responses from those who feel that they derive no benefit from public policies.

One of the potential benefits of neighborhood schools for minority populations is that they do make it easier to meet local needs. Courses such as African American literature or history, for example, are relevant to all students, but may be more heavily emphasized in schools in minority communities if parents express a particular interest. Teachers who specialize in teaching minority youngsters, moreover, can develop a greater understanding of the requirements of these youngsters. Once again, however, special attention must be given to the special needs of minority students. If we want qualified teachers in schools in black neighborhoods, we must make it in the interest of teachers to go to those schools and to remain in them—not punish them for the poor academic achievement of these schools' students, which seems to be Louisiana's current public school policy. If we have learned anything from our years of research, it is that student achievement is largely influenced by factors beyond the control of teachers. Still, teacher quality is a factor over which we do have some control, and added salary benefits for teachers who work in schools with large numbers of low-income or minority pupils can help to ensure that neighborhood schools benefit black families—even if these schools cannot level all of the inequalities of American society.

Magnet Schools

Neighborhood schools can help bring an element of stability back to our disrupted school districts. They also help to encourage support for public schools on the part of families that are financially and educationally best able to contribute to educational systems. By themselves, though, neighborhood schools are not likely to contribute to desegregation. Instead, our support for this strategy is based on a willingness to accept some degree of de facto segregation in schools in order to achieve other goals. There are, however, other policy options that may contribute to voluntary racial mixing, while striving to meet the varied interests of all families with children.

In all of the school districts that we looked at in the state of Louisiana, there was wide support for magnet programs. Indeed, in districts such as New Orleans, most of the few white students who remained in the public school system would only remain in the system as long they could obtain positions in magnet schools. Black parents generally supported magnet schools, although they sometimes objected that their own children were less likely to obtain admission to these programs than white children were. While we do not think that educational programs should be determined simply by consumer demand, policymakers in a democratic society should take very seriously the clear preferences and desires of the public.

Magnet schools in the United States are usually traced to an amendment to a piece of federal desegregation legislation, the Emergency School Aid Act (ESAA) of 1972. The ESAA was eliminated in 1981, but federal support for magnet schools was revived in 1985 under the Magnet Schools Assistance Program. The basic idea of the magnet school is to offer special, advanced teaching methods or specialized programs to bring non-minority children into minority-dominated schools voluntarily in order to reduce social isolation.

Magnet schools have been criticized on two grounds. First, it has been maintained that they do not really help achieve desegregation, that they simply create schools within schools by placing white children in magnet programs within majority-black schools. Second, it has been claimed that there is insufficient evidence that participation in magnet schools contributes substantially to academic achievement.[5]

From our viewpoint, these two criticisms touch on related matters. One of the central points in this book has been that the school performance of students is influenced by other students. Specialized programs are desirable, but the real virtue of competitive magnet programs, from the perspective of those who participate in them, is that students can go to school with other students who have managed to pass entry requirements to enter the programs. Whether or not the magnet schools themselves contribute to academic achievement, they provide places where high achievement is part of the social context. This means that, to some extent, magnet programs need to be schools within schools in order to provide an environment that can draw students who would otherwise enroll elsewhere. One of the virtues of magnet schools, in spite of a tendency toward internal segregation, is that they do help to keep white students from deserting public school districts with large minority populations. In addition, these schools can promote some degree of contact among students of different racial and socioeconomic backgrounds, particularly if students in nonmagnet components of magnet schools have access to resources and can participate in some of the magnet classes. We contend that it is better to have some degree of segregation within a school than to have blacks and whites concentrated in entirely different schools or even entirely different school districts—without the economic support of that segment of the community most able to provide it.

By themselves, magnet schools do not appear to be the cure for white movement out of minority-dominated school districts. Both Baton Rouge and New Orleans have had magnet programs since the early 1980s, and both have steadily lost white students. Neighborhood schools and magnet schools, then, should be seen as complementing each other. When neighborhood schools disappear, magnet schools become scarce resources that are desperately sought. As true racial mixing becomes increasingly difficult, since there are fewer and fewer whites in a school system, white students tend to concentrate in a small number of highly competitive institutions. Demand for entry into magnet schools by whites, on the average better prepared for tests and other qualification standards, limits the number of positions available to black students. With schools in their own neighborhoods, white families have two desirable options. They can either choose to try to get their children into magnet schools or they can enjoy the convenience and local control of their nearby institutions. In both instances they remain committed to public education.

It may also be helpful to approach the strategy of magnet schools from a new angle. Instead of simply placing particularly bright or talented white students in programs in majority-black schools, we recommend that school districts try placing bright, talented black students in majority-white schools. One of the consistent complaints of black parents regarding the magnet system is that it tends to offer special opportunities to whites. One way of addressing this objection would be to develop programs, specifically aimed at minority students, in the arts or sciences or for students who exhibit strong academic performance. This could be done in two ways. First, magnet programs established in predominantly white schools could have some residential requirements, so that these programs are open only to students from mainly black neighborhoods. Second, these programs could have income requirements. In order to obtain entry, students would have to pass fairly rigorous academic requirements and also be classified as low income. In states such as Louisiana, where the majority of low-income students are black, this would open positions in these magnet schools primarily to black pupils.

Minority-oriented magnet programs could conceivably help to combat negative stereotypes of black students that may be held by both blacks and whites. A danger of the traditional magnet program, which places academically or otherwise talented whites in a predominantly black school, is that this arrangement reinforces the view of scholastic performance as something "white." If those selected for strong academic skills are black, however, this can lead to a revaluation of these stereotypical views. Moreover, since this type of arrangement would bring the most gifted or dedicated black students into white schools, there would be little danger of the forms of white flight from declining schools that we have seen in this book. Also, since presumably there would be a stronger academic environment, these black students would be able to go farther, faster, than they might otherwise be able to in predominantly African American schools, where high achieving blacks are sometimes accused of acting white."[6]

Majority-to-Minority Programs

Neighborhood schools and magnet schools can still leave most black children in a district isolated in majority-black schools. To some extent, we simply have to live with this. If Americans have learned anything over the past half century, we have learned that we cannot create an egalitarian utopia by judicial or bureaucratic fiat. As we have seen throughout this volume, Louisiana schools continue to be largely segregated after three decades of disputatious, disruptive, and destructive struggles. Still, programs of small-scale, voluntary desegregation can ameliorate our racially unequal school systems.

Majority-to-minority programs have the potential to meet the aspirations of many black families while retaining the support of whites. These programs involve sending black students from majority-black schools into majority-white schools on a purely voluntary basis. In her work on the East Baton Rouge school district, Christine Rossell found substantial interest among black parents in participating in majority-to-minority programs. Her survey results showed that 35% of black parents in this district were willing to transfer their children to schools that were 75% white even if the children faced forty-five-minute bus rides each day. Half of these parents were willing to send their children to schools that were 75% white if this meant only a thirty-minute bus ride each day.

The goal of majority-to-minority programs should not be to create racial balances in schools. As we have seen, racial balances can very easily become imbalances as families respond to changing school compositions by moving, transferring, or shifting to nonpublic schools. Trying to change primarily white schools into schools with an idealized combination of blacks and whites tends to be a self-defeating effort. In addition, the chief goal of desegregation is ending the isolation of black students, which cannot be accomplished by simply transferring a large population of minority students from one school to another. This does nothing but move these students from one socially isolated school to another, with all the disruption that follows uprooting students from a familiar environment and dropping them into an unfamiliar one. Effective desegregation, then, must be based on the existence of majority-white schools into which black students can be integrated.

We recommend that a number of positions, well under the 30% threshold that we have suggested may lead to white flight, be opened to black students in schools serving majority-white neighborhoods. The precise number of positions will depend on the space and resources available. These places should be offered on a first-come, first-served basis to minority families who wish to see their children attend school outside of their own neighborhood. Note that this type of plan presupposes the existence of neighborhood schools in white neighborhoods into which some minority students can transfer.

Majority-to-minority programs may not be feasible in some locations, such as New Orleans and Monroe, in which there are too few white students remaining to have many majority-white schools. However, they continue to be a promising option in districts that still have white neighborhoods. In general, the degree to which districts emphasize efforts to place black students in majority-white schools or efforts to attract and hold white students must be a matter of demographics.

Residential Desegregation

Our schools are no longer segregated by law, but they continue to be segregated in reality because black and white families live in different places. Not only do they live in different communities, they live in different types of communities. According to U.S. Bureau of the Census estimates, a clear majority of African Americans (54.5%) lived in the central parts of cities in March 1998, while only 22.0% of non-Hispanic white Americans lived in central urban localities. This means that minority young people live in places where they are physically separated from the majority population. In contemporary American cities, jobs also tend to be scarce, so young people in urban centers have few opportunities to come into contact with people who have jobs and expectations for upward mobility. The sociologist William Julius Wilson has, as we pointed out, connected the phenomenon of concentrated poverty to the decline in marriage among African Americans, arguing that joblessness has removed the familial role of men in inner city areas.[7]

Part of the solution to the problems of our schools lies in recognizing that these problems do not originate in the schools but in the society outside of them. Schools are affected by these problems but cannot solve them. Breaking down segregation in the schools, from this perspective, is a matter of first breaking down residential segregation in American society. Attempts to ship minority students out of low-income, jobless neighborhoods each day to schools and then return them to those neighborhoods each afternoon can do little more than bring the problems of the neighborhoods into the schools.

Douglas S. Massey and Nancy A. Denton have argued persuasively that residential segregation in the United States is largely a product of discriminatory practices in housing markets and in governmental policies regarding housing.[8] We agree with Massey and Denton that eradicating housing discrimination must be a high priority. Local organizations that investigate and prosecute instances of discrimination in the sale and rental of homes should receive both state and federal assistance. Governmental agencies at all levels should undertake an active campaign to ensure that home loans by financial institutions become more racially egalitarian. Real estate agents should be thoroughly trained in disseminating information about housing in all residential areas to members of all racial and ethnic groups. However, even with all of these measures in place and enforced, there will be residential racial segregation as long as there remains a gulf between the incomes of racial groups, which is the case between whites and blacks in Louisiana.

Economic Development for Minority Communities

Even if there are increased opportunities for black Americans to find housing in white neighborhoods, they will not be able to move to desirable, middle class homes unless they can afford to do so. Moreover, it is unrealistic to expect that in the near future all people living in low-income, majority-black communities will leave their current settings. Many may not want to do so because of social or family ties. Therefore, the development of economic activities in minority communities is critical to establishing a social background that will serve students well in our schools.

Efficient, inexpensive public transportation throughout metropolitan areas can enable people to get to jobs, and it can bind suburban and urban areas more closely together. Minority communities tend to be located away from the suburban malls and office and industrial parks that hold many of the newly created jobs in today's economy. To take advantage of these jobs, people in minority neighborhoods must be able to get to them.

Both state and federal governments should provide incentives for job-creating investments in minority residential areas. Low-interest loans and tax advantages for businesses that locate in places with high unemployment can help stimulate economic activities where they are most needed. Training in basic skills should be available to all citizens so that they have the qualifications for the opportunities that exist, in their own neighborhoods or elsewhere.

The development of a government jobs agency along the lines of the Depression-era Works Progress Administration can serve the goals of job creation and training. This type of "make work" effort need not consist of digging holes in order to fill them in again, but it can entail building or rebuilding the physical infrastructures of low-income neighborhoods. New Orleans, for example, has such notoriously bad streets that drivers often feel that they need off-road vehicles for everyday urban driving. Hiring and training local jobless people to fill in the potholes and repave the surfaces would provide jobs and give work experience while at the same time making the city a more attractive place for business—and in the case of New Orleans—tourist activities. Putting thousands of healthy, unemployed individuals to work helping restore Louisiana's disappearing wetlands is another example of a way in which government can put many people to work, on the scale of the 1930s Tennessee Valley Authority, doing meaningful, community labor for meaningful wages.

The Reconstruction of Family

Traditional desegregation plans have tended to treat students as unconnected social atoms who can simply be moved from one educational institution to another with the expectation that school placement or events in schools can equalize opportunities. Human beings, however, are not separable from their social contexts any more than trees are separate from their ecological environments. They live in communities that shape their attitudes, their expectations, and their behavior. Even more fundamentally, they live in families. The family is the oldest of social institutions, and it continues to be the most basic.

There has been a tendency in the social sciences to present single-parent families as simply one among several alternative family types, an option that is just as valid as any other living arrangement. While this may seem like avant-garde thinking, the research evidence does not support this point of view. Though there may be some debate about why single-parent families are associated with academic and behavioral problems, the associations are clear. Students who come from single-parent families are at risk for underachievement in schools and for behavior that is poorly adapted to the school environment. There are certainly influences other than family structure that determine school outcomes. Having one good parent, moreover, can be preferable to two bad parents. When we concentrate students from single-parent families, though, we create a different order of problem. Although coming from a one-parent family may increase the school risks of each individual only very slightly, bringing together many pupils from this family type in the same school creates a seriously troubled academic environment.

We have argued in this book that family structure is both a school issue and a racial issue. There is good evidence that at least a large part of the reason students in majority-black schools, both black and white, generally show weaker scholastic performance than students in majority-white schools is that majority-black schools are, for the most part, schools with large proportions of students from single-parent families. In our examination of the schools in New Orleans, we saw the social disruption resulting from entire communities of children growing up in one-parent families. In our discussion of Lafayette, we saw that teachers who work in schools that concentrate students from one-parent families report serious disciplinary problems.

The connection between race and family structure creates problems for school desegregation. If going to school with black students means going to school with students from single-parent families, then it is entirely understandable that white families would want to avoid schools with large black populations. More importantly, though, racial differences in family structure perpetuate racial inequalities in school achievement and in life after school. Those from one-parent families begin their lives with a heavier burden than other children. Those who go to school with children from this family type encounter a troubled academic atmosphere.

If we are really interested in achieving racial equality of opportunity or in promoting a hopeful future for all children, we cannot take a laissez faire approach to our fundamental social institution. We need to recognize that the breakdown of the family is a serious social problem. Further, we need to acknowledge that it is a problem that most heavily affects minority children. Recognizing that the problem exists is the first step toward addressing it. Education has become a major political issue in the United States. Reconstructing the family is critical for meeting our educational challenges, and this topic should become at least as central as education to our political discourse—apart from a broader agenda to promote a particular political viewpoint.

Efforts at rebuilding the family must not take the form of blaming single mothers, unwed or divorced. The pressures that have led to an increase in one-parent households cannot be understood in terms of individual choices. Individuals in the same groups do not simply happen to make the same choices at the same historical periods by the miraculous coincidence of free will. We should also not ignore the difficulties facing single parents, many of whom are struggling to bring up children in poverty. Responding to the situations of these parents by telling them to get married would be unrealistic. Making child care available to every family, regardless of its structure, can, on the other hand, help cushion the hard shocks of raising children alone.

While public policy should help one-parent families, however, it should not simply accept this family form as the way of the future. Public assistance programs, now in a state of rapid and perhaps radical change, should emphasize putting low-income people into two-parent families as well as putting them to work. Family support funds available to couples with at least one working spouse can provide incentives for households headed by two adults.

Nongovernmental agencies should also be drawn into a concerted campaign to rebuild minority family life. Although the decline in marriage among black Americans may be causally ascribed to economic pressures, there is a normative element in any pattern of behavior. Active fatherhood should be promoted as a valuable and desirable state. Churches and mosques can contribute enormously to a family reconstruction campaign. Religious institutions have played a positive, leading role in almost all of the major episodes in black American history, and they can be central to creating strong families and communities as foundations for achieving racial equality.

We have tried too long to use our schools as instruments for solving the problems of the society outside the schools. There are some ways that schools can contribute to the goal of racial equality. Ultimately, though, segregated neighborhoods, unequal opportunities, and disruptive families and communities will affect schools more than schools will affect these conditions. The dream of educational desegregation can only become a reality to the extent that we overcome our troubled heritage of racial stratification in American society at large.

Appendixes

Notes

Index

Appendix A

Single-Parent Families and Educational Environment:
A Multivariate Analysis of the Relationship
of Indiscipline and Violence with Socioeconomic Levels and
Family Structures in Lafayette Schools

In Chapter 5, we saw that Lafayette students in schools with high concentrations of single-parent families do worse than those in schools with low concentrations. We have also seen that teachers, in responses to an open-ended question, overwhelmingly identified social disorder as the single greatest problem facing contemporary schools. We are left with the task of establishing a clear statistical connection between these two points, of providing evidence that single-parent families affect school outcomes by producing a school environment of social disorder.

In order to examine with a more sophisticated statistical approach than we used in the main text, we created a measure of school social disorder by using factor analysis to generate factor scores from two of the highly correlated ($r = .546$, factor loading $= .879$) survey items regarding the frequency of discipline problems and the frequency of violence in each teacher's school. The former item asked, "How frequent are discipline problems in your school?" Possible answers were "We never have such problems," "We seldom have," "We occasionally have," "We frequently have," and "Discipline is a constant problem." The latter item asked, "To what extent does discipline pose a problem in your school?" Possible answers were "No problem," "On occasions students may endanger others," "Students frequently endanger others," and "Students are never safe."

We then selected a number of theoretically meaningful possible determinants of teacher perceptions of school social disorder. We included indicators of the teachers' own backgrounds, experience, and school situations, since these may affect their perceptions. We also included teachers' reports of the residential and socioeconomic backgrounds of students, the family situations prevailing among their students, and levels of parental involvement in schools. In this way, we can use the reports of the adults most immediately involved in schools (the teachers) to examine whether social disorder in schools appears to be related primarily to the socioeconomic situations of their pupils or to school-level family circumstances. By including a measure of parental involvement we can consider to what extent the suspected effects of family structure on social order may be the consequence of a lack of parental participation in education. If disruption in the schools is a state that emerges from a concentration of single-parent families, it may be that this disruption results from gaps between home and school.

Table A.1 shows zero-order correlations among the variables that we use to examine the link between the social environment of schools and social disorder. Since we are looking at the reports of teachers, we think it important to include some teacher characteristics that may affect these reports. Education (measured by the highest degree obtained), race (0 for blacks, 1 for whites), and sex (0 for males, 1 for females) show no significant zero-order correlation with reports of social disorder. Years taught (measured by years of experience) is not significantly related to social disorder, but it is understandably associated with teacher level of education. Grade taught (with three levels: elementary school, junior or middle, and high school) is significantly related to reports of social disorder. Teachers in higher grades are also more likely to have higher educational credentials, and they are more likely to be male. Interestingly, neither class size nor school size (measured by reported numbers of students) is significantly related to social disorder as we would expect if discipline problems and violence were products of crowding.

These first variables indicate characteristics of the teachers and of the schools. The final variables indicate characteristics of the students themselves. Here we begin to see strong relationships with our measure of social disorder. Reported urban residence of students (most students live in rural or suburban areas = 0; most students live in urban areas = 1) shows a fairly strong positive relationship with reports of social disorder. Also, more urban school populations tend to have smaller class and school sizes, again suggesting that behavioral problems in city schools are not consequences of crowding. Teachers who report having students in comparatively high income brackets (most students are low income = 0; middle income or mixed = 1; high income = 2) report fewer problems of discipline and violence. Teachers with more experience are more likely to be in comparatively affluent schools, a probable consequence of the greater power of choice in teaching positions given to those with seniority. The more economically privileged a school, moreover, the smaller the school and its classes tend to be.

Our indicators of parental composition and parental involvement show the strongest statistical links with reported discipline problems and violence. The higher the reported proportion of students coming from single-parent families (almost all students live in two-parent families = 0; most live in two-parent families = 1; most live in single-parent families = 2; almost all live in single-parent families = 3), according to these educational professionals, the greater the level of social disorder in the schools.

Again, teachers with more experience are less likely to be in more troubled teaching circumstances, since they are less likely to report having high percentages of pupils from one-parent families. Those with higher percentages of pupils from single-parent households tend to teach smaller classes in smaller schools, once again making an overcrowding explanation implausible. Teachers who say that they have more students from families with only one parent are also more likely to teach students from an urban environment.

Finally, we see that the variable of teacher reports of parental involvement (parents not at all active in school affairs = 0; parents occasionally active = 1; parents usually active = 2; parents very active = 3) has the strongest zero-order correlation of all with reports of social disorder. The higher the grade taught, the less likely teachers are to see high levels of parental involvement. Parental involvement has no significant relationship with class size, school size, or urban residence of students. However, it is quite strongly associated with prevailing family structure, which suggests the possibility that single-parent families are connected to high levels of social disorder because single parents are less involved in the schools.

Table A.2 completes our analysis by using multivariate regression to

Table A.1. Zero-Order Correlations among Variables in the Analysis

	Teacher Education	Teacher Race	Teacher Sex	Years Taught	Grade Taught	Class Size	School of Students	Urban Residence Students	Income Level of Students	Family Situation Involvement	Level of Parental
School disorder	-.017	-.013	-.021	-.054	.135[a]	.026	.057	.221[a]	-.289[a]	.459[a]	-.473[a]
Teacher education		-.013	-.099[b]	.350[a]	.092[b]	-.087[b]	.020	.019	.055	-.017	.021
Teacher race			-.078	-.042	.074	.022	.023	-.020	.052	-.038	.037
Teacher sex				.042	-.244[a]	-.114[b]	-.243[a]	-.033	-.081	.134[a]	.055
Years taught					-.018	.030	-.036	.048	.102[b]	-.112[a]	.076
Grade taught						.046	.599[a]	-.085	.035	-.050	-.111[a]
Class size							.030	-.129[a]	.161[a]	-.203[a]	-.012
School size								-.202[a]	.164[a]	-.213[a]	0.021
Urban residence of students									-.134[a]	.257[a]	-.050
Income level of students										-.593[a]	-.524[a]
Family situation of students											-.520[a]

[a]p < .05
[b]p < .01

Table A.2. Standardized and Unstandardized Coefficients (in Parentheses) of Predictors of Reports of Social Disorder in Schools

	Step 1	Step 2	Step 3	Step 4
Education	.010	.017	.000	−.008
of teacher	(.012)	(.022)	(.0001)	(−.009)
Race	−.028	−.006	−.005	.003
of teacher	(−.055)	(−.012)	(−.010)	(.006)
Sex	.025	.024	−.006	.015
of teacher	(.068)	(.065)	(−.016)	(.040)
Years	−.038	.006	.027	.028
taught	(−.005)	(.001)	(.003)	(.003)
Grade	.179[a]	.058[b]	.121[b]	.089
taught	(.193)	(.151)	(.130)	(.097)
Class	.029	.078	.100[b]	.063
size	(.003)	(.009)	(.012)	(.008)
School	−.055	.048	.078	.074
size	(−.061)	(.054)	(.088)	(.084)
Urban residence		.218[a]	.135[a]	.149[a]
of students		(.277)	(.173)	(.190)
Income level		−.282[a]	−.032	.077
of students		(−.326)	(−.037)	(.089)
Family situation			.457[a]	.351[a]
of students			(.618)	(.479)
Level of parental				−.305[a]
involvement				(−.337)
Constant	−.351	−.642[b]	−1.763[a]	−1.079[a]
R^2	.024	.155	.275	.337

[a]$p < .01$
[b]$p < .05$

examine predictors of school social disorder. Step 1 regresses our social disorder factor on teacher characteristics and school characteristics. These explain very little of the variance (R^2 = .024), and only grade taught shows a statistically significant coefficient. Step 2 introduces the economic and residential variables: the extent to which teachers reported that their students came from urban areas and the reported economic backgrounds of students. Both of these showed strong, significant associations with social disorder in the schools. The more urban the pupil composition of schools, the greater the reported level of discipline problems and violence. The more economically advantaged the pupil composition, the lower the reported level of these problems. The variables in step 2 explain 16% of the total variance in reported school disorder.

Step 3 brings in our indicator of the family structures prevailing in schools: the extent to which teachers reported that their students came from single-parent families. The prevailing family structure is strongly related to social disorder (beta = .457). The coefficient for the income level of students becomes statistically insignificant, suggesting that there tend to be greater order problems in schools with large proportions of low-income students because these schools are likely to have large numbers of students from single-parent homes, not because students from single-parent homes tend to have low incomes. Further, the coefficient for urban residence decreases notably, indicating that part of the reason that urban schools have greater difficulties with discipline and violence is that urban students are more likely to come from households with only one parent.

Finally, step 4 looks at the question of parental involvement in schools. Are schools with large single-parent student populations associated with relatively high levels of poor discipline and violence because these schools can draw on little parental involvement and support? Apparently, this is not the case. A lack of reported parental involvement is certainly strongly linked to social disorder. Moreover, since the standardized coefficient for family structure declines by the statistically significant amount of .102 when the parental involvement variable is entered into the equation, it appears that some part of the association of family structure with disorder may be attributed to low levels of parental school involvement by single parents. However, the family structure variable continues to show a relationship to the dependent variable that is the strongest in the model.

We can draw a number of conclusions from our findings from these analyses of teacher responses in the Lafayette school district:

(1) Social disorder, in the opinions of the professional educators that we surveyed, is not only an important academic issue, it is the chief problem facing schools.

(2) A prevalence of single-parent families is closely related to the extent of social disorder in schools.

(3) Single-parent family structure shows a relationship to social disorder that is independent of the socioeconomic background of students.

(4) Prevailing family structure is a more important predictor of social disorder than student socioeconomic background.

Appendix B

*A Multilevel Statistical Examination
of the Harm and Benefit Thesis*

In Chapter 7, we offer a discussion of the academic consequences of desegregation. Here, we provide a more methodologically sophisticated analysis of the relationship between the racial composition of schools and the school performance of black and white students, using hierarchical linear modeling (HLM). In this analysis, we consider, first, whether the racial composition of schools is indeed related to the school performance of both black and white students and, second, why a relationship between school racial makeup and individual performance might exist. As possible explanations, we consider the poverty level of schools, the general level of familial educational and occupational backgrounds in schools, and the prevailing family structures of schools.

We have run separate models for black and white students in this examination. Using separate models has two methodological advantages. First, this provides us with a straightforward way of looking at predictors of academic achievement for two racial groups and of seeing how these predictors may vary according to race. Second, since there is a strong correlation between race and the other independent variables, using separate equations helps to reduce the problem of collinearity. We began by running a one-way ANOVA model in order to determine how much of the variance in test scores in our data was due to differences among schools and how much was due to differences among individual students.[1] Next, we ran models for both racial groups with only the individual-level predictors, poverty status (i.e., free and reduced lunch participation), parental educational and occupational level, and single-parent family background. This may be expressed by the equation:

$$Y = \beta_0 + \beta_1 + \beta_2 + \beta_3 + r$$

where Y = the predicted individual percent correct answers; β_0 = the inter-cept, or the overall average percent correct answers controlling for family background and socioeconomic level for each of the two racial groups; β_1 = the slope for poverty status; β_2 = the slope for parental educational and occupational background; β_3 = the slope for single-parent family back-ground; and r = the error term, that is, variations in individual scores not predicted by the independent variables. It is normally the practice to center independent variables in multilevel modeling, to set their means equal to 0. However, in this case it is more theoretically meaningful to enter our two dichotomous variables uncentered, since it is not clear what a mean that is halfway between black and white or halfway between a one-parent and a two-parent family would signify. The indicator of parental educational and occupational background is already "centered," in a sense, since a factor score already has a mean of 0.

In our next model, we included a level two variable, school racial com-position, centered around the grand mean. The connection of this model to the purely individual-level model may be expressed by the equations:

$$\beta_0 = \gamma_{00} + \gamma_{01} + u_0; \; \beta_1 = \gamma_{10} + \gamma_{11} + u_1; \; \beta_2 = \gamma_{20} + \gamma_{21} + u_2; \; \beta_3 = \gamma_{30} + \gamma_{31} + u_3$$

where γ_{00} = the mean achievement test score at schools with the average percentage of minority students; γ_{01} = the coefficient for the relationship between school racial composition and individual test scores; γ_{10} = the co-efficient for poverty status at schools that contain the average percentage of minority students; γ_{11} = the association between slopes of poverty status at different schools and percentage of minority students at those schools; γ_{20} = the coefficient for parental educational and occupational background at schools with the average percentage of minority students; γ_{21} = the asso-ciation between slopes of parental educational and occupational background at different schools and percentage of minority students at those schools; γ_{30} = the coefficient for single-parent family background at schools with the average percentage of minority students; and γ_{31} = the association be-tween slopes of single-parent family background at different schools and percentage of minority students at those schools. The error term of these equations, u, represents the variation among schools in average achievement level that is not predicted by the school-level predictor or predictors.

Once we have seen how the racial composition of schools is related to individual achievement and to the association of achievement with individual socioeconomic level and family structure, our next task will be to account for the apparent effect of racial composition. We will do this by entering the school-level socioeconomic variables into a model with racial composition first and then entering the school-level family structure variable into a model with racial composition. This will support one of the following views: that the association between racial composition and achievement can be attributed to the socioeconomic level of schools with high percentages of minority students; that this association can be attributed to the prevailing family structure in schools with high percentages of minority students; or that this association can be attributed neither to school socioeconomic level or prevailing family structure. We can express the first model with the following equations:

$$\beta_0 = \gamma_{00} + \gamma_{01} + \gamma_{02} + \gamma_{03} + u_0;$$
$$\beta_1 = \gamma_{10} + \gamma_{11} + \gamma_{12} + \gamma_{13} + u_1;$$
$$\beta_2 = \gamma_{20} + \gamma_{21} + \gamma_{22} + \gamma_{23} + u_2;$$
$$\beta_3 = \gamma_{30} + \gamma_{31} + \gamma_{32} + \gamma_{33} + u_3$$

where γ_{02} = the coefficient for the relationship between percent of low-income students in schools and individual test scores; γ_{03} = the coefficient for the relationship between mean parental educational and occupational background in schools and individual test scores; γ_{12} = the association between slopes of poverty status at different schools and percentage of low-income students at those schools; γ_{13} = the association between slopes of poverty status at different schools and the mean parental and educational background at those schools; γ_{22} = the association between slopes of parental educational and occupational background at different schools and the percentage of low-income students at those schools; γ_{23} = the association between slopes of parental educational and occupational background at different schools and mean parental educational and occupational background at those schools; γ_{32} = the coefficient for single-parent family background at schools with the average percentage of low-income students; and γ_{33} = the association between slopes of single-parent family background at different schools and the mean parental educational background at those schools.

When we enter school racial composition and school family structure together, we drop the two socioeconomic variables from the model in order to minimize collinearity and put in percentage of students from single-parent families as γ_{02}, γ_{12}, γ_{22}, and γ_{23}. Collinearity, of course, still remains a concern, since the basis of our reasoning in this study is the high degree of correlation between the percentage of minority students in schools and the percentage of students from single-parent families in schools. Therefore, in a final model we include percentage of students from single-parent families as the only school-level predictor. This methodological strategy will enable us to look at the relative predictive importance of school family structure compared to school racial composition and school socioeconomic level.

Table B.1 presents descriptive statistics for individual-level and school-level variables. Among black students, 70% were low-income, as measured by participation in the free and reduced lunch program, and 42% were from single-parent families. Note that the percentage of single-parent families is lower than that for black children in the U.S. in general. It should be kept in mind that these are tenth graders and that some selection has already occurred, since some students have dropped out of school. On average, black students answered 67% of the test questions correctly.

Among white students, only 19% were low income and 15% were from one-parent families. Clearly, both income level and family structure are highly correlated with race, one of the reasons we look at the two races separately in this analysis. On average, white students answered 79% of the test questions correctly.

The school-level variables are characteristics of the school contexts of black and white students, that is, of the 315 schools that contained at least one black student and of the 323 schools that contained at least one white student. Schools attended by black students contained, on the average, 43% black students. Of all African American tenth graders in public schools in Louisiana, 63% were in schools with a majority of black students (not shown in this table). Racial separation is no longer categorical, but African Americans tend to be in majority-black schools. Schools with at least one white student were, on the average 34% black. Other school-level traits are

Table B.1. Descriptive Statistics for Black and White Students Taking the Louisiana Graduation Exit Examination

	Mean	*Std. Dev.*	*Min.*	*Max.*	*N*
Individual Level					
Black					
Low income	0.7	0.46	0	1	18,314
Parental education and occupation	0	1	−3.03	3.99	13,967
Single-parent family	0.42	0.49	0	1	18,314
Percent correct answers	0.67	0.17	0	0.99	18,314
White					
Low income	0.19	0.39	0	1	23,739
Parental education and occupation	0	1	−2.74	3.96	21,742
Single-parent family	0.15	0.36	0	1	23,739
Percent correct answers	0.79	0.14	0	1	23,739
School Level					
Black					
Percent black	0.43	0.3	0.01	1	315
Percent low income	0.46	0.23	0	1	315
Avg. parental education and occupation	0	1	−4.52	4.94	315
Percent single parent	0.26	..16	0	1	315
Percent correct answers	0.7	0.08	0.31	0.94	315
White					
Percent black	0.34	0.27	0	0.99	323
Percent low income	0.43	0.22	0	1	323
Avg. parental education and occupation	0	1	−4.47	4.9	323
Percent single parent	0.23	0.13	0	1	323
Percent correct answers	0.79	0.06	0.42	0.92	323

similar, although the schools with at least one white student showed a higher average test score than the schools with at least one black student.

Table B.2 shows bivariate correlations for both black and white students and for the school contexts of black and white students. Again, this indicates that collinearity at the school level is an issue that will have to be dealt with carefully, by examining results when variables are included and excluded. The two rows at the bottom of Table B.2 consider how the percentage of students who are black is correlated with other school-level indicators at schools containing black and white students. In schools attended by both black and white students, higher percentages of black students are associated with lower test scores, higher proportions of low-income students, lower parental socioeconomic backgrounds, and greater percentages of one-parent families.

As a preliminary to analyzing our results, we ran two one-way ANOVA models in HLM2 (results not shown in the tables), one for blacks and one for whites, with the average percent correct answers on the Graduation Exit Examination as our outcome variable in each, individual students as level 1, and schools as level 2. For black students we obtained a variance component of .00208 for the overall average of scores (the intercept $[u_0]$) and a

Table B.2. Bivariate Correlations of Individual-Level and School-Level Variables in the Analysis for Black and White Students Taking the Graduation Exit Examination

	Percent Correct	*Low Income*	*Parental Education and Occupation*	*Single-Parent Family*
Percent correct		−.178[a]	.090[a]	−.296[a]
		−.348[b]	.037	−.566[a]
Low income	−.233[a]		−.196[a]	.243[a]
	−.297[a]		−.387[a]	.641[a]
Parental education	.219[a]	−.226[a]		.111[a]
and occupation	−.025	−.426[a]		−.061
Single-parent family	−.318[a]	.312[a]	−.002	
	−.570[a]	.544[a]	−.029	

Correlations with % Black (School Level Only)

	Percent Correct	*Low Income*	*Parental Education and Occupation*	*Single-Parent Family*
Blacks	−.336[a]	.731[a]	−.139[a]	.700[a]
Whites	−.323[a]	.642[a]	−.095[a]	.642[a]

Note: Numbers on the top in each cell represent correlations among individual-level variables; numbers on the bottom in each cell represent correlations among school-level variables.
[a] $p < .01$
[b] $p < .05$

variance component of .01548 (r) for the level 1 effect. By adding these together, we obtain a sum of .01756 for the total variance in black test scores. We can use these figures to decompose the variance, and we find that 88.15% of the variance in test scores among blacks is among individuals (.01548/.01756 = .8815) and that 11.85% of the variance in test scores is among schools (.00208/.01756 = .1185). For whites, on the other hand, we obtained a variance component of .00117 for the intercept (U0) and .01222 for the level 1 effect. By adding these two components together, we obtain .01339 as the total variance in test scores among whites. This means that 91.25% of the variance in white scores is among individuals (.01222/.01339 = .9125) and 8.74% of the variance in white test scores is among schools.[2] Apparently, then, there is something about the schools attended by blacks that makes schools a stronger predictor of achievement test scores for blacks than for whites.

Table B.3 shows results of an HLM model that includes only individual-level predictors of percent correct answers. We can use the coefficients to compare across equations (that is, to compare predictors for blacks with predictors for whites), but it is difficult to compare relative strengths of associations within equations. However, since the t-ratio is directly related to strength of association, we can use the t-ratios as rough indicators of relative strengths of association.

Both of the socioeconomic variables and the family structure variable are significantly related to test performance, and the relationships are in the expected directions. One point that does stand out is that parental educational and occupational level makes more of a difference for whites than it does for blacks: for some reason, a relatively high parental educational and occupational background does not seem to pay off for black students as well as it does for whites. Looking at the random effects, we see, first, that the variance component for low-income status is significant for whites, which means that the relationship between low income status and test scores varies significantly from school to school for whites, but not for blacks. We can also use the variance components for the intercept and for the remaining level 1error to calculate the percentage of reduction in error at both levels achieved by taking family structure and socioeconomic factors into consideration. For blacks, looking at family structure and socioeconomic factors accounts for only 3.4% of the school-level variance (.00208

Table B.3. Individual-Level Socioeconomic and Family Predictors of Achievement Test Scores of Black and White Students

Fixed Effects	Blacks Coefficient (S.E.)	T-Ratio	Whites Coefficient (S.E.)	T-Ratio
Overall intercept (β_0)	.739[a] (.004)	208.219	.811[a] (.002)	419.149
Low income (β_1)	−.022[a] (.003)	−8.33	−.019[a] (.003)	−7.158
Parental education and occupation (β_2)	.009[a] (.001)	7.137	.020[a] (.001)	23.437
Single-parent family (β_3)	−.024[a] (.003)	−7.137	−.030[a] (.003)	−8.898

Random Effects	Variance Component	S.D.	Variance Component	S.D.
Intercept (u_0)	0.00201[a]	0	0.00076[a]	0.027
Low income (u_1)	0.0001	0	0.00034[a]	0.018
Parental education and occupation (u_2)	0.00003	0	0.00001	0.004
Single-parent family (u_3)	0.00021	0	0.00069[a]	0.026
Level 1 error (r)	0.01515	0.12	0.01166	0.108

[a] p < .01

− .00201/.00208 = .0337) and only 2.1% of the individual-level variance (.01548 − .01515/.01548 = .0213). For whites, once we have taken family structure and socioeconomic factors into consideration, we have accounted for 35% of the school-level variance (.00117 − .00076/.00117 = .0350) and 4.6% of the individual-level variance (.01222 − .01166/.01222 = .0458).

We note that it is really only the coefficient for parental educational and occupational level that differs between the two groups and that this variable is by far the most important predictor of achievement for whites. Therefore, the evidence suggests that within schools some white students do better than others because of the socioeconomic status of their parents. Whites of some schools do better than whites in other schools, moreover, because some schools contain students from higher socioeconomic backgrounds, as measured by parental education and occupation. For black students, however, family socioeconomic levels are much less important.

Table B.4. Individual-Level Socioeconomic and Family Predictors of Achievement Test Scores of Black and White Students, with Racial Composition of Schools

Fixed Effects	Blacks Coefficient (S.E.)	T-Ratio	Whites Coefficient (S.E.)	T-Ratio
Overall intercept (g_{00})	.744[a] (.004)	211.038	.810[a] (.002)	415.461
Low income (γ_{10})	−.024[a] (.003)	−8.099	−.020[a] (.003)	−7.614
Parental education and occupation (γ_{20})	.009[a] (.001)	6.207	.020[a] (.001)	22.015
Single-parent family (γ_{30})	−.025[a] (.003)	−7.407	−.029[a] (.003)	−8.392
Percent black (γ_{01})	−.064[a] (.011)	−5.636	−.031[a] (.009)	−3.451
Low income by percent black (γ_{11})	.021[b] (.009)	2.393	−0.35[a] (.012)	−2.836
Parental education and occupation by percent black (γ_{21})	−.003 (.004)	−0.812	−.001 (.005)	−0.202
Single-parent family by percent black (γ_{31})	.005 (.009)	0.017	.020 (.017)	1.191

Random Effects	Variance Component	S.D.	Variance Component	S.D.
Intercept (u_0)	0.00169[a]	0	0.00072[a]	0
Low income (u_1)	0.00006	0	0.00032[a]	0
Parental education and occupation (u_2)	0.00003	0	0.00001	0
Single-parent family (u_3)	0.00019	0	0.00061[a]	0
Level 1 error (r)	0.01515	0.1	0.01166	0.11

[a] p < .01
[b] p < .05

Table B.4 brings the first school-level variable, percent black in each school, into the equations. The individual-level fixed effects remain relatively unchanged, and percent black has significant negative associations with the test scores of both black and white students. This means that we cannot attribute the negative association between test scores and minority-

Table B.5. Individual-Level Socioeconomic and Family Predictors of Achievement Test Scores of Black and White Students, with Racial Composition of Schools and Socioeconomic Composition of Schools

Fixed Effects	Blacks Coefficient (S.E.)	T-Ratio	Whites Coefficient (S.E.)	T-Ratio
Overall intercept (g_{00})	.742^a (.004)	189.137	.808^a (.002)	416.474
Low income (γ_{10})	−.023^a (.003)	−6.59	−.021^a (.003)	−7.141
Parental education and occupation (γ_{20})	.010^a (.002)	6.396	.019^a (.001)	18.168
Single-parent family (γ_{30})	−.027^a (.004)	−7.435	−.028^a (.004)	−7.432
Percent black (γ_{01})	−.061^a (.020)	−3.046	−.036^a (.011)	−3.262
Percent low income (γ_{02})	.013 (.029)	0.44	.019 (.016)	0.226
Mean parental education and occupation (γ_{03})	.011^b (.004)	2.595	.011^a (.002)	4.632
Low income by percent black (γ_{11})	.045^a (.017)	2.63	−.041^a (.017)	−2.439
Parental education and occupation by percent black (γ_{21})	.003 (.004)	0.353	.005 (.006)	0.406
Single-parent family by percent black (γ_{31})	.011 (.018)	0.539	.008 (.024)	0.744
Low income by percent low income (γ_{12})	−.056^b (.026)	−2.206	.012 (.024)	0.611
Parental education and occupation by percent low income (γ_{22})	−.017 (.012)	−1.436	−.009 (.008)	0.263
Single-parent family by percent low income (γ_{32})	−.002 (.026)	−0.078	.020 (.034)	0.556
Low income by mean parental education and occupation (γ_{13})	−.011^a (.004)	−2.913	−.002 (.004)	0.688
Parental education and occupation by mean parental education and occupation (γ_{23})	−.005^a (.002)	−2.647	.0001 (.001)	0.929
Single-parent family by mean parental education and occupation (γ_{33})	.005 (.004)	0.235	−.001 (.005)	0.769

Table B.5. *Continued*

Random Effects	Variance Component	S.D.	Variance Component	S.D.
Intercept (u_0)	0.00158[a]	0	0.00060[a]	0
Low income (u_1)	0.00006	0	0.00046[a]	0
Parental education and occupation (u_2)	0.00003	0	0.00001	0
Single-parent family (u_3)	0.00017	0	0.00091[a]	0
Level 1 error (r)	0.01515	0.12	0.01164	0.11

[a] $p < .01$
[b] $p < .05$

concentration schools to the fact that minority-concentration schools tend to come from low-income families with relatively low socioeconomic status or to the fact that the students, as individuals, are more likely to come from single-parent households. We also note that the percentage of black students has a greater negative association with the scores of blacks than with whites. Finally, looking at low income by percent black, we see that the greater the proportion of black students, the greater the negative association between low income and test scores for blacks. For whites, however, the greater the proportion of black students, the weaker the association between low income and test scores. This last contrast is an interesting one, but the theoretical significance of it is not yet clear to us.

Once we consider racial composition, proportion of reduction in error at level 2 increases from 3.4% to 18.8% for blacks (.00208 − .00169/.00208 = .1875). Clearly, differences between scores of black students in different schools are connected to the racial compositions of those schools. For whites, the increase in proportion of reduction in error is much less: from 35% to 38.5% (.00117 − .00072/.00117 = .3846).

Table B.5 includes the variables that indicate the socioeconomic level of the school: percent of low-income students and mean educational and occupational level of parents in each school. Percent low income shows no significant relation with test scores. The mean parental educational and occupational level of schools is positively related to performance. However, these socioeconomic variables do not account for the association between

Table B. 6. Individual-Level Socioeconomic and Family Predictors of Achievement Test Scores of Black and White Students, with Racial Composition of Schools and Percent Single-Parent Families in Schools

Fixed Effects	Blacks Coefficient (S.E.)	T-Ratio	Whites Coefficient (S.E.)	T-Ratio
Overall intercept (g_{00})	.742[a] (.003)	228.991	.809[a] (.002)	451.166
Low income (γ_{10})	−.024[a] (.003)	−8.075	−.021[a] .002)	−7.896
Parental education and occupation (γ_{20})	.009[a] (.001)	6.088	.020[a] (.001)	22.036
Single-parent family (γ_{30})	−.024[a] (.003)	−7.144	−.028[a] (.004)	−7.61
Percent black (γ_{01})	.016 (.016)	1.025	.015 (.011)	1.398
Percent single-parent families (γ_{02})	−.228[a] (.035)	−6.474	−.155[a] (.023)	−6.802
Low income by percent black (γ_{11})	.016 (.013)	1.188	−.011 (.016)	−0.704
Parental education and occupation by percent black (γ_{21})	.003 (.006)	0.492	.005 (.006)	0.868
Single-parent family by percent black (γ_{31})	.015 (.015)	1.019	.028 (.022)	1.271
Low income by percent single-parent families (γ_{12})	.018 (.029)	0.609	−.089[b] (.036)	−2.472
Parental education and occupation by percent single-parent families (γ_{22})	−.018 (.014)	−1.359	−.019 (.013)	−1.488
Single-parent family by percent single-parent families (γ_{32})	−.031 (.031)	−0.983	−.033 (.052)	−0.63

Table B.6. *Continued*

Random Effects	Variance Component	S.D.	Variance Component	S.D.
Intercept (u_0)	0.00120^a	0	0.00055^a	0
Low income (u_1)	0.00007	0	0.00026^b	0
Parental education and occupation (u_2)	0.00003	0	0.00002	0
Single-parent family (u_3)	0.00019	0	0.00075^a	0
Level 1 error (r)	0.01517	0.12	0.01166	0.11

[a] $p < .01$
[b] $p < .05$

racial composition and our indicator of academic achievement, since the coefficient of racial composition for both groups decreases only slightly. This finding suggests that we cannot attribute the lower scores of minority-concentration schools either to the socioeconomic characteristics of individual students or to the general socioeconomic levels of schools. We should note, however, that given the extremely strong correlation between school racial makeup and school poverty levels, poor schools do tend overwhelmingly to be schools with proportionately large numbers of black students.

Table B.6 provides an extraordinary contrast with Table B.5. When we take out the socioeconomic variables and include percent single-parent families in their stead, the coefficient for percent black becomes statistically insignificant and even positive in sign. In addition, percent single-parent families has a strong negative correlation with test scores for both blacks and whites. Looking at the variance components of the random effects, after we include the percentage of single-parent families in schools we can account for 42% of the variance between schools in test scores of blacks and 53% of the variance between schools in test scores of whites.

The proportion of one-parent families in schools is not only strongly related to individual test scores of students, regardless of their own family structures, it is also a powerful predictor of variations in scores from one school to another. Further, the family structure prevailing in schools appears to completely account for the negative association between racial composition and academic achievement.

Since racial composition and percent single-parent families are highly correlated, as we have seen, there may be some questions about distinguishing the association of each with the dependent variable. Therefore, in Table B.7 we present the results of an equation in which the prevailing family structure variable is the only school-level predictor. The percentage of one-parent families continues to display a strong negative correlation with the dependent variable after we remove racial composition from the equation. Further, looking at the variance components, we see that school family structure alone explains as much variance within and between schools as school family structure and racial composition together do.

The extremely high correlations among percent minority, percent low income, and percent single-parent family (see Table B.2) makes it difficult to look at schools at the far ends of racial concentration. That is, as schools approach 100% minority, there tends to be little variation in socioeconomic or family structure composition. Among the 347 schools included in this analysis, only 3 were both over 75% black and under 25% single-parent family. All of the schools that were over 90% black were majority-single-parent schools. Still, we believe that the evidence presented in the tables above strongly indicates that school family structure, rather than school racial composition, provides the best explanation for the correlation between the racial makeup of schools and the educational outcomes of individual students.

It is difficult to draw conclusions about causality from cross-sectional data. Nevertheless, our results do provide empirical support for a logical conclusion based on sound premises. This conclusion is consistent with the evidence we have seen throughout this book. The harm and benefit thesis that has tended to dominate thinking about desegregation maintains that the desegregation of schools benefits black students while doing white students no harm. However, our evidence suggests that the percentage of minority students in a school is negatively related to the performance of both black students and white students. This is extremely disturbing because it means that black and white families, to some extent, have contradictory real interests regarding their children=s schools. For black families, neighborhood schools in minority neighborhoods are apparently related to low levels of performance. The children of white families, though, generally do better (at least in terms of test scores) in schools in which there are

Table B.7. Individual-Level Socioeconomic and Family Predictors of Achievement Test Scores of Black and White Students, with Percent Single-Parent Families in Schools

Fixed Effects	Blacks Coefficient (S.E.)	T-Ratio	Whites Coefficient (S.E.)	T-Ratio
Overall intercept (g_{00})	$.743^a$ (.003)	237.535	$.810^a$ (.002)	457.798
Low income (γ_{10})	$-.023$ (.003)	-8.869	$-.020^a$ (.003)	-7.953
Parental education and occupation (γ_{20})	$.009^a$ (.001)	6.77	$.020^a$ (.001)	22.932
Single-parent family (γ_{30})	$-.024^a$ (.003)	-7.338	$-.029^a$ (.003)	-8.904
Percent single-parent families (γ_{01})	$-.202^a$ (.023)	-8.869	$-.137^a$ (.018)	-7.64
Low income by percent single-parent families (γ_{11})	$.045^b$ (.019)	2.367	$-.102^a$ (.028)	-3.677
Parental education and occupation by percent single-parent families (γ_{21})	$-.013$ (.009)	-1.537	$-.012$ (.011)	-1.174
Single-parent family by percent single-parent families (γ_{31})	$-.004$ (.020)	2.367	$.014$ (.038)	0.37

Random Effects	Variance Component	S.D.	Variance Component	S.D.
Intercept (u_0)	0.00120^a	0	0.00056^a	0
Low income (u_1)	0.00008	0	0.00025^b	0
Parental education and occupation (u_2)	0.00002	0	0.00001	0
Single-parent family (u_3)	0.0002	0	0.00055^a	0
Level 1 error (r)	0.01516	0.12	0.01167	0.11

[a] $p < .01$
[b] $p < .05$

comparatively few minority members. For the whites, then, neighborhood schools really do appear to be in the interest of their own children.

In probing the question of why the racial composition of schools is related to school performance for both black and white students, we have looked at some of the most obvious explanations that have appeared throughout this volume. Throughout Louisiana, and in each district we have considered individually, there are strong correlations among race, income level, family educational and occupational backgrounds, and family structure. These correlations also hold for the United States in general. Minority race, poverty, and single-parent families are so closely related in many of the most disadvantaged schools of the state as to be almost impossible to separate. However, in general, our analysis has led us to conclude that the concentration of students from single-parent families explains the low performance of black and white students in schools with large minority populations, although socioeconomic factors are still relevant.

This conclusion is a gloomy one for the effective desegregation of schools. Although the socioeconomic gap between blacks and whites has narrowed in some respects over the past twenty years, the family structure gap has, as we pointed out in the introduction, widened. Minority-dominated schools are increasingly likely to be schools in which children from one-parent families predominate. If middle class families seek the best available educational environments for their children, then desegregation of schools in districts with large minority populations can only be achieved by forcing these families to send their children to schools that do not provide optimal educational environments.

Notes

Introduction

1. Eric Foner, *Reconstruction: America's Unfinished Revolution, 1863–1877* (New York: Harper & Row, 1988). Foner's book is, in our view, the best treatment of how racial inequality was reimposed after the Civil War and essential reading for those interested in the historical background of racial stratification in the United States.

2. Carl L. Bankston III, "Demographics," in *African American Encyclopedia, Supplement,* edited by Kibibi Voloria Mack (New York: Marshall Cavendish, 1996), 1936–41.

3. Andrew Hacker, *Two Nations: Black, White, Separate, Hostile, Unequal,* rev. ed. (New York: Ballantine Books, 1995).

4. Carl L. Bankston III and Stephen J. Caldas, "Majority African American Schools and the Perpetuation of Social Injustice: The Influence of Defacto Segregation on Academic Achievement," *Social Forces* 72 (1996): 534–55.

5. Christopher Jencks and Meredith Phillips, editors, *The Black-White Test Score Gap* (Washington: Brookings Institution Press, 1998).

6. Alphonso Pinkney, *Black Americans,* 5th ed. (Upper Saddle River, N.J.: Prentice Hall, 2000), 102.

7. For the increase in single parent families, see U.S. Bureau of the Census, *Household and Family Characteristics* (Washington D.C.: U.S. Government Printing Office, 1994), Series P20, no. 477. In his otherwise valuable discussion of contemporary racial inequality, *Two Nations* (1995), Andrew Hacker gives a completely erroneous and misleading comparison of changes in black and white family structure. Hacker claims that the ratio of black to white single-parent families remained stable from 1950s through the early 1990s and that the ratio of black to white births out of wedlock declined during that period. Ratios should not be used for comparison because they always grow smaller as magnitudes increase (when I was 1 year old, my father was 21 times older than I was; when I was 20 years old, my father was only twice as old though we were not aging at different rates or growing closer in age). In reality, black rates of single-mother families increased from 1980 to 1990 from 45.9% to 58.4%, a rate of increase of about 1% each year. White rates of single-mother families during the same period, from 13.2% to 18.7%, a rate of increase of less than 0.5% each year.

8. William Julius Wilson, who has greatly influenced our thinking on this topic, presents

a good discussion of the debate in Chapter 4 of his book *When Work Disappears: The World of the New Urban Poor* (New York: Vintage, 1996). Wilson explains the decline in marriage among black Americans as a product of black male joblessness in inner city areas. While this seems to us a plausible explanation, it does have its problems. Notably, rates of single-parent families and out-of-wedlock childbirth among blacks are much higher than either poverty rates or unemployment rates.

9. Federal Bureau of Investigation, *Crime in the United States 1996* (Washington: U.S. Government Printing Office, 1997), Table 43, p. 233.

10. Gary Orfield, "The Growth of Segregation: African Americans, Latinos and Unequal Education," in *Dismantling Desegregation: The Quiet Reversal of Brown v. Board of Education,* edited by Gary Orfield, Susan E. Eaton, and the Harvard Project on School Desegregation (New York: New Press, 1996), 53–54.

11. Orfield, "Growth of Segregation" (1996), 53.

12. Stephen J. Caldas and John C. Kilburn, "A Parish Profile of the David Duke Vote: Sociodemographic, Economic, and Voting Propensity Predictors," in *David Duke and the Politics of Race in the South,* edited by J. C. Kuzenski, C. S. Bullock III, and R. K. Gaddie (Nashville: Vanderbilt University Press, 1995), 63–87.

Chapter 1

1. Solomon Northrup, *Twelve Years a Slave: Narrative of Solomon Northrup, Citizen of New York, Kidnapped in Washington City in 1841, and Rescued in 1853, From a Cotton Plantation Near the Red River, in Louisiana* (Buffalo: Derby, Orton, and Mulligan, 1853).

2. John H. Franklin, *Reconstruction After the Civil War* (Chicago: University of Chicago Press, 1961), 3.

3. Eric Foner, *Reconstruction: America's Unfinished Revolution, 1863–1877* (New York: Harper & Row, 1988).

4. Ted Tunnell, *Crucible of Reconstruction: War, Radicalism, and Race in Louisiana, 1862–1877* (Baton Rouge: Louisiana State University Press, 1984), 176–80.

5. Foner (1989).

6. Doug McAdam, *Political Process and the Development of Black Insurgency, 1930–1970* (Chicago: University of Chicago Press, 1982).

7. Donald E. DeVore and Joseph Logsdon, *Crescent City Schools: Public Education in New Orleans, 1841–1991* (Lafayette: Center for Louisiana Studies, University of Southwestern Louisiana, 1991), 41.

8. DeVore and Logsdon (1991), 56–57.

9. DeVore and Logsdon (1991), 76–81.

10. DeVore and Logsdon (1991), 89, 179.

11. Charles Vincent, *The African American Experience in Louisiana* (Lafayette: Center for Louisiana Studies, 1999).

12. Public Affairs Research Council of Louisiana, *Improving Quality During School Desegregation* (Baton Rouge: Public Affairs Research Council, 1969); T. Harry Williams, *Huey Long* (New York: Alfred A. Knopf, 1969), 704–5.

13. Personal communication, March 29, 1999.

14. Personal communication, February 18, 1999.

15. Quoted in Paul Teel, Susan Corl, and Stanley Coleman, *With All Deliberate Speed: Oral History, Drama, and the Desegregation of Southern Louisiana Schools* (unpublished grant proposal submitted to the Louisiana Endowment for the Humanities, 1996), 33.

16. Personal communication, September 1999.

17. Steve Landry, personal communication, March 24, 2000.

18. Charnell Oxford, personal communication, January 31, 2000.

19. John Dollard, *Caste and Class in a Southern Town* (New Haven: Yale University Press, 1937).

20. Personal communication, March 14, 1999.

21. Quoted in Teel, Corl, and Coleman (1996), 57.

22. Bart Landry, *The New Black Middle Class* (Berkeley: University of California Press, 1987).

23. Peter Blau and Otis Dudley Duncan, *The American Occupational Structure* (New York: Wiley, 1967).

24. Quoted in Teel, Corl, and Coleman (1996), 33.

25. Quoted in Teel, Corl, and Coleman (1996), 57.

26. Personal communication, November 17, 1998.

27. Quoted in Teel, Corl, and Coleman (1996), 14.

28. Quoted in Teel, Corl, and Coleman (1996), 56.

29. Personal communication, February 17, 1999.

30. Public Affairs Research Council of Louisiana (1969), 25.

31. James S. Coleman et al., *Equality of Educational Opportunity* (Washington: U.S. Government Printing Office, 1966).

32. Coleman et al. (1966).

Chapter 2

1. Peter M. Bergman, *The Chronological History of the Negro in America* (New York: Harper & Row, 1969).

2. Livia Baker, *The Second Battle of New Orleans: The Hundred Year Struggle to Integrate the Schools* (New York: Harper Collins, 1996), Chapter 3.

3. Ronald Perry, personal communication, April 9, 1999.

4. Thomas F. Pettigrew, E. L. Useem, C. Normand, and M. S. Smith, "Busing: A Review of the Evidence," *Public Interest* 30 (1973): 88–118.

5. Christine H. Rossell and David J. Armor, "The Effectiveness of School Desegregation Plans, 1968–1991," *American Politics Quarterly* 24 (1996): 267–302.

6. Rossell and Armor (1996).

7. Kern Alexander, *School Law* (St. Paul: West, 1980).

8. James A. Johnson et al., *Introduction to the Foundations of American Education*, 11th edition (Boston: Allyn & Bacon, 1999).

9. H. C. Hudgins, *Public School Desegregation: Legal Issues and Judicial Decisions* (Washington: National Organization on Legal Problems of Education, 1973).

10. Gary Orfield, "Turning Back to Segregation," in *Dismantling Desegregation: The Quiet Reversal of Brown v. Board of Education,* edited by Gary Orfield, Susan E. Eaton, and the Harvard Project on School Desegregation (New York: New Press, 1996), 1–22.

11. Sue Anne Pressley, "Charlotte Schools are Scrambling," *Washington Post,* November 8, 1999, sec. A, p. 3.

12. Quoted in Alison Morantz, "Desegregation at Risk," in *Dismantling Desegregation* (1996), 195.

13. James S. Coleman et al., *Equality of Educational Opportunity* (Washington: U.S. Government Printing Office, 1966).

14. James S. Coleman, "Rawls, Nozick and Educational Equality," *Public Interest* 43 (Spring 1976): 121–28; Carl L. Bankston III and Stephen J. Caldas, "Majority African American Schools and the Perpetuation of Social Injustice: The Influence of Defacto Segregation on Academic Achievement," *Social Forces* 72 (1996): 534–55; Stephen J. Caldas and Carl L. Bankston III, "The Effect of School Population Socioeconomic Status on Individual Student Academic Achievement," *Journal of Educational Research* 86 (1997): 206–14.

15. David J. Armor, *Forced Justice: School Desegregation and the Law* (New York: Oxford University Press, 1995).

16. David J. Armor provides an exhaustive list of research in this area in *Forced Justice* (1995).

17. James S. Coleman, "Racial Segregation in the Schools: New Research with New Policy Implications," *Phi Delta Kappan* 57 (1975): 75–78.

18. James S. Coleman, Sara D. Kelly, and John A. Moore, *Trends in School Segregation, 1968-1973,* Urban Institute Paper 722-03-01 (Washington: Urban Institute, 1975).

19. Thomas F. Pettigrew and Robert L. Green, "School Desegregation in Large Cities: A Critique of the Coleman 'White Flight' Thesis," *Harvard Educational Review* 46, no. 1 (1976): 1–53.

20. See Pettigrew and Green (1976), 6–7.

21. James S. Coleman, "The Role of Incentives in School Desegregation," in *Race and Schooling in the City,* edited by Adam Yarmolinsky, Lance Liebman, and Corinne S. Schelling (Cambridge: Harvard University Press, 1981), 182–93.

22. David J. Armor, "White Flight and the Future of School Desegregation," in *School Desegregation: Past, Present, and Future,* edited by W. G. Stephan and Joe R. Feagin (New York: Plenum, 1980), 206–14; David J. Armor, "School Busing: A Time for Change," in *Eliminating Racism,* edited by P. A. Katz and D. A. Taylor (New York: Plenum, 1988) 259–80.

23. David J. Armor, "An Evaluation of Norfolk Desegregation Plans" (unpublished study for the Norfolk, Virginia, Board of Education, 1982).

24. Leslie G. Carr and Donald J. Zeigler, "White Flight and White Return in Norfolk: A Test of Predictions," *Sociology of Education* 63 (1990): 272–82.

25. David J. Armor, "Response to Carr and Zeigler's 'White Flight and White Return in Norfolk,' " *Sociology of Education* 64 (1991): 134–39.

26. Just a few of the studies that attest to the phenomenon of white flight include Armor (1980); Christine H. Rossell, *The Carrot or the Stick for School Desegregationn Policy: Magnet Schools or Forced Busing* (Philadelphia: Temple, 1990); William A. V. Clark, "School Desegregation and White Flight: A Reexamination and Case Study," *Social Sci-*

ence Research 16 (1987): 211–28; James S. Coleman, Sara D. Kelly, and John A. Moore (1975); Reynolds Farley, Toni Richard, and Clarence Wurdock, "School Desegregation and White Flight: An Investigation of Competing Models and Their Discrepant Findings," *Sociology of Education* 53 (1980): 123–39; Steven G. Rivkin, "Residential Segregation and School Integration," *Sociology of Education* 67 (1994): 279–92; Christine H. Rossell, *Assessing the Unintended Impacts of Public Policy: School Desegregation and Resegregation* (Washington: National Institute of Education, 1978); Christine H. Rossell and J. M. Ross, "The Long-Term Effect of Court-Ordered Desegregation on Student Enrollment in Central City Public School Systems: The Case of Boston, 1974–1979" (unpublished report for the Boston School Department, 1979); Finis Welch, "A Reconsideration of the Impact of School Desegregation Programs on Public School Enrollment of White Students, 1968–1976," *Sociology of Education* 60 (1987): 215–21; Finis Welch et al., *New Evidence on School Desegregation* (Los Angeles: Unicorn Research Corporation, 1987); Franklin D. Wilson, "The Impact of School Desegregation Programs on White Public School Enrollment, 1958–1976," *Sociology of Education* 58 (1985): 137–53.

27. Stephen J. Caldas and Carl L. Bankston III, "The Promise and Failure of School Desegregation in Baton Rouge and New Orleans" (paper presented at the annual meeting of the Louisiana Educational Research Association, New Orleans, March 1999).

28. Lauren E. McDonald, "Boston Public School Decline: White Flight or Demographic Factors?" *Equity & Excellence in Education* 30, no. 3 (1997): 21–30.

29. Rossell is quoted in Kenneth Yost, "Rethinking School Integration," *CQ Researcher* 39, no. 6 (1996): 915–31.

30. Prince George's County Transportation Director Ken Savoid, quoted in *School Bus News,* September 2, 1998, p. 1.

31. McDonald (1997), 29.

32. James S. Coleman, *Social Climates in High Schools* (U.S. Government Printing Office, 1961); Christopher M. Jencks et al., *Inequality: A Reassessment of the Effect of Family and Schooling in America* (New York: Basic, 1972) Ulrich Neisser, "New Answers to an Old Question," in *The School Achievement of Minority Children: New Perspectives,* edited by Ulrich Neisser (Hillsdale, N.J.: Lawrence Erlblaum Associates, 1986), 1–17; Richard Selden, "Should Test Results Be Adjusted for Socioeconomic Differences?" *The School Administrator* 47 (1990): 14–18; James C. Hearn, "Academic and Non-Academic Influences on the College Destinations of 1980 High School Graduates," *Sociology of Education* 64 (1991): 158–71; Stephen J. Caldas, "Reexamination of Input and Process Factor Effects on Academic Achievement," *Journal of Educational Research* 86 (1992): 206–14; Stephen J. Caldas and Carl L. Bankston III, "The Effect of School Population Socioeconomic Status on Individual Student Academic Achievement," *Journal of Educational Research* 90 (1997): 269–78; Stephen J. Caldas and Carl L. Bankston III, "The Inequality of Separation: Racial Composition of Schools and Academic Achievement," *Educational Administration Quarterly* 34 (1998): 533–57.

33. U.S. Department of Education, National Center for Education Statistics, *The Condition of Education: 1994* (U.S. Government Printing Office, 1994); Andrew Hacker, *Two Nations: Black, White, Separate, Hostile, Unequal* (New York: Ballantine Books, 1995); Carl L. Bankston III and Stephen J. Caldas, "Majority African American Schools and the Perpetuation of Social Injustice: The Influence of Defacto Segregation on Academic

Achievement," *Social Forces* 72 (1996): 534–55; Carl L. Bankston III and Stephen J. Caldas, "The American School Dilemma: Race and Scholastic Performance," *Sociological Quarterly* 38 (1997): 423–29; Carl L. Bankston III and Stephen J. Caldas, "Race, Poverty, Family Structure, and the Inequality of Schools" *Sociological Spectrum* 18 (1998): 55–76, 1998.

34. U.S. Department of Education (1994); Christopher Jencks and Meredith Phillips, editors, *The Black-White Test Score Gap* (Washington: Brookings Institution Press, 1998).

35. Bankston and Caldas (1996); Lawrence Bobo,"Whites' Opposition to Busing: Symbolic Racism or Realistic Group Conflict?" *Journal of Personality and Social Psychology* 45 (1983): 1196–210; James S. Coleman (1975).

36. James S. Coleman, "Some Points on Choice in Education," *Sociology of Education* 65 (1992): 261.

37. J. Baird, personal communication, December 18, 1998.

38. Gary Orfield, "The Growth of Segregation," in *Dismantling Desegregation* (1996), 53–54.

Chapter 3

1. All of the statistics in this section are taken from the U.S. Bureau of the Census, *Census of Population and Housing, 1990,* Summary Tape File 3A.

2. This percentage of out-of-wedlock births is far below the average for white women for the U.S. as a whole. One of the reasons for this may be the small number of family households in New Orleans—both married and unmarried white families with children tend to settle outside of the city.

3. Donald E. DeVore and Joseph Logsdon, *Crescent City Schools: Public Education in New Orleans, 1841–1991* (Lafayette: Center for Louisiana Studies, University of Southwestern Louisiana, 1991), 225–26.

4. Livia Baker, *The Second Battle of New Orleans: The Hundred Year Struggle to Integrate the Schools* (New York, Harper Collins, 1996), Chapter 3.

5. DeVore and Logsdon (1991), 232; Baker (1996), Chapter 9.

6. U.S. Commission on Civil Rights, *The New Orleans School Crisis* (Washington: U.S. Government Printing Office, 1961), gives an overview of the crisis.

7. Baker (1996), 328.

8. Baker (1996), 378–79.

9. DeVore and Logsdon (1991), 245.

10. DeVore and Logsdon (1991), 258, 264.

11. Emile Lafourcade, "Race Ills Team Approved Here," *New Orleans Times-Picayune,* January 25, 1972, sec. 1, p. 12.

12. Emile Lafourcade, "Report Partly Unfair—Spears," *New Orleans Times-Picayune,* May 30, 1972, sec. 1, p. 4.

13. Morton Inger, *Politics and Reality in an American City: The New Orleans School Crisis of 1960* (New York: Center for Urban Education, 1968), 39.

14. Charlie East, "School Pairing Plan Is Filed," *New Orleans Times-Picayune,* Dec.. 2, 1972, sec. 1, p. 16.

15. Emile Lafourcade, "School Board OK's Transfer," *New Orleans Times-Picayune,* August 29, 1972, sec. 1, p. 7.

16. Emile Lafourcade, "No More Mixing Steps—Geisert," *New Orleans Times-Picayune,* September, 6, 1972, sec. 1, p. 7.

17. DeVore and Logsdon (1991), 266–70.

18. Newton E. Renfro, "Desegregation Plan Approved" *New Orleans Times-Picayune,* July 31, 1973, sec. 1, p. 1.

19. *New Orleans Times-Picayune,* "Desegregation Complete," October 22, 1978, sec. 1, p. 18.

20. *New Orleans Times-Picayune,* "School Doors Open," September 6, 1976, sec. 1, p. 24.

21. *New Orleans Times-Picayune,* "Desegregation Complete," October 22, 1978, sec. 1, p. 18.

22. Molly Moore, "Crisis in the Schools," *New Orleans Times-Picayune,* April 15, 1981, sec. A, p. 1ff.

23. Public Affairs Research Council of Louisiana, *Improving Quality During School Desegregation* (Baton Rouge: Public Affairs Research Council, 1969).

24. For a more detailed description of Vietnamese American students in New Orleans schools, see Min Zhou and Carl L. Bankston III, *Growing Up American: How Vietnamese Children Adapt to Life in the United States* (New York: Russell Sage Foundation, 1998).

25. All of the conversations and remarks reported in this section were recorded during the fall semester of 1994 unless otherwise noted.

26. This conversation is also quoted in Zhou and Bankston (1998), 134.

27. Chris Gray, "Leap Test Fails at Least One in Every N.O. School," *New Orleans Times-Picayune,* August 19, 1999, sec. A, p. 1 ff., quotation from p. 11.

28. Bruce Dansker, "Schools' Test Scores Improving," *New Orleans Times-Picayune,* July 29, 1982, sec. 1, p. 13.

29. Anand Vaishnav, "At-Risk Schools' Hard Part Starts Now," *New Orleans Times-Picayune,* September 25, 1999, sec. A, p. 1ff..

30. Chris Gray, "Third of State Students Miss the Mark on LEAP," *New Orleans Times-Picayune,* May 13, 2000, sec. A, p. 1ff.

31. Chris Gray, May 13, 2000, sec. A, p. 6.

32. Rhonda McKendall, "Whites Claim Racial Tension Plagues School," *New Orleans Times-Picayune,* June 26, 1986, sec. B, p. 35.

33. Steve Cannizaro, "Whites Lose School Bias Suit," *New Orleans Times-Picayune,* March 20, 1990, sec. B, p. 8.

34. Chris Adams, "Violence in the Schools," *New Orleans Times-Picayune,* April 2, 1992, sec. A, p. 1.

35. Grissett, Sheila, "Shots Frighten Lafon Students," *New Orleans Times-Picayune,* April 4, 1992, sec. B, p. 1.

36. Chris Adams, "Can Schools Save Black Boys?" *New Orleans Times-Picayune,* Feb. 2, 1992, sec. A, p. 1ff. Quotation from p. A-5.

Chapter 4

1. Stephen J. Caldas, "The Politics of Welfare Reform, Religion, Education, and Racism: Evidence from Three Southern Elections," *Southern Studies* 3 (1992): 1–14; D. W. Johnson, P. R. Picard, and B. Quinn, *Churches and Church Membership in the U.S.* (Washington: Glenmary Research Center, 1981).

2. All of the statistics in this section are taken from the U.S. Bureau of the Census, *Census of Population and Housing, 1990,* Summary Tape File 3A.

3. Percentages of children born out-of-wedlock are higher than percentages of children living in one-parent families for both racial groups. Living circumstances may differ from the circumstances of birth, due to adoption, raising of children by grandparents or other relatives, etc.

4. For an in-depth case study highlighting problems of freedom of choice, see Virginia E. Causey, "'Drafted into the Front Lines': Teacher Efficacy During School Desegregation in Columbus, Georgia, 1968–1975," *Research in the Schools* 6, no. 2 (1999): 9–24.

5. J. Baird and J. N. Luster, "Initiating School and District Level Change through Restructuring in East Baton Rouge Parish" (unpublished manuscript, Louisiana State University, 1990).

6. M. Thornton, "Administration Offers Alternative to Court-Ordered Busing," *Washington Post,* December 11, 1982, sec. A, p. 9.

7. Baird and Luster (1990).

8. "B.R. Parents Enraged by School Mix Order," *New Orleans Times-Picayune,* May 6, 1981, sec. A, p. 1.

9. Enrollment data cited throughout this section are from Louisiana Department of Education, *Annual Financial and Statistical Report* (Baton Rouge: Louisiana Department of Education, 1982–1998).

10. U.S. Bureau of the Census, *County Population Estimates for July 1, 1998, and Population Change for July 1, 1997 to July 1, 1998* (Washington: U.S. Bureau of the Census, Population Division, 1999).

11. Thornton (1982).

12. J. Baird, "Examining Parent Selection in the East Baton Rouge Controlled Choice Plan" (unpublished manuscript, Louisiana State University, 1990).

13. J. Baird, personal communication, December 18, 1998.

14. T. Guarisco, "Enrollment Drop Could Cost Schools $3.4 Million," *Baton Rouge Advocate,* Oct. 3, 2000, sec. A, p. 1.

15. Vincent Lagattuta, personal communication, August 24, 1999.

16. Donna Walden, personal communication, December 17, 1999.

17. U.S. Bureau of the Census, *County Population Estimates for July 1, 1998, and Population Change for July 1, 1997 to July 1, 1998* (Washington: Population Division, U.S. Bureau of the Census, 1999).

18. Charles Tolbert, personal communication, August 26, 1999.

19. Tolbert cited in K. King, "Expert: BR Losing Its White Students," *Baton Rouge Advocate,* July 13, 1999, sec. A, pp. 1, 4.

20. Charles Tolbert, personal communication, August 26, 1999.

21. K. King, "Half of EBR Magnets Failed to Attract 10 White Students," *Baton Rouge Advocate,* July 14, 1999, sec. A, pp. 1, 4.

22. Wade Smith, personal communication, January 27, 2000.

23. King, "Expert: BR Losing Its White Students" (1999), sec. A, p. 1.

24. King, "Half of EBR Magnets Failed to Attract 10 White Students." *Baton Rouge Advocate,* July 14, 1999 p. 1A, 4A.

25. Personal communication from researcher who wishes to remain anonymous, January 23, 1999.

26. Virginia. E. Causey, "'Drafted into the Front Lines': Teacher Efficacy During School Desegregation in Columbus, Georgia, 1968–1975," *Research in the Schools* 6, no. 2 (1999): 9–24.

27. E. Anderson, "Separate School Districts May Draw Court Challenge," *New Orleans Times-Picayune,* October 15, 1995, sec. A, p. 15.

28. Christine H. Rossell, "Improving the Voluntary Desegregation Plan in the Baton Rouge School System" (report to the court for *Davis et al. v. East Baton Rouge Parish School Board et al.,* October 27, 1999), 6, n.

29. Cited in King, "Expert: BR Losing Its White Students" (1999).

30. King, "EBR Awaits Holiday Count," *Baton Rouge Advocate,* August 20, 1999, sec. A, pp. 1, 14.

31. Guarisco, "Enrollment Drop Could Cost Schools $3.4 Million" (2000).

32. V. Ferstel, "Livingston School Enrollment Up 259," *Baton Rouge Advocate,* Oct. 4, 2000, sec. A, p. 4.

33. King, "Expert: BR Losing Its White Students" (1999).

34. Personal communication from Dr. Charles Tolbert, August 26, 1999.

35. K. King, "Parents Target Desegregation Suit as Obstacle," *Baton Rouge Advocate,* March 25, 1999, sec. A, pp. 1, 6.

36. Quoted on *Channel 2 News Ten at Ten* (Baton Rouge: WBRZ, August 19, 1999).

37. K. King, "Board Hopes to Entice White Students to Other Schools," *Baton Rouge Advocate,* August 29, 1999, sec A, pp. 1, 5.

38. William Julius Wilson, *The Truly Disadvantaged* (Chicago: University of Chicago Press, 1987).

39. R. McClain, "Ex-PAR Chief Doesn't Believe Education Can Reform Itself," *Baton Rouge Advocate,* April 25, 1999, sec. A, pp. 1, 16, 17.

40. Donna Walden, personal communication, December 17, 1999.

41. Quoted in King, "Expert: BR Losing Its White Students" (1999).

42. Louisiana State Department of Education, machine-readable data tape of test results of Louisiana Educational Assessment of Progress (Baton Rouge, 1990).

43. Stephen J. Caldas, "A Comparison and Contrast of the Desegregation Experiences of Three Louisiana School Districts: The City of Monroe, Ouachita Parish, and Lafayette Parish" (paper presented at the annual meeting of the Mid-South Educational Association, Point Clear, Ala., November 1999).

Chapter 5

1. Todd Billiot, "Judge: Rezone Schools," *Lafayette Advertiser,* May 20, 2000, sec. A, p. 1.

2. Jacques Henry and Carl L. Bankston III "Louisiana Cajun Ethnicity: Symbolic or Structural?" *Sociological Spectrum* 19 (1999): 223–48.

3. Stephen J. Caldas, "The Politics of Welfare Reform, Religion, Education and Racism: Evidence from Three Southern Elections," *Southern Studies,* 3 (1992): 1–14.

4. Stephen J. Caldas and John C. Kilburn, "A Parish Profile of the David Duke Vote: Sociodemographic, Economic, and Voting Propensity Predictors," in *David Duke and the Politics of Race in the South,* edited by J. C. Kuzenski, C. S. Bullock III, and R. K. Gaddie (Nashville: Vanderbilt University Press, 1995), 63–87.

5. Charnell Oxford, personal communication, March 27, 2000.

6. J. Philip Dismukes, *The Center: A History of the Development of Lafayette, Louisiana* (Lafayette: City of Lafayette, 1972), 39.

7. U.S. Bureau of the Census, *Census of Population and Housing, 1990,* Summary Tape File 3A.

8. Ibid.

9. Data on 2000–01 enrollments in Lafayette Catholic schools provided by the Catholic Diocese of Lafayette.

10. Home schooling data provided by Patsy Clardy, Louisiana Department of Education, and Louis Benjamin, Director of Census and Attendance, Lafayette Parish School Board.

11. C. Courville, "The Politics of Desegregation in St. Landry and Lafayette Parishes" (Master's thesis, University of Southwestern Louisiana, Lafayette, Louisiana, 1978).

12. F. Hardy, *A Brief History of the University of Southwestern Louisiana: 1900 to 1960* (Baton Rouge: Claitor's, 1973).

13. Courville (1978).

14. Caldas (1992).

15. Courville (1978).

16. Todd Billiot, "School Rezoning," *Lafayette Advertiser,* October 25, 1998, sec. A, pp. 1, 7.

17. Courville (1978).

18. See the discussion of white and black attitudes toward forcible desegregation in Christine H. Rossell, "The Convergence of Black and White Attitudes on School Desegregation Issues During the Four Decade Evolution of the Plans," *The William and Mary Law Review* 36 (1995): 613–63, and David J. Armor, *Forced Justice: School Desegregation and the Law* (New York: Oxford University Press, 1995).

19. J. Proctor. "Census Bureau Will Hire Up to 100." *Lafayette Advertiser,* November 11, 1999, sec. A, p. 4.

20. Billiot (1998).

21. John Miller (representative of parent group opposed to rezoning), personal communication, May 14, 1999.

22. R. Boyer, personal communication, December 2, 1999.

23. Todd Billiot, "Enrollment at 5-year Low," *Lafayette Advertiser,* October 18, 1999, sec. A, pp. 1, 7.

24. Personal communication from source who wishes to remain anonymous, October 29, 1998.

25. Personal communication from source who wishes to remain anonymous, November 11, 1999.

26. Personal communication from Lafayette Catholic school teacher who wishes to remain anonymous, November 9, 1999.

27. U.S. Census of Population and Housing statistics for Lafayette, 1980, 1990.

28. Carl L. Bankston III and Stephen J. Caldas, "Majority Black Schools and the Perpetuation of Social Injustice: The Influence of De Facto Segregation on Academic Achievement," *Social Forces* 75 (1996): 535–55; Valerie E. Lee and Anthony S. Bryk, "A Multilevel Model of the Social Distribution of High School Achievement," *Sociology of Education* 62 (1989): 172–92.

29. From Gallup Poll results reported in H. Shuman, Charlotte Steeh, and Lawrence Bobo, *Racial Attitudes in America,* Cambridge: Harvard University Press, 1985.

30. Stephen J. Caldas and Carl L. Bankston III, "The Promise and Failure of School Desegregation in Baton Rouge and New Orleans" (paper presented at the annual meeting of the Louisiana Educational Research Association, New Orleans, March 1999).

31. U.S. Census of Population and Housing statistics for East Baton Rouge Parish, 1970, 1980.

32. Quoted in K. King, "Board Hopes New Magnet Plan Passes Muster," *Baton Rouge Advocate,* October 28, 1999, sec. A, p. 2.

33. Personal communication, August 24, 1997.

34. A more detailed description and analysis of this survey may be found in Carl L. Bankston III and C. Eddie Palmer, *The 1996 Survey of Lafayette Parish Educators: A Report Prepared for the Greater Lafayette Chamber of Commerce.* (Lafayette: Greater Lafayette Chamber of Commerce, 1997; report available on request from the Greater Lafayette Chamber of Commerce).

35. Debbie Burrow, letter to the editor, *Lafayette Advertiser,* May 25, 2000.

36. "School Analysis Model Teacher Questionnaire" (unpublished survey, N. P. Moss Middle School, Lafayette, 2000).

37. Personal communication, February 19, 2000.

38. Todd Billiot, "School Board Makes Token Cuts from the Budget," *Lafayette Advertiser,* March 16, 2000, sec. A, p. 6.

39. Personal communication, March 15, 2000.

40. Personal communication, March 15, 2000.

41. John A. Bell, "Lafayette Parish Public School System Attendance Zone Modification, 1999–2000" (unpublished report, April 3, 2000).

42. Todd Billiot, "Judge: Rezone Schools" (2000).

43. Margaret Nett, personal communication, May 22, 2000.

44. David Thibodaux, personal communication, May 22, 2000.

45. Todd Billiot, "Phones Ringing Off the Hook," *Lafayette Advertiser,* May 26, 2000, sec. A, p. 1.

46. Billiot, "Phones Ringing Off the Hook" (2000).

47. Stephen J. Caldas, Roslyn Growe, and Carl L. Bankston III, "African American and

White Reaction to Lafayette Parish School Desegregation Order" (paper presented at the annual meeting of the Mid-South Sociological Association, Knoxville, Tenn., Oct. 14, 2000).

48. Haik, United States District Court, Western District of Louisiana, Lafayette-Opelousas Division, *Alfreda Trahan et al. v. Lafayette Parish School Board et al.,* civil action no. 10,903.

49. Curtis Brown, personal communication, October, 19, 2000.

Chapter 6

1. Louisiana State Center for Health Statistics, *1996 Louisiana Vital Statistics Report* (New Orleans: Louisiana Office of Public Health, 1996).

2. U.S. Bureau of the Census, USA Counties 1998, Louisiana, General Profile.

3. We define "segregated" in accordance with the definition used by the National School Boards Association, as a school that is over 60% minority.

4. "Jeff Anti-Bus Plea Rejected," *New Orleans Times-Picayune,* November 7, 1972, sec. 1, p. 18.

5. Suzie Siegel, "Black Students Bused in Jeff to be Transferred," *New Orleans Times-Picayune,* November 9, 1984, sec. A, p. 23.

6. U.S. Bureau of the Census, Census of Population and Housing, 1990, Summary Tape File 3A.

7. Quoted in Jeff Marcon, "School Board Stops Boundary Jumping," *New Orleans Times-Picayune,* River Parishes edition, September 8, 1988, Metro section BR 3, p. 5.

8. Quoted in Stephen Casmier, "St. John Schools Find Integration a Tough Order," *New Orleans Times-Picayune,* River Parishes edition, January 5, 1990, Metro section BR 1, p. 5.

9. Casmier, "St. John Schools Find Integration a Tough Order" (1990).

10. Stephen Casmier, "Sorrow and Joy Mingle in Death of Woodland School," *New Orleans Times-Picayune,* June 1, 1990, sec. B, pp.1, 2. Watkins quoted on p. 2.

11. Robert E. Pierre, "Desegregation Plan Draws Fire," *New Orleans Times-Picayune,* River Parishes edition, April 4, 1991, sec. A, pp. 1, 11. Noel quoted on p. 1.

12. Louisiana Department of Education, *Annual Financial and Statistical Report* (Baton Rouge: Louisiana Department of Education, 1989, 1997).

13. "Sex Education Curriculum to Be Replaced with Lesson in Abstinence," *New Orleans Times-Picayune,* November 23, 1991, sec. B4, p. 1.

14. "Caddo School Official Expects Student Exodus." *Times-Picayune,* May 14, 1981, sec. 1, p. 4.

15. Personal communication, October 1999.

16. *The Times Online,* http: //www.nwlouisiana.com.

17. "New School Mixing Plan Ordered." *New Orleans Times-Picayune,* May 20, 1980, sec. 1, p. 1.

18. United Press International, September 21, 1989.

Chapter 7

1. David J. Armor, *Forced Justice: School Desegregation and the Law* (New York: Oxford University Press, 1995).

2. Armor (1995), 61.

3. Arnold Rose, *The Negro in America* (Boston: Beacon, 1956).

4. Kenneth Clark and Mamie Clark, "The Development of Consciousness of Self and the Emergence of Racial Identity in Negro Children," *Journal of Social Psychology* 10 (1939): 591–99; Kenneth Clark and Mamie Clark, "Segregation as a Factor in the Racial Identification of Negro Pre-School Children," *Journal of Experimental Education* 8 (1939): 161–63.

5. Morris Rosenberg and Roberta Simmons, *Black and White Self-Esteem: The Urban School Child* (Washington: American Sociological Association, 1971); Judith R. Porter and Robert E. Washington, "Black Identity and Self-Esteem," *Annual Review of Sociology* 5 (1979): 53–74.

6. Nancy St. John, *School Desegregation* (New York: Wiley, 1975); Walter G. Stephan, "The Effects of School Desegregation: An Evaluation 30 Years after Brown," in *Advances in Applied Social Psychology,* edited by M. Saxe and L. Saxe (Hillsdale, N.J.: Erlbaum, 1986), 32–56.

7. Sandra Graham, "Motivation in African Americans," *Review of Educational Research* 64 (1994): 55–117.

8. John Ogbu, *The Next Generation: An Ethnography of Education in an Urban Neighborhood* (New York: Academic Press, 1984); John Ogbu, *Cultural Models and Educational Strategies of Non-Dominant Peoples* (New York: City College Workshop Center, 1989); John Ogbu, "Minority Education in Comparative Perspective," *Journal of Negro Education* 59 (1990): 45–57; Allan C. Ornstein and Daniel U. Levine, "Social Class, Race, and School Achievement: Problems and Prospects," *Journal of Teacher Education* 40 (1989): 17–23; Olga Reyes and L. A. Jackson, "Pilot Study Examining Factors Associated with Academic Success for Hispanic High School Students," *Journal of Youth and Adolescence* 22 (1993): 57–71; Signithia Fordham, *Blacked Out: Dilemmas of Race, Identity, and Success at Capital High* (Chicago: University of Chicago Press, 1996) ; Min Zhou and Carl L. Bankston III, *Growing Up American: How Vietnamese Children Adapt to Life in the United States* (New York: Russell Sage Foundation, 1998).

9. James S. Coleman et al., *Equality of Educational Opportunity* (Washington: U.S. Government Printing Office, 1966).

10. Eric A. Hanushek, "Assessing the Effects of School Resources on Student Performance: An Update," *Educational Evaluation and Policy Analysis* 19 (1997): 141–64.

11. Jens Ludwig and Laurie J. Bassi, "The Puzzling Case of School Resources and Student Achievement," *Educational Evaluation and Policy Analysis* 21 (1999): 385–403.

12. Dan D. Goldhaber and Dominic J. Brewer, "Does Teacher Certification Matter? High School Teacher Certification Status and Student Achievement," *Educational Evaluation and Policy Analysis* 22 (2000): 129–45.

13. A. S. Wells and Robert L. Crain, "Perpetuation Theory and the Long-Term Effects of School Desegregation," *Review of Educational Research* 64 (1994): 531–55.

14. Robert L. Crain, Rita E. Mahard, and Ruth E. Narot, *Making Desegregation Work: How Schools Create Social Climates* (Cambridge, Mass.: Ballinger, 1982).

15. James S. Coleman, "Rawls, Nozick, and Educational Equality," *Public Interest* 43 (Spring 1976): 121–28; Carl L. Bankston III and Stephen J. Caldas, "Majority African American Schools and the Perpetuation of Social Injustice: The Influence of Defacto Segregation on Academic Achievement," *Social Forces* 72 (1996): 534–55.

16. Stephen J. Caldas, "Reexamination of Input and Process Factor Effects on Academic Achievement," *Journal of Educational Research* 86 (1992): 206–14, 1992; Stephen J. Caldas and Carl L. Bankston III, "The Effect of School Population Socioeconomic Status on Individual Student Academic Achievement," *Journal of Educational Research* 86 (1997): 206–14.

17. Kern Alexander and M. David Alexander, *American Public School Law,* 4th edition (New York: Academic Press, 1998).

18. James S. Coleman, "Racial Segregation in the Schools: New Research with New Policy Implications," *Phi Delta Kappan* 57 (1975): 75–78.

19. Thomas Cook et al., *School Desegregation and Black Achievement* (Washington: U.S. Department of Education, National Institute of Education, 1984), 40–41.

20. Robert L. Crain et al., *Finding Niches: The Effect of School Desegregation on Black Students* (New York: Institute for Urban Education, Teachers College, Columbia University, 1993).

21. Jeannie Oakes, "Two Cities' Tracking and Within-School Segregation," *Teachers College Record,* 96, no. 4 (1996): 681–90.

22. In this discussion, we use relatively straightforward statistics that should be readily comprehensible to all readers. Those interested in a more sophisticated approach to the harm and benefit thesis should see Appendix B.

23. Virginia E. Causey, "'Drafted into the Front Lines': Teacher Efficacy During School Desegregation in Columbus, Georgia, 1968–1975," *Research in the Schools,* 6, no. 2 (1999): 9–24.

24. U.S. Bureau of the Census, Census of Population and Housing, 1990, Summary Tape File 3A.

25. Carl L. Bankston III and Stephen J. Caldas, "Race, Poverty, Family Structure, and the Inequality of Schools, " *Sociological Spectrum* 18 (1998): 55–76; Sandra Lee, "Family Structure Effects on Student Outcomes," in *Parents, Their Children, and Schools,* edited by Barbara Schneider and James S. Coleman (San Francisco: Westview, 1993), 43–75; Lynn M. Mulkey, Robert L. Crain, and A. J. Harrington, "One-Parent Households and Achievement: Economic and Behavioral Explanations of a Small Effect," *Sociology of Education* 65 (1992): 48–65; Gary Natriello, Edward L. McDill, and Aaron M. Pallas, *Schooling Disadvantaged Children: Racing against Catastrophe* (New York: Teachers College Press, 1990).

26. Gary D. Sandefur, Sara McLanahan, and Roger A. Wojtkiewicz, "The Effect of Parental Marital Status on High School Graduation," *Social Forces* 71 (1992): 103–21; Jiang Hong Li and Roger A. Wojtkiewicz, "A New Look at the Effects of Family Structure on Status Attainment," *Social Science Quarterly* 73 (1992): 581–95; Roger A. Wojtkiewicz, "Duration in Parental Structures and High School Graduation," *Sociological Perspectives* 36 (1993): 393–14.

27. Louisiana Department of Health and Hospitals, Office of Public Health, *1994 Vital Statistics of Louisiana* (New Orleans: Louisiana State Center for Health Services, 1996).

28. U.S. Bureau of the Census, *Population and Housing Characteristics: Louisiana* (Washington: U.S. Government Printing Office, 1990).

29. U.S. Bureau of the Census, *Income and Poverty Characteristics: Louisiana* (Washington: U.S. Government Printing Office, 1990).

30. Bankston and Caldas (1998).

31. Lee (1993).

32. Daniel P. Moynihan, *The Negro Family: The Case for National Action* (Washington: Office of Policy Planning and Research, U.S. Department of Labor, 1965).

33. William Julius Wilson, *When Work Disappears: The World of the New Urban Poor* (New York: Vintage (1996).

34. Brenda E. Stevenson, "Black Family Structure in Colonial and Ante-Bellum Virginia: Amending the Revisionist Perspective" in *The Decline in Marriage among African Americans,* edited by M B. Tucker and C. Mitchell-Kernan (New York: Russell Sage, 1995).

35. See Lee (1993); A. M. Milne et al., "Single Parents, Working Mothers, and the Educational Achievement of School Children," *Sociology of Education* 59 (1986): 125–39.

36. See Michael E. Lamb, "Nonparental Child Care: Context, Quality, Correlates, and Consequences," in *Handbook of Child Psychology,* 5th edition, edited by I. Sigel and K. Renninger (New York: Wiley, 1997), 73–134; Joseph H. Pleck, "Parental Involvement: Levels, Sources, and Consequences," *The Role of the Father in Child Development,* edited by M. E. Lamb (New York: John Wiley & Sons, 1997), 66–103.

37. See Sara McLanahan and Gary Sandefur, *Growing Up with a Single Parent: What Hurts, What Helps* (Cambridge: Harvard University Press, 1994).

38. Sanford M. Dornbusch et al., "Single Parents, Extended Families, and the Control of Adolescents," *Child Development* 56 (1985): 326–41; Darin R. Featherstone, Bert P. Cundick, and Larry C. Jensen, "Differences in School Behavior and Achievement between Children from Intact, Reconstituted, and Single-Parent Families," *Adolescence* 27 (1992): 1–12,; Irwin Garfinkel and Sara McLanahan, *Single Mothers and Their Children: A New American Dilemma* (Washington: Urban Institute Press, 1986); Sara McLanahan and Karen Booth, "Mother-Only Families: Problems, Prospects, and Politics," *Journal of Marriage and the Family* 51 (1989): 557–79; Jane L. Pearson, Nicholas S. Ialongo, and Andrea G. Hunter, "Family Structure and Aggressive Behavior in a Population of Urban Elementary School Children," *Journal of the American Academy of Child and Adolescent Psychology* 33 (1994): 540–48; Nancy Vaden-Kiernan, Nicholas S. Ialongo, and Sheppard Kellam, "Household Family Structure and Children's Aggressive Behavior: A Longitudinal Study of Urban Elementary School Children," *Journal of Abnormal Child Psychology* 23 (1995): 553–68.

39. Carl L. Bankston III and C. Eddie Palmer, "The Children of Hobbes: Education, Family Structure, and the Problem of Social Order," *Sociological Focus* 31 (1998): 265–80.

40. Lee (1993).

41. Natriello, McDill, and Pallas (1990).

42. Vivian Gunn Morris and Curtis. L. Morris, *Creating Caring and Nurturing Educational Environments for African American Children* (Westport, Conn.: Bergin and Garvey, 2000).

43. See Crain, Mahard, and Narot (1982).

44. Janell Byrd-Chichester, "Segregation: Then and Now," *NEA Today* 19, no. 1 (September 2000): 21.

45. Carl L. Bankston III, Stephen J. Caldas, and Min Zhou, "The Academic Achievement of Vietnamese American Students: Ethnicity as Social Capital," *Sociological Focus* 30 (1997): 1–16; Carl L. Bankston III and Min Zhou, "Valedictorians and Delinquents: The Bifurcation of Vietnamese American Youth," *Deviant Behavior* 18 (1997): 343–63.

46. Zhou and Bankston (1998).

Chapter 8

1. Rob Gurwitt, "The Case of the Missing Schools," *Governing* (September 1999), 21.

2. Christine H. Rossell, "Improving the Voluntary Desegregation Plan in the Baton Rouge School System" (report to the court for *Davis et al. v. East Baton Rouge Parish School Board et al.,* October 27, 1999), 29.

3. Stephen J. Caldas, Roslyn Growe, and Carl L. Bankston III, "African American and White Reaction to Lafayette Parish School Desegregation Order" (paper presented at the annual meeting of the Mid-South Sociological Association, Knoxville, Tenn., Oct. 14, 2000).

4. Jeanne Weiler, "Recent Changes in School Desegregation," *Urban Education Digest,* April 1998, ERIC (http: //eric-web.tc.columbia.edu/digests/dig133.html).

5. See Susan E. Eaton and Elizabeth Crutcher, "Magnets, Media, and Mirages: Prince George's County's 'Miracle' Cures," in *Dismantling Desegregation: The Quiet Reversal of Brown v. Board of Education,* edited by Gary Orfield, Susan E. Eaton, and the Harvard Project on School Desegregation (New York: New Press, 1996), 265–89. Eaton and Crutcher's critical view of magnet schools is weakened somewhat by the fact that they look at only a single school district.

6. Signithia Fordham, *Blacked Out: Dilemmas of Race, Identity, and Success at Capital High* (Chicago: University of Chicago Press, 1996).

7. William Julius Wilson, *The Truly Disadvantaged: The Inner City, the Underclass, and Public Policy* (Chicago: University of Chicago Press, 1987); William Julius Wilson, *When Work Disappears: The World of the New Urban Poor* (New York: Vintage, 1996).

8. Douglas S. Massey and Nancy A. Denton, *American Apartheid: Segregation and the Making of the Underclass* (Cambridge: Harvard University Press, 1993).

Appendix B

1. Anthony S. Bryk and Stephen W. Raudenbush, *Hierarchical Linear Models: Applications and Data Analysis Methods* (Newbury Park: Sage Publications, 1992).

2. See Bryk and Raudenbush (1992), 17–18, 61–62.

Index